ANNIE REICH:
Psychoanalytic Contributions

ANNIE REICH:

Psychoanalytic Contributions

INTERNATIONAL UNIVERSITIES PRESS, INC.

New York

Reich, Annie.
    ANNIE REICH: psychoanalytic contributions.
    Bibliography: p.
    1. Psychoanalysis—Cases, clinical reports, statistics.
    [DNLM: 1. Psychoanalysis. WM 460 R344p 1973]
    RC506.R39   150'.19'5   72-8790
    ISBN 0-8236-0149-8

Contents

Foreword

ANNIE REICH died on January 5, 1971, at the age of 68. This volume represents her life's work, the careful observations of an exceptionally gifted psychoanalytic clinician. The very first paper, "Analysis of a Case of Brother-Sister Incest," shows her unique qualities. She was a keen observer with profound empathy for her patients. She never became lost in psychoanalytic jargon, and described her patients so vividly that they came alive in her presentations. Annie Reich was first and foremost a brilliant clinician. Insofar as she advanced theoretical conclusions, they were always based on well-documented clinical observations.

The papers which are assembled here embrace a wide range of topics. There are clinical papers, such as the one "On the Genesis of a Pregenitally Fixated Neurosis" and "A Clinical Contribution to the Understanding of the Paranoid Personality." Especially beautiful, are the papers on extreme submissiveness and narcissistic object choice in women, papers which show Annie Reich's deep understanding of the psychology of women.

As it is to be expected from a therapist of her stature, she has made valuable contributions to problems of psychoanalytic technique. "On the Termination of Analysis," "A Special Variation of Technique" and "Special Types of Resistance in Training Analysis" belong in this category. Annie Reich's papers on countertransference are of particular interest. She uses the term countertransference to include all those tendencies in which the activity of analyzing has an unconscious meaning for the analyst. Such tendencies, if they remain undiscovered, can interfere with the analyst's work; on the other hand, they may provide him with an added impetus for being involved in, and dedicated to, the taxing demands of his profession.

The first paper on countertransference (1951) was presented at the Midwinter Meeting of the American Psychoanalytic Association in December, 1949. It was in some respects a pioneering work, since at that time not much attention was being paid to the role of countertransference in the analyst's work. Years later (1960), Annie Reich took up this subject again in "Further remarks on countertransference." In the intervening years between the publication of these two papers, the subject provoked much discussion in the psychoanalytic literature. Annie Reich's second paper contains a lucid critique of attempts to use the emotional interplay between analyst and patient to evade the proper and intricate analytic work. She argues most adamantly against those authors who advocate acting out on the analyst's part and who propose the use of cathartic episodes as important therapeutic tools. She demonstrates that such attempts can have only transient influence at best, and that they can never replace the working through process.

In her last paper, "Empathy and Countertransference," Annie Reich returns to the vital problem of
analytic epistomology: how does the analyst gain insight in his patient's unconscious processes? What is
the nature of the analyst's intuition or empathy? She
reaches the conclusion that a temporary identification
takes place between the analyst and his patient. The
analyst has to shift from this intuitive understanding
to an evaluating, intellectual attitude. Annie Reich
scrutinizes the difficulties which interfere with an analyst's empathy—among them countertransference reactions. Again she points out that countertransference
is not a source of true insight into the patient's emotional life. Her clarification of, and distinction, between
empathic understanding and acting out in countertransference are convincing and valid.

Annie Reich's papers avoid easy schematization.
They convey the infinite variety of the analytic experience, the richness of problems and puzzles which make
the analyst's work so interesting. And this is the beauty
of her papers: she shows us how much a fresh approach, an unceasing wonderment can contribute to
making our work into thrilling pursuit of understanding "the secret chambers of the heart" (H. G. Wells).

George Gero, M.D.

Acknowledgments

O UR MOTHER died, after a lengthy illness, while preparing this book for publication. The book would have died with her were it not for the energy and dedication of a number of people who felt that to continue the task would serve as a true act of commemoration. The effort in managing all the details of translation and organization of someone else's work was very great and we are truly grateful for the deep feelings that motivated mother's friends to undertake this task. We would like to thank Mrs. Mary Mills for bringing the unfinished state of this work to the attention of Edith Jacobson and Viola Bernard. Dr. Bernard undertook the tremendous organizational task of collating the book. As coordinator and general "expeditor," she contacted and worked with all concerned, including Dr. George Gero, the publisher, the translators, indexer, typist, and ourselves. Dr. Jacobson undertook the chore of checking and supervising all the translations for scientific accuracy, adding corrections where needed. Dr. Gero not only contributed a fine foreword, but was helpful in deciding on the order in which the papers should be placed and in providing general scientific supervision. In addition, we would like to thank Jeanette Taylor, who typed the entire manuscript; Eva Kessler, who translated three of the papers from the original German; and Godfrey Cobliner, who reworked them. Our special thanks are due to Paula Gross, who was mother's secretary for many years, who translated the presentation on "Masturbation and Self-Esteem," and who provided Dr. Bernard with relevant materials and information.

Eva Reich Moise, M.D.
Lore Reich Rubin, M.D.

x •

1

Analysis of a Case of Brother-Sister Incest

(1932)

HERTA IS a working-class girl, 20 years old, a frail creature with delicate, pleasant features. Her undernourished appearance and slightly stooped posture somewhat diminished her charm. At the beginning of treatment, she was in a state of depression, obsessed by the fear of going mad. She observed her mental state incessantly, picking up tales about cases of mental illness from every quarter, and comparing them with her own history. She gave no credence to the physician's reassuring statements regarding her state of mind; on the contrary, she feared the doctors would lock her up in a mental institution. Furthermore, she was troubled by many fears of physical illness and bodily damage. She could not stand being in a closed room, was frightened of the dark, of being assaulted, etc. In addition, she suffered from a series of psychosomatic ailments such as palpitations, dizziness, sleeplessness. Altogether, she presented the picture of a severe anxiety neurosis. This condition set in about three months be-

Translated by Eva Kessler from *Internationale Zeitschrift für Psychoanalyse*, 18:109–120.

fore treatment was initiated. Its onset was signaled by a severe hysterical attack—the final breakdown of a tortured human being, a last escape from a tragic fate.

From her sixteenth to her twentieth year, Herta had had an incestuous relation with her one-year-older brother whom she had come to know when she was 15. Her brother had spent his childhood at the home of relatives, and she had been unaware of his existence up to that time.

The lovers lived in constant fear of being found out. They were caught in a web of lies and guises, separated from and cast out by everyone. Besides, they were naive enough to assume that the absolute frigidity of the girl, quite natural under these circumstances, would keep her from becoming pregnant, a popular, widely shared superstition. When Herta's pregnancy became apparent, the two young people were at the end of their wits and decided to commit joint suicide. Kind people in whom they confided in utter despair took care of them. They procured a refuge for the girl for the period of time before the delivery, helped the couple to play out a skillful comedy in front of relatives and authorities, and thus kept them from being discovered.

During the months of her pregnancy, which Herta spent in hiding, she began to suffer from certain anxiety states. She was afraid she might go blind or break down and faint, and she suffered from a strong, completely unfounded jealousy toward the brother, who, she felt, was neglecting her.

After a normal delivery, Herta felt relatively well. Three months later, the child died of pneumonia, which was, after all, fortunate for the girl. Herta received the news of the child's death in the hospital, to which she had been confined for several weeks because of a serious pyelitis. The atmosphere in the hospital was a rather religious one; neither the nurses nor the other patients had any idea that the quiet, modest girl, who looked like a child, had only recently become a mother under such circumstances. She was regarded as the epitome of virginal virtue, a factor which greatly provoked her guilt feelings. Meanwhile, her jealousy toward the brother had increased tremendously. In nearly paranoid fashion, she believed to have discovered signs that he was having relations with other women, and she felt deserted as the unwed mother of a fatherless child. The authorities tried to press her into revealing the name of the child's father—she feigned not to know it. Feeling exceedingly guilty toward her own mother, she thought the latter had cast her out. On that critical day, she had a strong longing for her mother, and she later said, "If my mother had been at my side everything would have turned out differently." The news of the child's death caused a storm of conflicting emotions in Herta. The feeling of liberation was contrasted by a very real grief at the loss—a grief to which she did not dare abandon herself. Overshadowing the feelings for the child, however, the thought obsessed her: "Now, I am going to die too, and my brother will be free to love someone else." She felt that this was more than she could take.

Herta was given injections because of the kidney ailment. For some time she had been afraid of these injections. Although some weeks earlier a clumsy and even rude physician had hurt her badly by a poorly administered injection, she did not mind that. She started to fear the injection only when another physician, whom she liked, gave them to her. Apparently, it was a repressed affection for this physician which caused her anxiety. On that day, when the injection was about to be given, the girl was suddenly overcome by intolerable anxiety and had the feeling she was going mad. All of a sudden, she found herself screaming loudly and her entire body shaking with convulsions. She tried to get hold of herself, but to no avail. This, in turn, increased her anxiety. She feared that she would be taken to a mental institution at any moment. After a few hours, the attack subsided, but the anxiety remained. Only after a period of several months of analytic work did this anxiety give way to a milder form of anxious depression.

Let us now try to reconstruct the childhood history as it came to the fore in the course of a two-year analysis. That may help us to understand the attack, the neurosis, and the development of the patient's character.

Herta's childhood had been that of a typical working-class girl. It was full of frustrations, of hunger, of disappointment, and of more severe rejections than those usually experienced by middle-class children; on the other hand, it was more filled with strong sexual temptations and satisfactions. Her childhood was marked by constant oral deprivation, except for her infancy, about which little is known. The child spent the first two years of her life with foster parents in the country. Allegedly, they treated her lovingly and took good care of her. Perhaps separation from these affectionate foster parents was of decisive importance, but this is a mere assumption. At the age of two, Herta was brought to her grandmother with whom she stayed for another two years. The grandparents had been people of "better" standing, civil servants with stern religious-conservative convictions. This, however, did not keep the honorable post office supervisor, her grandfather, from deserting his wife for some girl. Herta's mother, at the age of 15, started a love affair with a handsome but brutal and hard-drinking workman despite, or just because of, her strict education. She gave him three children out of wedlock—Herta is the second one—before he finally decided to marry her. The grandmother, though deserted, materially ruined and embittered, clung to the views and life style of her social class. She was hard, coldhearted, intolerant, and tried to teach Herta good manners and decent behavior by way of beatings and scoldings. The child was not permitted to move around, to protest; she was supposed to play quietly at her grandmother's feet in her little store. She had no smile for Herta, no kind word—nothing but grumpy faces and, added thereto, strict sexual prohibitions. Herta recalls only warnings not to get involved with men; but there can be no doubt that, at that time, strict prohibitions of masturbation were issued. The memory of one incident is significant: by an awkward movement of her grandmother, the child was pushed against the hot stove and burned her ear. She screamed, and the grandmother forced her to stop screaming.

An unmarried son, her favorite, living at her grandmother's home, sometimes gave sweets to the little girl, requesting her to masturbate him as a reward. It may well be that fellatio took place too. The child, fully understanding the crass discrepancy between the orders of the grandmother and the actions of the uncle, reacted with strong anxiety and, at the same time, with feelings of deep mistrust towards the prohibiting adults. She never gave up that attitude. Similar experiences were added like links in a chain. A short time later, a man led her from the street into the entrance of a house and requested her to masturbate him. In the course of time, more and more exhibitionists approached her; several times, in a way not to be mistaken, she was asked to submit to sexual intercourse. Later on, Herta probably looked for such situations, but originally, it was her social situation that exposed her to such temptations.

At the age of four, when war broke out, Herta came home to her parents. The father had been drafted. The family was living in great distress and need. Besides Herta, there was Paul, three years old, her companion in the miserable years to come, and George, two years old, the mother's darling. This last child was the only one of all the children whose need for love had been satisfied, and the only one who did not become neurotic. He seemed to have been the object of Herta's oral envy. Direct memories to this effect are lacking, but again and again Herta would repeat how dearly she had loved little George, and how amiable he had been. George was allowed to stay with the mother who took him to work with her, while Herta and Paul were sent to kindergarten. At that time, Herta was already intimidated and defiant. She was unkempt, dirty, always hungry. The mother made her dresses out of old material; they made her look ugly and ridiculous. The children in kindergarten made fun of her. She did not want to wear the dresses, she cried, but the mother beat her and compelled her to continue wearing the dresses. Of course, Herta did not understand that her mother, tortured by worries, had no recourse; the only thing she saw was that mother herself was still wearing "beautiful" dresses.

Herta caught lice. They shaved her head. Everybody ridiculed her, and her mother joined in. Herta became mean and more defiant than before. In kindergarten, she was beaten quite frequently, and nobody cared for her. She stopped going to kindergarten. She would leave the house at the usual hour, and, even in the cold of winter, she would roam the streets with her little brother until it was time to go home. She lived on garbage which she picked up in the gutter. Her mother did not notice all this.

When the father came home at the end of the war, the economic situation improved somewhat. However, the father drank and would come home completely inebriated at least once or twice a week. In his drunkenness, he had attacks of pathological jealousy, cruelly swearing at the mother in the presence of the children, speaking cynically about their sexual life, beating her brutally, demolishing furniture, etc. Herta was terribly afraid of her father and feared he would kill the entire family. She took her mother's part. She tried to protect the mother with her frail body, herself between father and mother, knowing it was not she whom the father wanted to beat. But the father, blind with rage, rained blows on Herta's head as well. The child not only felt the pain, but was terrified that she would be crippled by the beating. In the analysis, the long-forgotten words suddenly cropped up, "Father, don't beat me on the head; it will make me a nitwit." Hence, her later fears of going mad went back to the fear of being beaten into a nitwit by her father.

She had welcomed the father initially and was prepared to love him. She expected him to make up for the disappointments she had suffered from the mother. She became the father's favorite child; he gave her little presents. At that time—she was 6 or 7 years old—she had a dream which she recalled: *Kaiser Karl enters her room through the window and is very sweet to her.* Having observed the scenes between the parents, she knew what happened when father loved you. We can assume that such beatings frequently turned into sexual acts, and that the man, in his insensible drunkenness, was not disturbed by the children's presence, thus strengthening the child's notion of the sadistic nature of coitus. We did not succeed in ever uncovering a recollection of such sexual relations between the parents, but her later anxiety attacks contain all elements of such scenes.

Herta's anxiety arose mainly in situations which awakened the wish to be raped—a wish which must have been formed through these experiences—whenever she met a man who might conceivably be cast in the role of rapist: the physician who gave her injections, a man in the streetcar who gazed at her fixedly, and the like, made her think of being overwhelmed and crippled. In later years, this original fear blended with syphilophobia: sexual activity makes one contract syphilis which brings about softening of the brain and death in a mental institution—just like her mother's grandfather who indeed had died in a mental institution. Her masturbation anxiety during puberty also belongs in this category. She resumed masturbation at the age of seventeen, during the incestuous relationship with her brother, which left her completely anaesthetic. Her brother, to whom she confessed this, made her take an oath to give up masturbating, or else she would fall seriously ill. Not able to keep the oath, she went on masturbating, but with greatly disturbed gratification, obsessed by the fear of going mad.

Her anxiety attacks occurred mainly in closed rooms where she had the feeling of being hopelessly trapped, just like in the bedroom at home, when she had known that flight from the raging father through the only exit of the room was impossible. As mentioned, this fear, together with the severe guilt feelings about incest, had to lead to frigidity. She became extremely anxious during intercourse, mainly on account of the man's excitement which disgusted and horrified her because it reminded her of her father's rage. On the other hand, she was, of course, fixated to the brutal father. She managed to enrage men with whom she got involved by tormenting them and deliberately fanning their jealousy, to the extent that her brother, as well as the friend with whom she became involved during the analysis, after separating from her brother, repeatedly threatened her with a gun.

She chose the new boy friend entirely in the image of her father. She decided to "go with him" when she was told he was rowdy, a gambler, a seducer of women. It was her ambition to make him give up these bad qualities and to make him over into a new person. In the very same way, as a little girl, had she felt that it was within her ability to transform her father into another person and make him stop drinking. In her opinion her mother had handled her father wrong. At the age of 15, during an absence of her mother, she had indeed been able to keep her father sober for several weeks. Keeping house for him, working until late at night, she had treated him lovingly. The thought that she was able to be a better wife to the father was quite conscious—not so the attendant sensual component. The little girl's situation was a complicated one: she was deeply attached to the father and she understood his rages as a justified reaction to the sexual rejection by the mother. She wanted to take her mother's place and to do a better job of it. On the other hand, her conscious personality took sides with the responsible, respected mother, who was a human and worthy person, and to whom she was bound by a deep oral longing for love. The primarily sensual ties to the father were not ego-syntonic; only the hatred toward him was permitted to become conscious. Repeatedly, she asked her mother simply to do away with the brutal father, to stab him in his sleep.

The mother did not reward the child for taking sides with her. Tired and overworked, she nagged and criticized the love-hungry child instead of giving her affection. She wanted to make a good, industrious well-bred girl of Herta. Herta had to stay home to take care of the newly-born brother, to wash the dishes, to do the cooking, while the brothers were at liberty to play in the street and in the fields. This inequity was all the more intolerable for the child because she was just beginning to attain a position among her brothers and friends which might compensate her for many frustrations. Herta exercised an unlimited power over her younger brothers. Like a queen, she governed the little circle. All the boys loved her, waited on her, fulfilled her every wish. If one of them did not obey he would be beaten, just like her mother was beaten by the father. Her power was based on making the boys believe that she possessed a nut in which there lived a tiny elf, Tom Thumb, who, being a mighty spirit subject to her command, could produce, by magic, whatever she wanted. For hours, she would sit huddled in a corner with the other children narrating fantasies of her wonderful kingdom. Curiously enough, the other children believed every word she told them, although she could never prove her power. High up on top of a mountain, she would build a wonderful castle for herself to which no adult would ever be admitted. There Herta wanted to live, the only girl with all the little boys. Tom Thumb would provide all manner of delicacies for them. But the most wonderful part was that they would all sleep in a bedroom with red velvet walls and no windows; there, every night, the little boys would be allowed to indulge in sexual games and mutual masturbation with the little queen.

The element of the windowless room provides material for her claustrophobia of later years. The voluptuous fantasies resulted not only from experiences with the uncle and observations in the parental bedroom, but also from several sexual experiences Herta had when she was seven in a Hungarian village where she had been sent as a starved city child. There, on Sunday nights, male servants and maids would meet for orgastic celebrations, which the child watched furtively. She clearly recalls having observed coitus of her foster parents. Evidence that she realized what was going on is provided by a game the little girls used to play at that time; they put little pieces of wood into each other's vaginas.

These excessive sexual experiments and temptations gave rise to all kinds of fears which were further aggravated by the foster parents' unreasonable warnings. Whenever a training problem came up, Herta was told gypsies would steal her away, cut her up, and eat her. Indeed, gypsies did prowl in the region. One of them had approached the child with his penis exposed and had unmistakably invited her to sexual intercourse. Herta's later experiences, insofar as they repeated the earlier ones, confirmed that sexual intercourse was dangerous and frightening, thus increasing her susceptibility to anxiety. In the Tom Thumb fantasy, the fear was overcome successfully. The possession of this magic spirit had made her more powerful than all the others, and the blind devotion of her admirers compensated for the love the adults had never bestowed upon her. No doubt, Tom Thumb represented the longed-for penis lifting her high above her real station. Tom Thumb was the size of a thumb, and was capable of making himself grow and shrink. With the help of this fantasied penis, Herta attained power over her brothers and could thus satisfy her instinctive oral craving for love.

Herta's wish to be a boy was conscious. As a girl one is a second-class person. One is limited in one's freedom, at the mercy of men. She had seen that in her mother. As a girl one was not loved. It seems that Herta connected her lack of a penis with the many frustrations she suffered from her mother. We can assume that she considered the lack of a penis as the penalty for her many sexual sins. The Tom Thumb idyll, which undid the irretrievable loss in fantasy, and which, magically, provided her with every imaginable satisfaction, was disrupted repeatedly by her mother, just because Herta was a girl. She was not supposed to roam the streets with the boys; she was supposed to stay home and to work. If she did not obey orders, her mother beat her despite the fact that Herta risked life and limb fighting father on her behalf. But Herta could not renounce the love of the many little admirers. Nobody else loved her. She had no penis and no child (the recent birth of the youngest brother had been a new disappointment for her. Mother had given birth to the baby, not she herself; for her it meant nothing but work; and while she tried so hard to win her baby brother's love, he nevertheless preferred mother). Thus nothing was left for her. She was consumed with envy of everyone who had more, on whom more love was bestowed. Later, when the Tom Thumb fantasy no longer worked, she stooped to intrigues and mean tricks to maintain her power over the children.

All the while Herta was filled with fantasies of a great future. She would be a movie star; all men would lie at her feet. In the meantime, she succeeded in getting a good bit of sexual satisfaction: at 10, she let herself be masturbated by her brother George every night, feigning to be asleep so that she could not be implicated. The family of six slept together in the only room of the apartment, Herta in one bed with two brothers. It had to happen. The same thing was repeated the next year with a neighbor's child. At that time the family was very close with the boy's parents and, for some time, the two couples slept in one apartment, while the seven children slept in the other. Wild things went on among the children. Besides genital games they staged wild anal orgies. The older ones compelled the youngest boy to eat bread covered with excrement, and similar things.

Outwardly, Herta developed more and more into a "good" girl. The mother had no reason to be dissatisfied with her. Herta was industrious and obedient, and her entire instinctual life went on behind her mother's back. The outward change in her character—she had completely given up her defiance—was the result of strong guilt feelings toward the mother. There were different levels in Herta's relation to her mother, but the main point is that she never stopped loving her mother and longing for her to return that love. The mother remained the oral love object. In later years, Herta repeated this side of her relation to her mother in her relation to all women who could conceivably serve as mother substitutes. She approached every apprenticeship, every job, ready to love her (female) employer, and with excessive expectations that now, at long last, she would find love and affection. But, of necessity, after a short time she was disappointed. Nobody could give her the amount of love she craved. Interpreting minor reprimands as expressions of cold lack of affection, she reacted more or less openly with plain hatred. Thus, disappointment turned oral love into oral hatred.

Herta's mother had disappointed her repeatedly. At her first menstruation, the mother sent her to school without sanitary napkins so that the blood dripped to the floor. When, thereupon, Herta held her underwear together with safety pins which tore the underwear, the mother beat her. This affect-laden recollection clearly demonstrates the essence of her reproachful attitude toward the mother. She interpreted menstruation and her lack of penis as punishments for her sexual crimes, for her rivalry with the father, and for her death wishes toward the mother. This third component of her relation to the mother, stemming from the oedipal situation, was reactivated in her relations to all mother-substitute persons. Regularly, she had to find out that the originally beloved teacher or employer had relations with men whom she favored over her. Her jealousy was twofold: she felt deserted by mother and rivaled with her for the man. As soon as Herta would find out the bitter facts, her behavior toward the particular woman changed completely: while she had originally approached her openly, ready for love, she now became stubborn, defiant, mean, thus provoking real rejections besides the imagined ones.

Herta's superego was formed entirely in the image of her mother. She admired her mother for bearing her father's brutality with calm unconcern, without losing her courage and love of life, and without stooping to petty intrigues like Herta. At the same time, Herta had reason to mistrust her mother. She knew that her mother had committed adultery while her father was in prison for theft. While the mother had told her that girls do not need sexual pleasure, that that is something reserved only for men, she claimed sexual freedom for herself. All the distrust formerly awakened by the experiences at the grandmother's home came to life again. In the last analysis, this distrust was based on the sharp contrast between her social situation and the moral demands made on her and, as mentioned before, was one of the main factors undermining her positive relations to women. It kept her mother's demands from quite reaching her, because she constantly doubted the honesty and the validity of these demands. Thus Herta's identification remained superficial. The superego remained isolated, resulting in a split of her personality into a reactive personality, created by guilt feelings, and a hidden, wild, instinctual personality. This split became particularly apparent in Herta's mendacity which was only partly conscious. A psychic mechanism enabled her, under definite circumstances, to isolate certain layers of her personality from consciousness. It was a kind of short-term repression which dissolved when the environment made a deceit unnecessary. This mechanism worked the following way: in the course of the analysis, she had really forgotten those thoughts for which she felt guilty towards me as the mother image; it was in fact impossible for her, in spite of all her efforts, to recall them. But similar processes went on outside the analysis; indeed they made it possible for her to maintain a sort of general psychic equilibrium. No sooner would a thought emerge than she would forget it, lest it become associated with other conscious elements.

During Herta's puberty, her mother blocked one path which have led to consolidation of both halves of Herta's personality. She cut off her daughters's tender relationship with a boy, which could have led to ego-syntonic instinctual satisfaction, on the grounds that "it is not proper for a 14-year-old girl to go steady with a boy." The contrast between the petit bourgeois morality and the many seductions in the life of the patient was grotesque. It is self-evident how much hatred, rage, and hence also guilt were aroused by these experiences.

Shortly thereafter, Herta was again sent abroad with

a children's group. She came under the care of particularly bigoted, hard-hearted people—a new edition
of the grandmother. They curbed her with beatings,
scoldings, threats, and aroused in her the strongest
guilt feelings, originating mainly from her death
wishes against the foster mother. She returned home
outwardly even more perfectly the image of a "good
girl" than before. Quiet, timid, well-mannered, she
worked late into the night. It seemed as if Herta did
not share the other girls' interest in flirting and boys.
The mother was satisfied; Herta stayed home and had
no boyfriends.

In the meantime, however, Herta had been seduced
by her 17-year-old brother. She undoubtedly played a
rather active role in this situation. What a
break-through of instinct! What a defiant, hypocritical
disguise! In order to preserve her relationship with her
brother, she became enmeshed in a web of lies. This,
in turn, increased her guilt feelings. The brother represented the original incestuous object, the father, and
concomitantly, the man subject to her command, just
like the little brothers in former times. She ruled and
tortured him. He had to turn over all his earnings to
her, receiving from her as a favor only enough to cover
his barest needs. Already in early childhood, she had
made up her mind that that would be the way she
would treat her husband; she would not let herself be
exploited like her mother. Incessantly, she demanded
and received presents from him, mainly chocolate. He
had to account to her for his every action every minute
of the day, for she was terribly suspicious and always
in fear of being deceived or deserted. In her jealousy,
she developed paranoid traits and invented a thousand

intrigues (this will be particularly apparent in her later relation to the friend) in order to isolate her brother from others and to keep him all to herself.

Herta was not faithful herself. In order to be quite safe in any contingency, she liked to have several irons in the fire. Fear of desertion was the prime mover of her behavior, making her cling to the brother despite the fact that he repelled her, particularly when he desired her sexually. She was disgusted with him when he was excited. The old fear of the father was revived. The more ardent her brother became, the colder her reaction, but again and again, she would arouse his desire to a frenzy by means of cunning enticements only to deny herself to him. Occasionally, she would give in, but only when she feared she might lose him because of her excessive refusals. This sadistic behavior was her revenge for everything she had had to suffer, for the disappointments the mother and father caused her, for not possessing a penis. In the course of the analysis, all this became conscious to her as an active castration wish. She wanted to castrate the man orally during the sexual act, to bite off his penis. In this her oral instinctual tendency combined with her sadistic drive.

The more intense her castration wish became, the more Herta would fear the man's revenge. This fear, an essential component of her frigidity, originated in early childhood. She had always been afraid of crippled men. Again and again, jealousy occasioned her sadistic activities. It was intolerable for her to cede to a rival. For this reason, she was unable to give up the relation to her brother although it had long been torturous to her. Three times she had broken it off; three times she resumed it, as soon as she noticed that he was freeing himself from her and getting interested in other girls. The same pattern characterized her relationship with her boyfriend, long after his brutal attitude had destroyed her genuine love for him. Initially, the jealousy was based on the rivalry with her mother, when the latter had been the stronger rival. At deeper levels, the jealousy corresponded to the oral envy of the child and the penis envy that ensued from it. It was the jealousy that caused Herta's strongest conscious guilt feelings. In fact, the deepest instinctual tendencies of her personality were expressed in this attitude.

Herta's attraction for men was so great that they were not able to get away from her without breaking down completely. Both her brother and her boyfriend repeatedly tried to commit suicide. Herta suffered severely from her own behavior. Again and again, she stressed that she was just as uncontrollable a person as her father, that she was just as jealous as he, which she considered her greatest crime, and that everything would be all right if only she could be like her mother. It appears that her ego identification had been with her father, while her superego was developed in the image of her mother. This identification with the father was based on the oral fixation to the mother which, later on, was transformed into a phallic-sadistic one. In the last analysis, the torments she dealt out to men were intended for the phallic mother. To castrate the phallic mother was simultaneous revenge and instinctual satisfaction. Castration loomed as punishment; it pervaded the entire register of her anxieties.

All these various tendencies broke through in Herta's hysterical attack. The death of the child mobilized the old feeling of oral loss and revived the longing for mother. But the mother was not present. Herta's disappointment turned against her brother in the form of aggression. That added up to the forbidden sexual impulses toward the physician. Thus the attack represents, on the one hand, the sexual intercourse with the father, resulting in her destruction, and on the other hand, castration of the brother (mother) and his revenge. When the attack had subsided, the fear of the doubly motivated castration and destruction was established as a lasting state of mind in the form of fear of going mad.

Because of the split in Herta's personality which I described above, the analysis had to overcome great difficulties. She had a powerful mother transference toward me and, for several months, presented to me only the superego part of her personality with all the guilt feelings; i.e., she suppressed what really moved her, she lied, she dissimulated. Only when, after three quarters of a year, I threatened to break off the analytic treatment if she would not give up her relation to her brother, did she bring a flood of confessions, and her instinctual structure was gradually revealed. Despite the most intensive interpretation of the mother transference, Herta did not stop dissimulating throughout the entire analysis; again and again she withheld current material until she finally brought it to light when it already belonged to the past. For extrinsic reasons, the analysis had to be broken off at the end of two years. Herta had been relieved of a great part of her anxiety and from time to time, in her love affair with her boyfriend, she succeeded in having an orgasm. But she had no less an impulse-ridden personality than before. In the course of the analysis, she had come to realize her wish to be a man and her castration wishes too, which probably has been of essential help to her. But, despite the fact that these were the main topics of our interchange during the analysis, we did not succeed in resolving either the sexual fixation on the father or the oral relation to the mother. The duration of the treatment, apparently, was too short for attaining this goal.

In summarizing we see the following picture: a simple genital father relation, completely in accord with the usual hysterical structure, superimposed over a deeper oral disturbance of the relation to the mother. While the relation to the father is expressed in hysterical anxiety and disturbance of genital object relations, the oral structure leads to deep disturbances of the ego in the sense of being impulse-ridden, to a far-reaching isolation of the superego, and to a personality split.

This development of the vicissitudes of instinctual life and of the ego cannot be considered as an isolated one: it is characteristic of the libidinal development of children of those working-class strata bordering on *Lumpen proletariat.* These are children to whom the parents, crushed by need and misery, never gave the care they needed; children, who, without any supervision, grew up in the streets; children who, in consequence of the terrible housing shortage, from early childhood on had not only witnessed the sexual activity of the adults, but who, on top of that, were exposed to a great number of sexual seductions. In no way does this mean that these children grew up with no limitation on their instinctual impulses at all; on the contrary: by sudden, contradictory, moral prohibitions and frustrations they were more shocked than they would have been in an atmosphere of consistent and constant limitation of their instinctual drives. Regularly, we find in these children the overflowing orality which cannot be satisfied, and which leads the way to addiction, impulsiveness, criminality, waywardness. Abundant sexual activity, disturbed by deep guilt feelings, cannot, of course, provide satisfaction. It only acts as a constant stimulation, increasing the intolerable excitement. These are the people who fill the juvenile prisons; they are the nucleus of the inmates of reformatories. Individual analysis cannot cure these mental mass epidemics caused by the structure of society.

2

On the Genesis of a Pregenitally Fixated Neurosis

(1932)

THE ANALYSIS of a depressive hypochondriacal patient gives me the opportunity to contribute material to a discussion of the problems of masochistic character.

After having unsuccessfully undergone various other
therapies, a young man, 24 years of age, tried analysis
as a last resort. He had been ill since early childhood,
and suffered from numerous intensive fears, the content
of which, in the last analysis, was always a physical
damage. Under the influence of his religious upbringing, it was usually the fear of punishment in hell
which, for many years, stood in the center of his neurosis. For days he would stay alone in his room, imag-
ining the tortures inflicted upon him in the other
world because of his sins. He saw himself cut to pieces,
burnt, pierced by a glowing iron, buried alive. His
imagination was exceedingly fertile, inventing the most
refined methods of torture. Similar dangers, in various

Translated by Eva Kessler from *International Zeitschrift für Psychoanalyse*, 18:388–400.

other forms, were threatening him from all sides. He was afraid of being run over by an automobile, of being ground into pap, of being crippled by a car; murderers were waiting for him in the dark entrance hall of the house to attack him from behind; he expected to succumb to a heart attack at any moment or to fall down and break his neck. But he did not react to these fears like a phobic who would try to avoid dangers; on the contrary, he wallowed in his fears. He would constantly observe his state of mind, ponder over his suffering, watch his body. He was so involved with his own person that he nearly completely lost contact with the outer world. His behavior was both hypochondriacal and masochistic. Let us first consider his hypochondriacal traits.

As could be expected in a person suffering from such intensive fears of castration, the sexual life of the patient was thoroughly disturbed. Despite his fervent longing for love, he had never become involved with a woman up to the time of the analysis. Whenever he tried to approach a woman, his symptoms intensified vehemently. Since early childhood, he had masturbated excessively while being tortured by severe guilt feelings. These masturbatory activities could bring no sexual satisfaction to him as an adult: on the one hand, the guilt feelings kept him from experiencing pleasure; on the other hand, he was not seeking purely genital satisfaction. Under the influence of his fear and of his pregenital fixations, the quanta of excitement were shifted from the genital to other organs. These were, in turn, libidinally hypercathected (*überbesetzt*), became the focus of his self-observations, and reacted with various states of tension and spasms.

Thus he suffered from severe symptoms of congestion, he was constantly excited, and he could not sleep at night. The tortures of hell which he so feared were to be Divine punishment for his masturbation.

The patient's hypochondriacal symptoms must, in the first place, be understood as phenomena of the blocking of organ libido (in the sense of Ferenczi, 1912). As is typical for hypochondriacal phenomena, the fantasies accompanying the symptoms were mainly of a pregenital nature (see W. Reich, 1926).

Let us consider the two most important organic symptoms. The first one consisted of a feeling of pressure and tightness in the chest; it increased to feelings of choking. Basically, this represented the realization of one of the punishments in hell. A fantasy accompanying the symptoms provided an insight into their meaning: he collapses at work; everybody comes running; even the boss bends over him, helps him, fondles him. Hence the symptom expresses his fear as well as a passive homosexual tendency. Characteristically for the patient, this tendency is not permitted to be expressed except in connection with suffering.

This symptom subsided when the patient had recognized these facts, but another one became all the more intensified: when in company, especially in the company of girls, and the patient wanted to show himself in a favorable light, the muscles of his face, of his torso, and of his upper extremities became so tense that his smile was distorted into a grimace, and his movements turned awkward and clumsy. At the same time, he was afraid of becoming completely and irreparably paralyzed. He blushed. He was extremely shy, to the point where it was torture for him to be in the company of others. It became impossible for him to take an examination. He could not be successful in any occupation. In a nearly paranoid way, he thought everybody knew what was wrong with him, everybody observed him, everybody scoffed at him. The situations in which the symptoms appeared with the accompanying blushing clearly show that they are the expression of exhibitionist impulses. The fact that the inhibition of the exhibitionistic impulse took the form of increased muscle tonus leads us to assume a strong sadistic component. The symptoms centering around the mouth suggest a strong oral-erotic tendency.

These pregenital tendencies were met by strong anticathexis leading to their repression. This repression, utilizing the motoric facilities of the muscles, produced the awkwardness, the feeling of paralysis, the inappropriate movements; in short, it produced dystonus (see Fenichel, 1928). The physical disturbance extended to the sensory sphere as well, mainly to the sense of depth. It produced feelings of alienation from certain parts of the body, from mild parasthesia to the feeling that the organ no longer belonged to him.

The patient's inability to have an erection belongs in this sphere. In one way or another, he had been afflicted with it since puberty, frequently to the point where he felt he did not possess any genitals at all. The feelings of alienation extended to the entire lower part of his body: he did not have a feeling of himself; everything seemed to have gone dead as if it were wooden; he had no abdomen; he had no legs.

The following episode was particularly illuminating in pointing up the dynamics of this process. At one time, the patient, clad only in bathing trunks, took a sunbath in the company of a friend. The situation was favorable for mobilizing passive homosexual wishes. Immediately, the patient's castration anxiety was activated. He was lying with his legs apart, the sun shining on his genitals. All of a sudden, he was seized by the feeling that his sex organs had melted away in the sun. What had happened? The defense against the homosexual impulse had encroached on his sense of bodily self. As the impulse was repressed, his sense of depth was simultaneously affected and repressed. The entire experience made him feel as though the castration had already taken place, and he reacted with vehement anxiety.

There were other changes in bodily sensation whose structure was more complicated because they were based on early identifications. When, in the course of the analysis, his castration fear was activated, he felt as if he had been "cut in two"; his feet were on one side of the room, his head on the other. At another occasion he felt as if he consisted of two parts loosely connected at the neck. The patient was deeply shaken by these experiences and cried like a child when he was overcome by them. By tracing these anxious experiences back to their infantile origins, we succeeded in making them disappear. In both cases, he had identified with the hated object. He experienced on his own body what he would have liked to do to the hated object.

From time to time he suffered from general states of depersonalization. He felt alienated from himself, he asked himself "Who am I? What shall I do?" These too were defense mechanisms in reaction to breakthroughs of impulses.

During the analysis, the patient's consciousness was frequently swamped by homosexual and other perverse fantasies, which his ego tried to resist. The feelings of alienation helped him to bear such intolerable situations. The intensity of sudden breakthroughs of sadistic impulses and murderous tendencies was dampened by feelings of alienation. At such times, the patient was so full of doubt as to his own personality that the rage subsided, the danger was overcome. One time, the patient stood next to the analyst ready to pay his monthly bill. He claimed that I had not said "Thank you," and was seized by the impulse to choke me. This affect probably was due to the fact that he had to pay me at all. At that very moment, depersonalization set in: the murderous impulse was superseded by brooding, self-observation, doubt. The depersonalization was not the result of an ego detachment, of a withdrawal of libido; it resulted from the repression of the sadistic impulse.

Feelings of alienation and states of tension gave abundant material for anxious hypochondriacal self-observation. The patient saw himself ending in a mental hospital. Yet he was also convinced that he had the most interesting neurosis in the world and that his tragedy was equal to the *Divine Comedy*. His general behavior mirrored this overvaluation of his illness, his fantasy that his suffering was the only narcissistic reserve left to him in the despair of his impotence, his inability to work, and his isolation.

The patient adopted a very masochistic attitude in his life as well as in the analysis. He filled the sessions with unending complaints about his state of mind, which he expressed in a dying voice. In the same way, he found no other subject for his conversations with other people than complaints. He constantly reproached: "nobody is helping me"; "look how I am suffering"; "why don't you help me"; "it is your fault that I am suffering; you do not love me." He always felt he was treated unkindly, he was tortured, he was rejected. In the transference, he continually criticized the technique of the analysis. Through such behavior, he provoked actual rejections. He would ring up the psychoanalyst six times on a Sunday although he had been told the first time that she was out of town. Each disappointment brought about an intensification of his complaints. With obvious satisfaction, he showed off the worsening of his condition, apparently intending to torment others by arousing their guilt feelings. Superficially, this attitude was intended to compel others to love him. He acted on the assumption that the other person had only to see his suffering in order to afford him automatically the love he longed for. He assumed that suffering gives you a claim on love. The analysis was able to uncover the role sadism played at deeper levels in this attitude. His masochism, having the effect of sadistic torment of the object, was intolerable for everyone with whom he got involved. By reproaching the object, he shifted the responsibility and the guilt for his sadistic attitude on the other person, pretending that the latter had provoked him. That he was really acting out sadistic impulses is evident from a fantasy he had in childhood whenever his father beat him: The father, after crippling him by his beatings, breaks down himself, and repents. Further evidence that the main purpose of his masochism was to torment the object was presented in the course of the analysis. Whenever we succeeded in making one of his symptoms disappear, he was in no way happy, would not admit that he had improved, and would find something new to blame the analyst for.

The analysis of this attitude led us right back to his childhood. The patient had grown up in rather modest circumstances, the only son born after four girls. The father was a compulsive neurotic, a hard and petty man, who lived only for the fulfillment of his religious duties. He was unloving and and inordinately strict with the boy, and beat him senseless for the slightest offense. The patient remembers these scenes as indescribably horrible. The father, his face red and distorted with anger, would allow no one to care for the child lying on the floor. At the end of such scenes, the boy would creep into a corner and cry for hours on end, becoming ever more deeply immersed in his despair, hoping his mother would come at long last and take him in her arms, or even that the father would finally take pity on him and be kind to him. It was then that he had the fantasy of his penitent father caring for him and bringing him presents.

Here, the patient's masochistic pattern is already fully developed. By suffering he wants to force others to love him and reap his revenge on them. As time went on, he began to recollect that very frequently sexual games had been the cause for the beatings. There was a strict prohibition of, and severe punishment for, touching the penis. It was likewise strictly forbidden to the then three-year-old child—the beating scenes took place between his third and seventh year—to approach the mother physically. The father did not allow him to sit on her lap, to nestle against her, etc., because, he said, the boy was too old for such things. In fact, the child had a strong need for the mother's tenderness, so that his overtures to her were probably very striking. We were not able to find out whether the father had ever threatened to castrate the boy. In any event, the child had always taken the father's attitude as a consistent horrible threat of castration.

The boy also suffered from a severe phobia. When he was naughty, his sisters would threaten him with the "black man" who would come and get him, cut him up, destroy him. Their practical joke consisted of calling the bogey man by telephone and then pretending to have a conversation with him through the locked basement door. While the boy was frightened into a state of panic, the sisters were royally amused by the performance. His later fear of being scoffed at and ridiculed was traced back to this scene. In yet another way, the sisters became the co-executioners of his castration. From time to time, they accused the boy of sexual "crimes," whereupon the father gave him a horrible beating. There was plenty of opportunity; up to his seventh year, the patient shared a bed with his mother and sisters. While during the day, the father used to threaten him with the most horrendous punishments for every physical approach, at night the boy was allowed to nestle against the women's bodies. It gave him the greatest pleasure to embrace his mother, to touch her breasts, and to touch her genitals with his feet, as if by chance. While the mother was asleep, he masturbated, pressing his penis against her body in great excitement, all the while beset by fear of his father. He had the feeling that the father was eavesdropping on him "from behind the door"—the element, "from behind the door," stemming directly from his fear of the black man. He expected the monster to attack and annihilate him at any moment. This same fear reappears subsequently in his fear of hell, which is a later form of the masturbation anxiety. He imagines the avenging God as a father, bigger than life-size, waiting behind the clouds for the moment when he can pounce upon the poor sinner.

Thus the fear of the father was concomitant with strong sexual desire for the mother. The ensuing development was a peculiar derivative of the Oedipus conflict. An intensive hatred of the father was bound to develop in reaction to this fear. For hours on end, the child would imagine how he would torture the father, how he would kill him, even cut off his penis. The way to the woman lay only over the body of the father. In the course of the analysis he dreamed that *his father dropped dead to the floor and that, at the same moment, he the patient, seizes a girl.* It is a characteristic masturbation fantasy of early puberty in which phallic-aggressive tendencies break through, forming the beginning of normal masculine development. At that time, he saw himself *riding on horseback through a dark tunnel, his sword drawn, mowing down the heads of devils right and to the left.* But neither in childhood nor in puberty could he maintain this sadistic-phallic attitude for any length of time. Under the influence of such contrary educational tendencies he could not, in his childhood, arrive at a successful resolution of infantile sexuality. Regressive processes set in, giving an even more pregenital and sadistic character to the genital drives, and thus activating ever greater masses of anxiety. Even in early childhood, the patient's masochistic fantasies and attitudes provided the only (insufficient) possibility for discharge of dammed-up libido. The particular complication, resulting from the simultaneity of temptation and prohibition, seems to be responsible for the relentlessness and indomitability with which drives and effects manifested themselves in patient's life, particularly for the intensity of his anxiety and sadistic impulses, hence too for the particular therapeutic difficulties involved in his case. The sequential patterns of childhood were repeated during puberty. Under the continued influence of sexual prohibitions, the phallic attitude had to be relinquished. It gave way to increased tortured brooding and organ-libidinal symptoms. At the same time, his attitude became more strongly sadistic. He buried himself willingly in his neurosis, and fully expected that his great suffering would so endear him to a girl that her love would flow over him like a miracle.

The same process which prevailed in the patient's puberty was repeated continually in his adult sexual life. Again and again, he dreamed of a masculine-genital approach to women. But this genital striving was disturbed because it was tied to pregenital tendencies. Besides anxiety and brooding, he was subject to narcissistic-aggressive fantasies. He saw himself as a genius, a great artist, a statesman, a Don Juan, irresistible to thousands of women. His genital strivings were predominantly exhibitionistic and sadistic. He wanted women to admire him, in particular, to admire his genitals. He would exhibit himself and masturbate at the window. He had fantasies of brutal rape, of hurting and soiling women. But an overpowering anxiety and awareness of his impotence impeded the realization of his wishes. Thus the road to masculinity was closed to him. The patient, reacting with crying and moaning, provocatively exhibited his suffering. He wanted to be fondled and caressed like an infant. Moreover, he had the intense wish to suck at the breast of the analyst, to look at her genitals and her anus and to suck them too. In such phases, his perverse fantasies became more and more abundant. From time to time, he was overcome by homosexual impulses of a particularly embarrassing and humiliating character. He wanted to suck at a dirty, diseased penis. At such times, he could barely stand the presence of a man, so afraid was he of acting upon his desires. But his perverse fantasies did not remain passive for any length of time. Under the influence of acute frustration in the transference, the wildest aggressions broke through, containing elements of all the pregenital phases. He wanted to punish the rejecting love object with all the tortures of hell of which he himself was afraid. He found the highest satisfaction in these cruel fantasies. One fantasy in particular played a major role: he would tear the clothes off women's bodies, grab them by the feet and tear them to pieces, would lacerate their anus, pierce their womb, penetrate their bodies and devour its contents, eat their excrements, tear off their breasts, and so on. At the same time, his sexual curiosity became overpowering. He longed to watch fat old women during their excremental activities. In fact, for several months he watched the most intimate activities of an old woman living across the way, through opera glasses.

His sadistic impulses became so strong that he had

to restrain himself forcibly so as not to attack others. He felt his restraint physically. He felt himself clenching his fists in his pockets; it was the only way he could keep his hands off the object. He felt himself biting his lips; it was the only way he could keep himself from biting the object to pieces and devouring it. Suddenly it became clear that the states of tension which had been tormenting him were mainly the physical expression of his suppressed coprophagic and cannibalistic tendencies.

What had really happened? Just as in his childhood, the patient, out of fear, had left the genital phase and regressed to pregenital levels the markedly sadistic structure of which could be understood from the analysis of the childhood situation. The childhood castration fear not only expressed itself directly as fear of the father and of the black man; it also became the motor force behind the patient's extraordinarily intensive sexual exploration. The nightly intimate physical closeness to mother and sisters had stimulated his curiosity excessively without fully satisfying it. Mother and sisters avoided showing themselves in the nude to the child. At one time or another, he had undressed one of the sisters, for which the sisters had reported him to his father. His ideas of the female body certainly were very vague. He could not imagine that women had no penis. On the other hand, he was bound to become aware of this, in the course of his innumerable contacts with his mother and sisters. Out of fear for his own penis, he now built theories about the fate of the female penis, based on old libidinal interests; confirming these theories became of vital importance for him. To this curiosity, fed by excruciating anxiety was added hatred for the disappointing, castrating mother who had rejected his love. Hence, the particularly sadistic character of his sexual curiosity.

At first he thought women's breasts ended in a penis. His observations of cows had led him to this idea. With the keenest of interest, the boy had watched a cow being milked at her four "penises." Once, he was permitted to join in the milking, but the animal, sensing the unaccustomed hand, kicked him. In his contact with mother, he had already experienced woman's jealous care of her breast-penis. According to the then prevailing custom, he had been breast-fed for a very long time. In all probability, weaning had been quite sudden. Nothing further is known about this period, but his feeling that mother withheld her penis, which he wanted to suck, from him for lack of love, is, in the last analysis, based on his oral fixation. The same is true of his wish to bite every disappointing object to pieces, to devour it. The penis to him seemed created solely for the purpose of being sucked at. He had a vivid recollection of mother washing him, kneeling in front of him. He would exhibit his penis and try to touch her face with it in order to make her suck at it. The touching of the mother's breasts, moreover, was the very thing that his father had strictly forbidden. We can assume that he had frequently tried to do this in the daytime too, thus causing the father's intervention.

Another of his theories was that mother had shoved her penis or her penises into a hollow of her body, that she could, all of a sudden, thrust them forward. Mother possessed a sinister hollow between her legs, a cloaca; she could project an enormous penis out of it.

Or, there was a kind of vagina between the breasts with a penis hidden inside. Mother's entire body enclosed a sinister hollow, a labyrinth, a town with many streets wherein one could get lost; horrible devils and hideous rats and snakes lived there. It was this monstrous body of mother's that the boy wished to penetrate to solve the mystery at any price. If mother did not let him enter voluntarily, he would have to subdue her by force, tear off her clothes, disembody her, split her open from top to bottom, just like the cow he had seen hanging at the slaughter house, split lengthwise by an axe.[1] His own penis had to be the tool for this gruesome execution. But the mother would destroy the child's little penis with her own enormous one. There were dreadful tongs at the entrance to the mother's womb, an enormous guillotine which would castrate the child.[2] It was only natural that the patient, thus doubly threatened by father and mother, had to renounce his potency.

Dreams reported by the patient during that period of analysis clearly illustrate the fear of the mother's genital:

1. He lets his penis hang down through a hole in the floor. There is a sausage-cutting machine downstairs; it will cut his penis into thin slices.

2. He sticks his head into a room through an open door. There is a red velvet drapery at the door. All of a sudden he is guillotined.

3. A woman loses a set of false teeth out of her vagina.

---

[1] This was the model for the state of depersonalization in which he felt himself consisting of two halves, only loosely connected at the neck.

[2] Regarding the oral-sadistic fantasies of forceful entrance into the mother's womb and destruction of its contents, see Klein (1928).

The idea of a retractable penis can be traced back superficially to the boy's observations of a stallion. At deeper levels it is based on anal elements. The mother, herself an anal character, had contributed to the child's anal eroticism and even satisfied it to some extent. Every time the child had a bowel movement, the mother considered it as a gift to her, impatiently expected and joyously received. On innumerable occasions, she gave him an enema. She thus contributed to the fixation to which the patient's libido could withdraw later on. The mother had given a particular amount of satisfaction in this area; small wonder that the love-hungry child remained fixated there. Later on, he expected men to provide the same pleasure as mother. Thus the patient fantasied sucking at a black, hard penis covered with a sticky matter, which he attributed to a friend. The associations led directly to the rubber attachment of the irrigator.

At the age of three and a half years, the child listened stealthily to mother having a bowel movement. It seemed to him mountains and rivers were rushing forth accompanied by thunderous noise. This led to the fantasy that, at that moment, mother had ejected her enormous penis. This was the basis for his interest in the excremental processes in women, in the anus and feces. This, combined with his oral tendencies, is at the root of his coprophagic strivings, his cunnilingus and anilingus fantasies, and the particular form of his homosexual wishes to suck at a dirty, diseased penis.

From here on in, the structure and genesis of his homosexuality become clear. All the pregenital tendencies originally directed toward the phallic mother find expression in his homosexuality. He desires mother's penis for two reasons: on the one hand, he wants it to give him oral and anal pleasure, as he experienced from the irrigations; on the other hand, he was desperately seeking proof that there was no castration. The mother denied him the needed penis, apparently through sheer lack of love, for she must have possessed many penises. Mother would have to be killed, torn to pieces, to enable the patient to pull her penis out of her body. He turns away from this wicked mother; he turns to a man—the possessor of the penis.

In childhood, he had observed with great interest that his father and his kindly uncle possessed the desired organ. He hoped that father would provide what mother was no longer willing to give him—oral and anal satisfaction and, most of all, the assurance that castration was impossible. Who could be better equipped to give such assurance than the father, the avenging castrator himself? Besides, the boy had long since found out that being a girl protects you from father. His sisters were not threatened, not beaten. To be a girl did not have to mean to be without a penis. According to his theory, girls merely hid their penises. Thus he offers himself as love object to his father expecting oral and anal satisfaction from him.

Freud (1931) stresses the importance of the preoedipal relationship to the mother for the development of female sexuality, and illuminates the continued effects of drives directed toward the mother in heterosexuality. It seems that this pregenital relationship to the mother, whom he imagined to be phallic, was of fundamental importance for the patient's homosexuality. This relationship was transferred to the father only secondarily. Fenichel (1931) also describes such a change of object in a man, a carryover of preoedipal love into the oedipal phase.

The following question comes up: why did the patient choose the *masochistic* form for his homosexuality? We can safely assume that he provoked his father into beating him by his misbehavior. We know for certain that, at the age of eight, he had the strong desire to be spanked publicly on the naked buttocks by a strict schoolteacher, the image of his father. Behind this stood the wish for anal surrender.

We were not able to prove that this behavior was in part dictated by a wish to be punished. He accepted the beatings; they even calmed him down, because they were only thrashings and not the castration he feared so much. Nor were we able to prove that the combined anal pleasure and pain caused by the enemas caused him to remain fixated to this pain-pleasure. Rather, two main factors seem to have been decisive for the breakthrough of the patient's pregenitality in masochistic form: (1) his inordinate longing for love and, respectively, his excessive fear of loss of love, expressed in insatiable masochistic demands; and (2) a boundless sadism which could only break through if turned against himself.

In his article on the masochistic character, W. Reich (1932) points out that this unsatisfied yearning for love, which he considers a typical characteristic of masochism, is a reaction to massive anxiety provoked by a sadistic upbringing. We find, in our case, a confirmation of Reich's theory. Only the assurance that the child is loved and has nothing to fear helps alleviate the severe anxiety; the masochistic attitude is a pathological attempt to find this assurance.

Reich stresses three libidinal factors as the basis of masochistic character: anality, exhibitionism, skin eroticism. Although we draw no generalizations we must, in our case, single out orality as being in the foreground. We see the patient's insatiable, indomitable need for tenderness as characteristic of persons who suffered early oral deprivation, while Reich attributes this very trait to skin eroticism. The importance of anality and exhibitionism, however, is corroborated in our case. We must assume that anal fixation played an even greater role than we could prove on the basis of the material revealed during the relatively short analysis.

The second decisive factor is the excessive sadism of the patient. We have tried to understand its dual genesis: as a reaction to sadistic treatment by the father and as resulting from pregenital tendencies toward the mother. The patient's sadism was expressed in various forms: directly, in sadistic fantasies; in reverse form, in anxiety and masochistic fantasies; and, finally, as real torment of the environment, cloaked in masochistic behavior. Rarely could the patient afford the luxury of open sadistic fantasies, for these fantasies were almost immediately followed by their counterpart, the fear of hell. Only for brief moments could the patient enjoy his pregenital sexual goals in fantasy: sadistically overpowering women, tearing them apart, cutting them to pieces, castrating his objects, eating bodies and excrements, etc. Only a few moments later he would be transformed from the tormenting subject into the tormented object. In his fear of hell, he himself experienced the tortures he intended for his victims. Then, in his fear, he enjoyed the distorted satisfaction. From this, we can understand that he sought the fear and wallowed in it. In his own torment, he simultaneously enjoyed the torment of his victims and reactivated the primary oral-anal relationship to mother. The two extremes, revelling in perverse, or even psychotic, fantasies and drowning in wild fears are one and the same, are two sides of the same experience, and the patient vacillated incessantly between them. The fact that his aggression was turned against his own ego protected him from the breakthrough of criminal impulses against the environment, from the possibility that his aggression might again turn against the object, from the threat of psychosis which commonly attends this kind of libidinal structure. The patient's narcissism, so close to megalomania, and his severe depressions show that he was only a short step away from psychosis. In fact, he had highly developed mechanisms of oral incorporation which are characteristic of melancholia. But introjection was not complete; object relations were not totally lost. A trifling impulse could turn his massive sadistic libido against the outer world again. The patient was in constant fear of this, and frequently resorted to sudden states of depersonalization in order to master the situation. The fact that the patient's libidinal position is not exclusively pregenital indicates the reversibility of this process. We observed significant phallic strivings too, which counteracted the definitive introjection and protected the patient from becoming psychotic.

That the patient's fear indeed resulted from an introjection of the object is evident from the following.

His fear of hell became exacerbated at two different times: once, when he was eight years old, and again, at the age of twenty. The first time it subsided spontaneously at the end of a few years; the second time it lasted, undiminished, from his twentieth year up to the time of the analysis. The occasion had been the same in both instances. When the patient was eight years old his father fell ill with a severe neurosis. His symptoms were mostly hypochondriacal, and very similar to the anxieties of the patient. The father, assuming that he suffered from incurable stomach and heart ailments, had severe death fears. The second time, a feared and admired friend, definitely a father image, became seriously afflicted with similar symptoms. The patient's attacks of choking replicated the father's illness exactly. The patient probably attributed the father's illness to his own death wishes, but he was unable to enjoy the triumph over his father. He had destroyed the father; he had incorporated him. He himself had become the father now. He suffered along with his father, experiencing the latter's afflictions in his own body. God had taken over the role of the avenging father, that is to say, the father had not only been incorporated into the ego, but into the superego as well. And thereupon, the superego was again projected onto the outer world, punishing the patient by causing him the same pain the real father was suffering, while the patient felt guilt at having inflicted the pain on his father. In addition, there appeared the entire inventory of punishments in hell, long known to the boy from the religious indoctrination he had received at school.

The reversion of the aggression against his own ego

made any self-healing impossible, for it would have constituted real revolt against the father's sexual prohibitions.

Actual sadistic torment of the object, cloaked in masochistic behavior, could be carried out without fear of the consequences because it was, so to say, an unbloody revenge. Had the masochistic maneuver been successful, had he attained his goal of receiving love and tenderness, he would have been enormously relieved. The patient would no longer have had to fear the father or hate him. He would not have had to punish father in himself and could thus be saved from self-destruction. To be sure, there were more appropriate ways of bringing about reconciliation with the father, but the inappropriate masochistic manner offered the advantage of simultaneous sexual satisfaction, for in the fear of hell the patient experienced not only revenge and punishment, but libidinal gratification as well. And that is what made the patient's conflict insoluble, what made it so difficult for the therapist to influence him.

Let us summarize the libidinal development of this case in a short survey. An extraordinarily great number of pregenital satisfactions fixated the patient to the mother. Nevertheless, he attained the genital phase in a predominantly exhibitionistic manner. Sadistic punishments by the father interrupted early genital development and threw the child back into pregenitality. The old anal-sadistic tendencies were revived and aggressive and libidinal tendencies toward the father were combined. This process was vastly intensified by intimate physical contact with the mother and continued violent punishment by the father. The enormous sadism resulting from this situation could find expression only in the form of masochism, turned against the self. Thus we get the impression that the patient's sadism resulted primarily from orality, which may have been primarily constitutional, and which may have been increased by experience. Reaction to his brutal upbringing furthered the patient's sadism. A primary masochistic striving, turned outward only secondarily, could not be ascertained. In this case, Freud's (1905b) original formulation, that the masochistic perversion is an expression of sadism turned upon the self, suffices (p. 158).

The analysis succeeded not only in uncovering these mechanisms, but also in making the patient experience them affectively. Unfortunately, the analysis had to be broken off for external reasons before we had attained palpable therapeutic success. The patient left, deeply shaken, to continue the analysis with a lady colleague. A few weeks after this change, he was able to pass his examinations. I am not in a position to state to what extent he has lost his symptoms and given up his masochistic attitude.

3

A Clinical Contribution to the Understanding of the Paranoid Personality

(1936)

I AM going to report some clinical material gathered during the analysis of a psychosis. This material and some conclusions we can draw from it do not so much add anything essentially new to our knowledge of psychoses, as they confirm the discoveries with regard to paranoia made by Freud (1911, 1914, 1924a, 1924b), Tausk (1919), and, above all, Abraham (1924). The fact that in addition to the above-mentioned publications, there exists, at least in the German literature, only one work by E. Bibring (1929) dealing with the problem of paranoia, which contributes clinical material in support of Abraham's statements, appears to me to make my observations worthy of reporting.

Abraham (1924), referring to the theories of Stärcke (1919) and Ophuijsen (1920) concerning the scybalum nature of the persecutor, observes:

Translated by Eva Kessler from *Internationale Zeitschrift für Psychoanalyse*, 22:315–337.

When the paranoiac has lost his libidinal relations to his object and to all objects in general, he tries as far as he can to compensate for the loss which to him amounts to a destruction of the world. As we know since Freud's analysis of the case of Schreber, he proceeds to reconstruct his lost object. We may now add that in this process of reconstruction the paranoiac incorporates a part of his object. In doing this he undergoes much the same fate as the melancholiac who has introjected the whole of his object by a process of incorporation. Nor can he, either, escape his ambivalence in this way. Like the melancholiac, therefore, he tries to get rid of that part of his object which he has taken into himself. And on the psychosexual developmental level on which he is this can only be an anal process for him. To a paranoiac, therefore, the love-object is equivalent to faeces which he cannot get rid of [p. 489].

A case published by Bibring (1929), clearly identifies the persecutor with the patient's image, projected into the outer world, of his own buttocks. In the case which I examined, it was the scybalum itself that assumed the role of the persecutor.

The material in the above-mentioned cases was gathered from psychiatric observations. In the case at hand, extraordinarily favorable circumstances made possible analytic insight into the structure and genesis which is usually precluded either by narcissistic blockage or by disintegration of the personality.

Maybe there is still another direct approach to the archaic world which finds expression in psychosis. It is revealed to us by the games and fantasies of infants, but in language which is hard to understand at first. Through interpretation, we have to translate it into the language of adults. In doing this we run the risk of making mistakes in our translation, i.e., we might project the familiar, differentiated contents of our thinking into the child's diffuse world of thinking. Reading the publications of the English school of child analysis, one frequently cannot dismiss the impression that such mistakes of translation did indeed occur.

What, in my opinion, makes the present material valuable is the formal fact that these deepest layers, which we are used to reconstructing by complicated interpretation from scanty, distorted residues, are in my case quite on the surface. They are clearly formulated, so that we need not rely on our more or less correct understanding and on our art of interpretation. Well organized ego parts next to unequivocally psychotic symptoms, deepest ego and libido regression next to good intelligence and ready cooperation produce a remarkable situation: the patient talks about the impressions, the thoughts, the fantasies of the second year of his life just as consciously and naturally as about the happenings of the day before. Not being able to give a very detailed report, I cannot even approximately convey the uncanny impression which such utterances of the patient generate.

The patient is a 20-year-old schizophrenic whom I have been analyzing for two years. At the age of 16, he went through a schizophrenic episode following a trauma, a bite by a dog. It began with a severe attack of anxiety in the waiting room of the Pasteur Institute, where he was going to be vaccinated against Lyssa. At that time, he had the feeling that the configurations of the miserable needy people, waiting with him to be vaccinated, "were overflowing into him." From then on he felt his own person and also the outer world changed in an awful way. The delusion of "assuming another person's configuration" remained his central symptom until it was resolved in the course of the analysis. It became necessary to commit him to an institution for several months. Later on, he quieted down a little; periods of delusions about changes in the world were followed by periods of more normal reality orientation. In the latter periods he was well organized, accessible, clear, but obsessed by manifold compulsions and by a tendency to brood excessively. Outwardly, he gradually achieved an appreciable degree of dissimulation. He was able to graduate from high school and is now attending the university. The first impression is that of a nice, friendly boy, but, after some time, one notices his excessive and unnatural readiness to agree with his interlocutor; one observes the empty, exaggerated surrender in his smile and that, despite his friendliness, he is quite inaccessible and rigid. He approaches people for only a short time, is almost completely isolated, and remains lonely with his fantasies. Furthermore, until recently, there always were periods full of wild and uncontrolled aggression.

He is very intelligent, but that does not keep him from being, at the same time, quite involved in magic thinking. For example, the telephone rings during his analytic session, whereupon he shouts at me: "Of course you did that on purpose in order to disturb me!" Intellectually he knows perfectly well that I cannot possibly have caused the telephone call. But these two convictions have nothing to do with each other. They exist side by side in a most peculiar way, without influencing each other.

His pregenital instinctual aims and anxieties are completely conscious, and he expresses them without inhibition. The fact that they are unrealizable, impossible, inhuman, does not preclude them. Yet he does not feel that these ideas are fantasies, are ego-alien; he views them as plain, fully accepted reality. Some examples: he says, "I would like to tear a person into small pieces, then dress these, mix the whole thing, and devour the pap." Or, "I would like to live like a wild animal, urinating and leaving my excrements wherever it happens, wallow in it if I please." "I walk around among people and things whom I want to eat. That is why I am so lonely." "Give me something, give me something quick, I have to have something, I want to eat your genitals, your breast. Why should I have nothing at all, and you keep all the sexuality for yourself?" Before the beginning of the summer vacation, he said, "I must quickly give you something of myself to eat in order to prevent you from leaving. One has to give a person a piece of one's breast in order to be loved."

These examples might provide an approximate picture of the patient's drive structure and of his conduct. I shall now proceed to a report on his central symptom, the "assuming of another configuration."

Sometimes he has a perfectly normal picture of the world; but, all of a sudden, the person with whom he is talking turns into a terrible monster. For example: "There are feces in the wrinkles of his face; the eyes are gushing out of their sockets; he is as thin as a skeleton, as a mummy; he is entirely an ill-smelling mass." The changes simultaneously taking place in the patient's personality are exactly the same. The figure of the horrible object diffuses into him. "I have been damaged forever. I am completely putrefied; my teeth have all rotted away; my face looks like raw meat, like nothing but scars after an operation, like one single giant scar," etc. When I object that there is no truth in all this, that he can look into the mirror and convince himself of the incorrectness of his statements, he simply shrugs his shoulders. He knows it still is so. The contents of his statements are not always the same, but there are always delusions of being damaged with no possibility of correction. He is castrated, as a whole, a female, a male genital, a dead body and, in the last analysis, always a piece of feces.

He has worked out a series of defensive measures against these awful happenings, which require all his strength. They consist in a magic undoing of the injury. Thus he frantically tries to imagine that he is exceedingly tall, intelligent, powerful; or he attempts to feel like an admired object in the outer world, assuming the configuration of the admired object. The attempt to enhance his own ego by exerting himself is matched by that of enhancing the objects, to see in them heroic persons, geniuses, perfect human beings. But the defensive nature of his effort to desexualize the relation to the object comes out clearly in that he cannot keep up this attitude for any length of time. After a short while, the enhanced objects turn back into hideous monsters. Let me give only this very sketchy report on the symptoms.

What are the situations causing the delusional change in the objects? We understand that, as soon as the approach to an object leads to libidinal excitement, the world of the adult collapses suddenly, and reality testing ceases. Ego and id regress to an archaic level. What is the nature of the drives that are so disastrous to the patient? In the course of the analysis, we were able to discover several overlapping attitudes toward objects: a defensive, oral-anal-sadistic one, a warded off passive-homosexual trend also based on pregenital mother relations; and, late in the analysis, a genital-heterosexual wish that was more deeply repressed than the others and threatened by the most intense fear of castration. But I will not deal with this last aim in my report because it became tangible only after the symptom of taking on a configuration had been completely resolved.

We had to overcome the most serious resistance, expressed in wild aggression, before discovering the patient's homosexual fantasies in the course of the analysis. In the beginning, he had the fantasy of genital intercourse with the father, their phalluses touching, the stronger phallus of the father destroying the boy's weaker one; or of anal intercourse, where the scybalum as the father's phallus would enter the patient causing a dreadful bleeding wound. In order to escape castration, the wish for passive surrender was changed into strongly sadistic wishes for incorporation. The father's scybalum, respectively the father's penis, was to be devoured and destroyed. Before and at the beginning of the analysis, these oral-sadistic and coprophagic wishes dominated the manifest features of the patient's illness. I have previously given examples of the patient's openly cannibalistic and coprophagic fantasies.

Connected with this regressive debasement of the instinctual aim, we find withdrawal of libido from the real object and ego regression which make it possible for the patient to equate the object's organ with the entire object. This constitutes the essence of the fantasy that the object is horribly changed or, as the patient calls it, the fantasy of "stool-man." The monster is the father, but he bears the characteristics of the scybalum.

Abraham (1924) taught us to understand how this equating, or rather this fusion of the object and the part of the body, occurs: it represents an introjection of the desired organ in place of the lost object and a re-projection of the introject into the outer world. The patient experiences this remarkable process of the bodily passage of the object with an amazing consciousness.

As soon as he cathects an object libidinally, the object turns into a ghost. But this ghost does not come into existence in an instant; it has, so to say, a history. It is the final result of a complicated process, of which we witness the last phase. To give but one example out of the wealth of material: one day the patient arrives for his treatment greatly upset and reports:

Today I have been damaged for the rest of my life because I was compelled to talk with my grandma for a prolonged time. She is an emaciated skeleton, a ghost; her intestines are hanging out. I did not want to speak to her, but I had to force myself to be politely sympathetic. It is as if I had to eat her up, one more spoon for mama, one for papa, one more for grandma. I have always felt a disgust for all food, for pap and the like. One must not eat them; talking with grandma is just the same. All of a sudden it changes, and then I have to eat, to devour, and then I like to talk to her, and then I have grandma inside myself, and then I become grandma. Then I am just as ghastly as she is; everybody looks at me the way I formerly looked at grandma. But then I must defend myself; I must push the hideous out of myself, I must fight her within myself.

The mechanism by which the introject is, in turn, ejected from the body is likewise somatically prescribed. It is orally incorporated and anally ejected. But then the scybalum comes back to life; it assumes the features of the just-devoured object, but in a distorted, ugly form. Thus, it is the patient's fault that the objects are so horribly changed, crippled, transformed into feces. He devours them, chews them up, but they "stir around, bustle in his body," as he once said. They "threaten him from inside"; they "infect him with their own defects." He assumes the configuration of the objects. The experience of undergoing a change, which makes him feel forever damaged, is exceedingly unpleasant for him. For this reason he wants to remove the objects from his body again; he wants to get rid of their configuration. Thus, as Abraham points out, it is the negative side of the ambivalence which makes the patient eject the object, and thereby provokes its projection.

The re-ejected objects have turned into feces, into a purulent ill-smelling mass. Besides, they have been crippled; their limbs are missing or are attached in the wrong places; their faces are deformed. These ideas are based on the fantasy that the objects have been chewed, torn into small pieces; they cannot be put together again. The monstrosity of the stool man corresponds to the monstrosity of the bite. [1]

Like his grandmother, all sick and somehow ugly people excite the patient sexually. Exaggerating their defects gigantically, he feels himself to be the cause of their physical defects. All these people have gone through his body; they are his products; they were produced by the fusion of the external object with the projected idea of his own scybalum. But the objects he has crippled threaten him with their vengeance. They persecute him; they want to do to him what he did to them; they want to murder him, to devour him; they want to turn him into feces.

Fear of the revenge of the ill-treated objects compels him to reincorporate the already transformed objects. Thus the shape of the injured object diffuses into him anew, and the punishment has been inflicted. This compels him once more to renew his projection—and thus the vicious circle goes on ad infinitum. But there is another side to this process; it has, simultaneously, a punishing and a gratifying character. The stool represents the incorporated object for the patient. The sensation he feels during its alleged entry is exceedingly pleasurable for him and, he believes, caused by the object. Once the stool is ejected and he is thereby separated from the object, the aim of his sexual desire is to unite with the stool-persecutor anally or orally, to reincorporate him anally, just as he had wanted to incor-

---

[1] The genesis of such fantasies of dismembering by chewing has been stressed by Malcove (1933). According to the theory of various English authors, they are the main motives for the most diverse efforts of restitution.

porate his father's phallus. Thereupon, defense turns love into abhorrence, sexual longing into a feeling of persecution. The final overpowering, i.e., reunion with the persecutor, is horribly feared, yet reenacted repeatedly.

Corresponding to the depth of his regression, the patient's instinctual aims are polymorphous-perverse. Besides his wish for anal surrender to the father, we also find the homosexual tendency, in debased form, as the wish to be devoured and turned into scybalum. Thus complete annihilation and deepest gratification are identical. Fear and gratification are not to be separated; active and passive instinctual aims continally alternate with each other. The configuration shifts from the object to the patient, then again from the patient to the object without any distinguishable sharp boundaries in this chaotic mix-up of self and object.

Let me give a short summary: As soon as the patient's sexual excitement reaches a certain pitch, his fear of castration compels him to ward it off. Instead of manifesting an object-libidinal, genital, or anal tendency, he regresses to tendencies of incorporation which are mainly aimed at the phallus or the scybalum of the father. When this happens the real object ceases to exist, the stool-persecutor represents an already damaged, threatening, projected introject which he strives to destroy and to regain simultaneously by a renewed act of incorporation.

At this point, I think I should report some facts of the patient's infantile life history. I shall confine myself to facts which are essential for the understanding of the case.

We were able to uncover a series of traumatic situations of danger and frustration which explained so severe an oral-sadistic fixation. Two serious illnesses toward the end of the second year had produced a tremendous fear of losing the contents of his body; this, in all probability, made a normal overcoming of the orality impossible. Whooping-cough accompanied by steady vomiting, lasting several weeks, and a severe intestinal infection, accompanied by painful and uncontrollable diarrhea, had made the "outflowing" a terrible, threatening danger to his life. He considered his body to be an empty bag filled with blood, feces or sweets; the slightest injury could lead to everything running out.

Besides his fear that the contents of his body would flow out, the patient also had an intense fear of starving. He imagined that starvation would take the form of drying-up, shrivelling, being turned into feces. The fear of starving was probably a consequence of the first severe oral trauma he had suffered. His mother did not have enough milk. For two months he starved, not getting enough milk from his mother's breast. Furthermore, in later times, his mother was frequently absent. This meant object loss in addition to oral frustration. At all events, his mother continued in the role of the frustrating person. He was conscious of and did not repress the reproach that, "there was never enough to eat; she always grabbed it from me and ate it all." I must emphasize that there never was such a thing as real need in the patient's life.

We cannot be sure whether this first trauma or the later illnesses were the decisive factors. Anyhow, the child remained fixated at the oral-sadistic stage. Food and objects could never be held apart; they were equated. Solid food was considered to be parts of other people's bodies; mushy food was considered to be feces or vomitus. A severe eating disturbance was bound to develop in order to rationalize the fear of starvation and the never repressed, severe fear of being devoured.

A little later, strict training in cleanliness provided the foundation for the patient's anal fixation. Severe punishment for soiling caused constipation, which his governess fought with excessively frequent enemas, to which he reacted with intense fear of bursting.

When he was three and a half years old, a tonsillectomy was performed on the child under narcosis. The tonsils, that is, something "edible," had been "torn out of his body." This brought the fear, which by now was also related to the genitals, to its culmination. The extension of the fear to the genitals was due chiefly to the fact that, corresponding to the patient's age, there was a physiological heightening of his genital excitability. He had genital sensations and probably had heterosexual fantasies while masturbating. On the other hand, these fears were also caused by the sight of the female genitals which he considered to be an anal wound, through which the woman lost her blood and her excrements. At that time, he already felt threatened by the evacuation of the excrements.

During this period, the child experienced the beginning of a positive oedipal relation despite all his fears. But an important change in his object environment took place; the boy's father returned from the war. The child turned to him, fully ready for love. But, inhibited by severe genital and pregenital fears, he did not achieve masculine identification with his father. Instead, he started competing passively with his mother for his father's love. It so happened that, at this time, he listened stealthily to a primal scene which he perceived as an oral- and anal-sadistic act. That was the decisive fixating experience. The father tears off the mother's imagined penis and devours it. With his penis, he then pierces a hole in the mother and inflicts upon her the anal wound which the child, horrified, had had the opportunity to observe earlier. Thereupon the stool comes out, covers the mother's body until she is completely turned into feces and is devoured by the father. Hence, surrender to the father was terribly dangerous: it meant castration, it meant being turned into feces, it meant being devoured.

Under the impact of this experience the child indulged in copious pregenital activity. He repeatedly committed coprophagic acts and developed a strange form of anal masturbation wherein the penis was smeared with feces and thus converted into stool. In this way, his own scybalum became a substitute for the father and united with him in a regressive, nonthreatthing precious. Thus he took over the strength of the father and united with him in a regressive, nonthreaening way. [2] But this sexual activity was blocked by a prohibition of the beloved governess: feces are poisonous; the penis would rot away; he would fall ill.

Thereupon, he gave up masturbating, to which he reacted with the following anxiety dream:

He defecates lying in bed, and takes the feces in his hand in order to eat them. At this moment, the

---

[2] Nunberg (1938) has called attention to the genesis of a certain form of homosexuality resulting from incorporative tendencies.

scybalum turns into a horrible man, whose body consists of excrement. The limbs are missing; there is only a torso and a head with top hat; a leg grows out of the middle of the chest. Something terrible is happening.

As an aftermath of that dream he became intensely afraid of his own stool. It would come to life as it did in the dream, and turn into a terrible persecutor. Defecation turned into a hostile act against the "stool-man" as he called the ghost. By closing the anus during defecation, he decapitated the stool-man; by flushing the toilet, he annihilated the adversary whose terrible revenge he feared.

Presently, the fear extended to the genital which, equated with the stool, he now perceived as an autonomous living being rather than as a part of himself, as a "genital-man" who was capable of separating from his body at any time. The stool-man, by the way, possessed distinct characteristics of the genital: no limbs, a top hat on his head, a single leg sticking out of the chest.

From then on, the child's condition deteriorated steadily. For many months, he hallucinated extensively, mainly at night, that the killed stool-man returned as a ghost to threaten him.

This childhood psychosis subsided gradually, but it left behind serious defects. Object relations remained disturbed, the ability to play and learn was strongly diminished, and superego formation was impaired. Repression remained inadequate, and pregenital instinctual breakthroughs were not uncommon. To this were added considerable contradictions in the boy's education: on the one hand, the father's strict demands, on the other hand, far-reaching favors, even seductiveness on the part of the mother during the prepubertal and pubertal periods. After the boy's exhausting struggle to break the habit of masturbation at the beginning of adolescence, the psychosis broke out again, in the same form as in his childhood: the ghostly persecutor of his adult life is identical with the stool-man of his childhood. The mechanisms of the childhood psychosis are the same as those of his adult life.

The psychotic episodes in childhood and adolescence have the same structure. In both instances severe castration anxiety brings about regression to an anal-passive fixation to the father. But the regressive process does not stop here: a further sliding back into archaic, oral- and anal-sadistic phases ensues. This regression is far-reaching and affects ego and id simultaneously and extensively, with drastic consequences. Together with the efforts at self-healing, which we will discuss later, it leads to a state which we designate as psychosis. Reality is not completely lost in the process. Object relations are not given up completely, but, in accordance with the regression, they become wishes for incorporation, predominantly destructive—and thereby reality is transformed into something frightening which cannot be mastered. The world consists of nothing but objects that can be devoured and objects that devour. The borders between self and outer world are fluid. What is frightening in the inner self suddenly becomes menacing from without. The horrible qualities of the object are perceived in one's own body. The talion principle reigns: "an eye for an eye, a tooth for a tooth." No reasoning, no insight into causal connections, no protection by a loving object can help the patient to cope with this frightful world.

But even the primitive ego does not surrender without putting up a defense. It is not a matter of the ego being simply overwhelmed by the id; rather, the ego takes up the defense against the instinctual drives with primitive means in an attempt to avoid anxiety. But the primitive ego has at its disposal only primitive means of defense—means clearly derived from the id. Indeed, the regression goes back to a point where separation of the ego and the id has not been completed.

While the picture was made more complicated by these different forms of defense, they afforded an opportunity for exceptionally close study of the peculiarities of so primitive an ego. That is why I would like to recapitulate these mechanisms in some more detail.

The situation from which the entire process originated was the fear of the real objects. It returned, in a changed form, as fear of the persecutor. If he introjects the objects, the patient escapes this fear. Thus to assume the configuration of another serves as a defense. Having become the other person, he is now just as formidable as the object and need not be afraid anymore. Anna Freud (1936) described this mechanism as identification with the aggressor. Similar attitudes are known to us in the magic of the primitives.

The unpleasurable hypochondriacal sensations which the patient experiences when he feels overcome by the configuration of the object indicate that the damage has been done, that the castration has occurred. This, it seems, is easier to tolerate than the fear of impending castration. Moreover, when he becomes the other person, the object no longer exists for him in the outer world, the object world ceases to exist, and the patient suffers a narcissistic regression. He tries to remain in these narcissistic states, in which, as he puts it, "everything has already jelled." This narcissistic-hypochondriacal attitude constitutes his basic mood which is, from time to time, interrupted by delusional phases wherein the hypochondriacal feelings are usually present in abortive form. He claims: "I have been injured for all time." His efforts at restoration govern the manifest clinical picture entirely. Their true aim is to establish a feeling of omnipotence.

Narcissistic states in psychotics frequently have a megalomanic, exceedingly pleasurable character, but only when the object libido, falling back on the ego, is used to enhance primary narcissism. In our case, no such fusion was achieved. On the contrary, the conflict between self and object continues intrapsychically. This is expressed in hypochondriacal unpleasure. The conflict between self and object is repeated in the conflict between ego and superego. This corresponds to the fact that the patient's upbringing forced him to reject anality, so that the transformation into scybalum was insufferable for him. Stärcke (1919) also held that the reversal of the libido direction in paranoia arises from the negative attitude toward anality forced upon the patient by the environment. There are short periods in our patient's life when, apparently under the influence of powerful sexual excitement, the ego is flooded by the drives; in these moments he experiences uninhibited autoerotic eruptions and can enjoy infantile anal feelings of grandeur free of conflict. Thus, on a Sunday, when he had no analytic session, he wrote a special delivery letter containing nothing but the following words: "Is one not bound to be a genius when one can produce pieces of scybalum as big as I can?"

But the fear of the avenging objects is too great and the patient's superego is too strong to let such states last for any length of time. Instead of anal delusions of grandeur, the patient experiences delusions of inferiority. Instead of autoerotic eruption, a damming-up of organ libido sets in which the patient experiences as physical transformation.

Tausk (1919) has set up a scale for various gradations of these organ-libidinal feelings of change; (1) a plain feeling of change; (2) on further intensification, a feeling of alienation where, as a defense, the dammed-up organ is no longer perceived. Finally, the intolerable tension compels the patient to project, and here again, two stages are distinguishable. In the first, the organic sensations are caused by an external object; in the second, the entire sick organ is projected into the outer world and perceived as an apparatus of influence. Bibring (1929) puts it more generally when he states that projection of the intolerably, dammed-up erogenous zones and their fusion with the object takes place. In the case of our patient projection of the feces led to the formation of the man of scybalum.

Bibring (1929) believes we should insert one more step into this series, namely the organ megalomania which he places before the alienation. In our case, we can observe the formation of this organ megalomania in *statu nascendi*. For a long time the patient strove to "ennoble" certain parts of his body—to "vault" the back of his head, to "enlarge" his brain, to "raise" his forehead, and so on. Undoubtedly, all this represents an interpretation of body sensations in an ego-syntonic sense, based on a damming up of narcissistic organ libido. In other words, there is active, voluntary creation of delusions of organ grandeur. Analysis of the psychic contents of this organ megalomania led back to pregenital fears which had been activated by regression of the ego and of the instinctual drives. The underlying fear of castration was the basis for his fear of loss of body contents. To be deserted, to be destroyed, to be killed, to be castrated, to be emptied, not to have enough food—all these fears were summarized in the one fantasy of being transformed into feces. Feces represented the destroyed matter, the formless, the poisonous. The decisive castration threat of his childhood had been that feces must not touch the genital, or else the genital would rot away.

It had been, at the same time, an important instinctual aim to reincorporate the stool, and with it the lost object and the lost bodily substance. That led repeatedly to coprophagic acts, and to the strange anal masturbation. Rubbing excrement on the genital was a weak substitute for eating excrement. Lewin (1930) pointed to the fact that the rubbing in of excrement originally had the oral meaning of percutaneous incorporation. In this the genital stood for the entire body.

But it is in vain to try and overcome the loss of object and substance by coprophagic actions, for it is precisely the scybalum which is the main object of fear, the poison. Attempts at restoration can, therefore, succeed only if they are characterized by a special exclusion of and defense against anality and by an accentuation of genitality. The organs are being "ennobled," enlarged, embellished.

Thus, to have a large brain means, in a displacement from bottom to top, that the genital does not consist of feces, but it is beautiful and undamaged. In this way the most important demand of the superego is fulfilled and, simultaneously, the oral loss is restored; there is no longer any need to be afraid. The conflict with the object occasioned by the oral refusal, and expressed by the anal threat, has been resolved. Ego and superego and ego and object have been reconciled. Thus hallucinated gratification of the central id tendencies, of the wishes for incorporation, has taken place. Hence, a single bodily sensation expresses the solution of a whole series of conflicts which existed originally between ego and object and now take place within the ego. The wealth of conflict solutions experienced in the organ sensation, seems to explain why the sensation is interpreted as a feeling of grandeur.

The "ennoblement" of the body, by the way, is only one of many forms of restitution. In accordance with ego regression, they all have a magic quality. The body is made intact again by the incorporation of select food, by the retention of stool, by the possession of penislike objects, etc. Most of these mechanisms are based on the archaic belief that one is what one eats. Transferred to the mental sphere this means, one is what one thinks. That is why the patient attempts to cultivate exalted thoughts in himself, to feel like a genius, to think uninterruptedly, etc. The patient's good intellectual development springs from these sources. Hence we see that psychical as well as material things matter to the patient, but for him they are all concrete. Thoughts, words, noises, images—all are things. If he hears a noise—and he is especially afraid of noises because he connects them with the primal scene—sharp objects penetrate him. If one speaks to him, one feeds him words. When he speaks, he makes you a present of his words. If he reads a lot, his head fills up, etc.

But the most remarkable substance—and here I return to the organ megalomania—is the libido. The libidinous excitement too is perceived as a substance within the body. When he "vaults the back of his head," he has a sensation of fullness in his head. When he is sexually excited, he feels the excitement as precious matter in his body. In his words:

> I was always so tired because my entire body was tense; I wanted that tension. I did not want it transmitted to the genital because it might escape from there; it might run out with the ejaculation; the entire sexuality might get lost. I have always frantically endeavoured to increase the sexuality, to keep it in suspense. That exertion was so great I had to withdraw from the outer world.

Thus he feels the excitement in his body as a precious possession which is being threatened. That is why, as he puts it, he wants to have his sexuality in safe keeping, just as he likes to keep four fountain pens in the closet at home in case he loses one. In the same way, he would like to store "his sexuality" with an object of the outer world in order to keep it safe.

To me the feeling that the excitement is something substantial seems to be the verbal expression of an alienation of the organs which has already taken place or which is threatening to take place. The alienated organ becomes lost to the patient in the same way as the stool, the penis, the contents of the body, can become lost. Desperate clinging to the organ megalomania is intended as a protective measure against alienation. But it may well be that in our case, like in that described by Tausk (1919), too great an increase in the damming up impels the patient to project. The patient describes this experience in the following words:

> I throw my excitement upon somebody else; I elevate somebody else with my sexuality. Then it will be safe; then nothing can happen to it. A woman, a movie star, a teacher, all that appears to be so magnificent, so fabulous, so glorious, shining like brass, like God himself.

Thus the feeling of grandeur which he can produce in himself, but which, as we will see later, he cannot retain, is projected upon an object. That much we have understood. The longed-for grandeur means not to consist of feces, to be an intact genital, i.e., to be superego. The projection of libido transforms the object into this desired genital. The object becomes large and desirable, while the patient himself is impoverished. "Within me and around me everything is dark. But outside, far outside, it is all light. I am like a poor beggar. My richness, my excitement, my genital, all that is outside. I am empty."

The parallelism of this process of projection to the one I described first—the transformation of the objects into horrible ghosts—is evident. Just as the delusion of inferiority is the opposite of the megalomania, so the exalted objects are, so to say, persecutors with reverse signs. While he experiences the ejection of the "stool-man" undistorted as defecation and, at the same time, as a hostile act, the somatic nature of the process of projection is no longer clear here; rather, it is distorted, disembodied as a feeling of exaltation perceived as a gift to the object. Here, the stool is projected as a product of sadistic destruction and, at the same time, as the main erotogenic zone; there, it is the intact genital, elevated to the superego. The frankly sexual nature of the persecutor is clear: the terrible objects are simultaneously the sexually exciting ones. But the patient is attached in desexualized subservient admiration to the forcibly exalted objects; he wants to be loved by them. In a way characteristic for him, he tries to assume the configuration of the exalted objects, to become their like. He is subservient to them, tries to think their thoughts, to use their words, but achieves only an empty parroting. He clings passionately to the fantasy of the exalted objects; not for a moment does he want to think of anything else lest the configuration of the object be lost.

Thinking gives him magical power: as long as he thinks of something he is identical with what he thinks of. This represents a desexualized act of devouring: to assume the configuration of the object is desexualized incorporation; thinking is a mitigated form of devouring. To be sure, thoughts for him are also substances; thoughts make the brain grow. If he were to stop thinking of the object for only a moment, it would be lost; something he wished to devour would escape him, and he would fail to incorporate the wonderful object.

If he achieves reincorporation of the object, if he can get back the borrowed libidinal cathexis, as it were, a strong feeling of omnipotence sets in which is linked with intense pleasure. At such times, he feels he is the richest man in the world, he is an unheard-of genius, he is a great statesman, etc. But if he fails, the configuration of the ghost diffuses into him again.

This feeling of grandeur is very labile; it takes tremendous strain and effort to hold on to it. The patient must constantly feel like the exalted object; if he slackens in this concentration for only a moment, the configuration of the hero abandons him, and the hero turns forthwith back into the ghost. Out of the wrinkles of the face he admired a moment ago, feces now stare at him. The ideal figure which, on the one hand, carries phallic traits, and, on the other hand, is felt to be asexual, has again turned into a grossly sexual stool-man. And thus the gruesome circuit starts anew.

The patient's efforts to desexualize the relation to the objects fails all the time. The break-down of the feeling of grandeur and the retransformation of the object into feces signifies an instinctual drive breakthrough. The fact that the patient tries frantically to cling to the noble feelings indicates in itself that constant anticathexis is taking place: he has to think of the good object without interruption. If it is correct to assume that thinking is a diminished form of devouring, then there must be reason for being afraid of the retransformation of this sublimated method of incorporation into the unsublimated, destructive, oral-sadistic method. And in fact, omnipotence is threatened mainly by the breakthrough of sexual thoughts and excitement. The sight of some defective objects, or even the thought of them suffices to activate at once an intensive sadistic wish for devouring and destroying. Everything defective disturbs omnipotence because it immediately triggers the wish to destroy completely what is already half destroyed by devouring.

One example: the patient sits in a movie theater; he feels enthusiasm for the hero, for the beautiful woman. But he is not able to see the whole screen because it is, in small part, concealed by the head of a person sitting in front of him. He had just been feeling happy as the hero of the movie, but now he is injured forever. A picture which cannot be seen in its entirety is defective for him. This gives rise to his cravings for destruction. He fantasies that he tears the limbs out of the movie-hero's body and devours them piece by piece.

In a new projection, he constantly blames the people of his environment for having damaged him, for having disturbed his omnipotence. "How would it have been if my mother had not entered my room today! In that case I would have been an unheard-of genius, a famous man. But now she has injured me forever." It is mainly the mother whom he thus blames, as if he wanted to say: "My mother is to blame for all my defects, for the defects of my body as well as for the defects of all things. She did not give me enough nourishment, she tears out of my body what I have incorporated, she thus compels me to get back by force what I was robbed of."

For a better understanding of this labile feeling of grandeur I would like to insert a short report on the infantile antecedents of these processes. The infantile image of the exalted object was the fantasy of God. He imagined him as a gigantic tumbler—that is, as a gigantic phallus. The tumbler had been his favorite toy. The fact that it would always rise again transformed it into an indestructible penis capable of steadily repeated erections. And thus it became a talisman against the child's fear. Some time later he fantasied God in a splendid wide coat, like a priest. But if one tore the coat off God, a horrible, naked, dirty, sexual devil appeared. Therein we see the same debasement of the desexualized object as he produced later on. The shape of the divine tumbler is round and smooth like a phallus, but the naked devil with limbs, tail and horns, etc., has "furrows." They are the imprints of the intestinal inlets on the stool. This means that God turns back into the stool-man. The facial wrinkles smeared with feces also mark the retransformation of the hero into the persecutor.

The God-Phallus is identical with the genital-man, with his penis which separates from him, becoming independent. Hence it is the genital parallel fantasy to the stool-man. The almighty divine tumbler thus is simultaneously the boy's own little penis. This penis no longer belongs to his body. The father has robbed him of it, has incorporated it, and has thus assumed the configuration of the penis. He is fused with the penis. Thereafter, when the boy masturbates, he feels he is robbing the genital-man-father of the pleasure, for his lust belongs to the other person, just as his penis does. In this, I think, we can see one of the sources of the peculiar idea that the excitement is of substantial nature.

The God of his childhood as well as the exalted objects of the adult represent objects which have incorporated the genital; and this genital is equated with the patient's entire body. In his article, "The body as Phallus," Lewin (1933) has pointed out that this equation of penis and body, based on an earlier act of incorporation, has the consequence that the wish to penetrate the mother's womb with the phallus is transformed into the wish to return to the mother's womb with the entire body. This shows itself in the fear, i.e., the wish to be eaten.

The exalted objects and God thus represent the mother, into whose womb the child has returned. That is the decisive point. The objects with whom the patient is reunited are desexualized, or better, they are no longer sadistic, no longer frustrating objects. If the object loves him, being devoured, being fused with the object, is a longed-for instinctual aim. But if the object is a threatening, a punishing one, being devoured represents a horrible danger, and the wish to be incorporated turns into fear.

Let me clarify this by means of a little example: The attachment the patient had developed to me in the course of the analysis is a deep, oral mother attachment. He cannot exist without me. Whenever I have to interrupt the analysis for a only a few days, he suffers deep feelings of being deserted and anxiety. He feels as if he were quite alone in a dark room, in a cave whose walls· are made of excrement. He drowns in excrement. By deserting him, I have turned into a wicked, sadistic mother; the reunion does not bring happiness, but danger. Sometimes he would say that only my presence could protect him from being devoured by a terrible giant (= the stool-man). Being devoured by the ghost means: to be chewed up, to be crushed, to be turned into excrement. Being devoured by the father is a debased substitute for the homosexual fantasy, but this too represents an awful, horrible reincorporation which rouses the most gruesome anxiety in him.

But when his relation to me was friendly he would say, "I would like to be entirely inside you; then you will always be with me and love me. I would like to drink milk from you so that I would have everything. Please, oh please devour me. You will swallow me up entirely, I shall be inside. And then nothing can happen to me ever again."

In his periods of omnipotence he sees this fantasy fulfilled. By a nondestructive mechanism, he has been reunited with the lost object, which is no longer awful and hostile; on the contrary, it loves him, it gives him everything he desires, he need not be in fear anymore. Everything that had been taken away from him, everything he had projected, has returned to him. There is no conflict anymore between ego and object, between ego and superego. He has become identical with both. It seems that the almighty God in the outer world, who had gained his omnipotence by incorporating the child's organs, represents a reversal of the original situation when the child was omnipotent, because it had incorporated the organs of the object and thus had become identical with it. It seems quite possible to me that this is the typical way for the child to form the idea of the omnipotence of adults.

Our patient does not succeed in remerging with the object. He cannot maintain the state of omnipotence. He is fixated at the oral-sadistic level whose instinctual aim is the incorporation of a destroyed object. In order to save himself from all distress and anxiety, he tries to regress to the level which is one step deeper, to the oral-sadistic level, which is relatively unperturbed by frustrations. He fails in this regression presumably because the frustrations generating the fixation are too intense. How he experiences the failure of the regression is described above. Again and again, he feels disturbed in his strivings by the outer world; he feels "damaged by the mother." Again and again, "defects" remind him of the frustrations he had suffered and provoke his own oral sadism.

At one time, when he experienced great gratification in reality, he succeeded in this regression and, simultaneously, in the restoration and reconciliation: At the age of sixteen he was seduced by a much older woman and experienced his first coitus. The woman appeared to him to be wonderful and magnificent; in her arms he felt completely at one with her. She was he and he was she. The separation between self and object was annulled; there was no danger, no destruction. He was reunited with his mother.

But this love object was suddenly snatched from him by interference from the outer world. He reacted to the loss as if the whole world had been destroyed. Suddenly, not only the people, but the things too were changed, everything became alien. He did not understand anything. Everything made him wonder that the single parts made up a whole and just this whole. To him a human being consisted only of single parts, of blood, muscles, and atoms. A compulsion to think set in: He had to make things "conscious to himself," i.e., everything he perceived had to be named—"This is a flower; this is a table." The entire world had fallen to pieces because he had chewed it up, had dismembered it. By rendering them conscious, by conceiving things "whole and intact," he tried to restore the world's completeness.

This making-chewed-up-things-whole-again plays a major role in the theories of the English school. It is not only held as the basis of numerous symptoms, but also as an impulse for the most complicated sublimations. The increased ability to think which the patient retained after this period must be considered one of his few successes at sublimation.

Dismemberment of the whole world seems to reproduce his original reaction to the primary loss of the object and the oral disappointment. He had early fantasies that the entire world was edible but, at the same time, consisted of feces. He had lost the object and oral pleasure too early and, therefore, he had destroyed the whole world.

Had the patient succeeded in regressing to deeper, nonsadistic stages, the differentiation between self and object would probably have been eliminated permanently, and the patient would have sunk into a permanent narcissistic state. The end of the world, as we know it from classic paranoia, for example, the Schreber case (Freud, 1911), is indeed a regression to still deeper, probably to a stage of complete object loss. But our patient never reached the point where the world came completely to an end, where the object was permanently lost, where a continuous psychosis broke out. Presumably, the reason for this is that there was no sudden outbreak of psychosis in a personality which, until then, had been intact, but that there was developmental arrest of the ego and of the instinctual drives. The fact that the patient had at his disposal a mechanism which we might call flight into reality was perhaps one of the decisive factors that prevented the formation of a continuous delusional system. The second level of projection described by Tausk (1919), wherein the entire organ is projected on the outside object, corresponds to the patient's transformation of objects into feces. He can protect himself although against these by way of new incorporations alone, he can use another method against the persecutor of the first kind, that is, against the objects of the outer world which disturb his omnipotence: he reproaches and blames the real object for his illness, is defiant, and plays the savage man by identifying with the attacking persecutor. This leads to uninhibited outbursts against the outer world, to polymorphous-perverse breakthroughs, and to coprophagic orgies experienced with immense gratification, free of guilt feelings and conflict. This is followed by complete relaxation like at the end of satisfactory coitus. Surprisingly after such an excess, a sudden change takes place in the patient's relations to reality. Several times, I observed that periods of especially disquieting world and ego transformation, which made me fear he would sink into a complete catatonic state, culminated in a pregenital breakthrough which quite suddenly restored a relatively normal relation to reality.

The perverse instinctual act, or a somehow adequate autoerotic substitute activity, exercised in reality, thus prevents the narcissistic damming up of libido and, beyond that, the delusional transformation of ego and object. This transformation consists in warding off the wish for incorporation, which until then had been alive as such, and in withdrawal of libido from the real objects. The magic incorporation of the objects replaces real devouring. Thus the delusional construction has the same function as the neurotic symptom. It serves the defense and the gratification simultaneously. By transposing the instinctual activity into fantasy, it acts as a defense; in its content, it represents an instinctual wish as already fulfilled (the defense fails insofar as fantasy and reality get mixed up again).

Our problem is how to understand the nature of this magic incorporation. It seems to be the result of a deep regressive transformation of the ego. Its most important criteria, put briefly, are: (1) Ego and outer world are no longer distinctly separated. The outer world which brings pleasure belongs to the ego; unpleasurable parts of the ego belong to the outer world. (2) Instead of gratifying his wishes by changing reality, the patient hallucinates the gratification. (3) Causal connection is foregone; primary-process and magic, prelogical thinking are in effect. (4) Therewith the ego lose the ability to test reality; the world is perceived according to the representation of the own ego, and even the patient's instinctual aims are attributed to the outer world. The talion principle reigns; it turns the wish to devour into fear of being devoured. (5) The introjection does not protect against anxiety. The object that had been feared in the outer world is later feared inside his own body. (6) Projection and introjection are the defensive means of the primitive ego.

Ego regression and instinctual regression are but two sides of the same process. It is regression to the time of finding the object, when the differentiation between self and object was first developing, corresponding to the instinctual aim of incorporation, an instinctual aim whose content it is to turn outside into inside. Ego and id are not yet quite separated. Ego mechanisms still clearly show their instinctual drive origin. In the reported circular course between ego and object, between introjection and projection, the origin of this process from devouring and expelling is still perfectly clear.

A further archaic, magic form of defense is the warding off of an instinct by the instinct itself. To overcome the fear of an injured object, this object is completely destroyed. In the last analysis, this is a turn from the passivity to activity: The patient, instead of submitting to castration, turns castrator. Or, he is afraid of turning into feces. As a defense against anxiety, he smears himself with feces. The execution of the fantasy conquers the anxiety.

Not only do we clearly see that the defense mechanisms originate from the instinctual drive but even so exclusive an ego function as perception clearly shows its descent from the instinctual drives. Let me give an example:

Because the analysis had been interrupted for several days, the patient had again got into serious conflict with me. After several days of vehement reproaches, he suddenly started crying, turned to me and said: "I am so afraid, I would like to palpate your face with my hands; it is so strange, only hills and hollows, they do not belong together. I would like to lick it all off, to take it into my mouth; I am sure it tastes like milk." A little later, "I have lost the feeling for the size of things. Everything seems quite small to me, the houses, the trees, the cars. I would like to put all that into my mouth."

It is as though he had regressed to a time when the integrated comprehension of an object as a totality had not yet been attained, when the object was as yet not perceived as a person, but only as diffuse edible matter. Even more, looking at these parts is like sucking them in, taking them in through the eyes. Eyes are a substitute for the mouth. They are not yet the main pathway for the perception of reality; everything still has to be taken into the mouth. The mouth is not only the most important erotogenic zone, it represents the principal means of communication with the outer world. The eyes are only just beginning to contest for this role with the mouth.

This description of the archaic ego does not claim to be complete; these were the features that suggested themselves when I received the material of this case.

Concurrent with many archaic features retained by the ego, superego formation remained defective. Two factors caused the failure of the boy's superego formation: first, the mother's continued seductions made normal resolution of the Oedipus conflict impossible; second, by his passive-homosexual attitude and by his severe pregenital anxieties, the child was pressed into oral-sadistic incorporation of the father instead of identification with him. Instead of internalizing the father's demands, instead of turning him into his ideal, instead of developing according to the father's wishes and thus, simultaneously, winning his love, the introjection remained a coarse sexual coprophagic act. In the course of the normal formation of the superego, parts of the object libido are ordinarily desexualized and incorporated into the ego to serve the cathexis of objects. This did not happen in our case. The act of introjection remained an act of unsublimated gratification. Projected into the outer world as a persecutor, this pseudo superego confronted the boy as a horrible phantom, in no way different from the fears of retaliation which had already haunted the two-year-old boy when he killed little animals; they would then come into his bed at night. These fears of retaliation have their origin in an instinctually determined misunderstanding of the outer world; but, despite their fantastic contents, they pertain to something real and not something "inside." It is preferable, therefore, not to attribute them to the superego as yet.

Besides this pseudo superego, we find genuine superego parts apparently originating from identifications with the governess who had prohibited the patient's coprophagic activities. This relation had been predominantly tender, thus making it possible for the child to effectively internalize the educational demands. The effects of these normal superego parts are evident in the patient's seemingly successful adaptation to reality which I stressed at the beginning. He can be affectionate, kind, ready to help. In the course of the analysis, these traits came more and more to the fore. In spite of occasional instinctual breakthroughs, he is usually reliable and punctual. His strivings to improve conform to a high degree to the demands of society. Although based on narcissistic longing for grandeur, they nevertheless enable him to work, to pass examinations, to enjoy music and good books, etc. Apparently, those parts of the superego which are based on identification with the governess are essentially more resilient. They reach far into the megalomania. To be sure, these various parts of the superego can supersede each other. What was sublimated can easily turn into the archaic. Besides, projections onto objects of the outer world appear very readily. Toward these superego objects, he does not act out of guilt but out of anxiety, which remains as castration anxiety. Thus he once said to me: "If you are angry at me, a piece is torn out of my body!"

While the normal, desexualized superego reproduces the internalized demands and prohibitions of the educating persons, the first stages of the superego correspond only to the fear of avenging reality. They are only loosely connected with the ego and can, therefore, easily be isolated and ejected. Contrary to this theory, the English school considers these first stages as already genuine superego.

In this connection, I would like to mention that, as obvious as it might seem, I do not think this case could serve to confirm the theories of Melanie Klein and her followers regarding the instinctual structure and the instinctual conflicts of the infant. Melanie Klein (1932) considers mechanisms similar to those established our analysis to be the norm of development, but she places them back into a much earlier age, into about the second half of the first year, and she traces them to games and fantasies without the help of direct recollections. Both the clinical picture and course of our case differ widely from the picture of typical neurosis and even more from that of normal development. The severity and peculiarity of the patient's state of mind make us draw the compelling conclusion that cases in which, in consequence of special fates, oral sadistic conflicts of such intensity come to the fore result in a psychosis or something similar to a psychosis. It seems more than improbable that similar instinctual conflicts of even approximate intensity should take place in normal development. We were able, in our case, to uncover severe traumata resulting from frustration which can be made responsible for the intensity of

the oral sadism. But we seriously doubt that the
conflicts of the normal child, centered around orality
and the trauma of weaning, have a similarly sadistic
character. True, ambivalence is always based on the
destruction of the object in the course of incorporation,
but the subjective need to destroy results only from
accumulated frustrations.

In no way did we find an outbreak of the Oedipus
conflict in as early a period as Klein claims to have
discovered, followed by such special instinctual tendencies as the urge to tear the father's phallus out of the
mother's womb. Such special fantasies seem to have
been placed back into early, still undifferentiated periods.

Finally, I would like to say a few words about the
course of the analysis. Right away, the analysis was
placed into the series of narcissistic mechanisms of
improvement and restoration. Hence we were assured
of the patient's eager cooperation.

A very patient analysis of his pregenital anxieties
gradually succeeded in resolving his rage, his defiance,
his urge to destroy and to devour as a defense against
underlying passive homosexual tendencies. When he
gave up this defense the attitude of the patient
changed most impressively. One was able to establish
contact with him; he became human, so to say; he
began to have insight into reality; he learned to differentiate between inside and outside, fantasy and reality, present and past. The delusional phases receded
more and more. They did not break out except in periods of resistance. The stereotypical "I have been injured" turned into "I am scared."

Around that time, the patient began to have regular relations with prostitutes; he gave up his pregenital excesses. To be sure, at the beginning these genital acts served only the discharge of the homosexual fantasies, but gradually we succeeded in a very thorough analysis of his fear of castration. That, to a certain degree, cleared the way to women for him. He was able to turn to his studies with renewed interest, and he succeeded in establishing new sublimations.

We found out that his castration anxiety culminated in the fear of bursting during ejaculation. His ability to shift libido to other organs of his body and to transform it into narcissistic body sensations had its origin in various practices of his puberty aimed at preventing ejaculation. The organ sensations disappeared with the restoration of his genital excitability.

The analysis has not yet been finished, but its therapeutic chances seem to be favorable. Technically, this analysis proceeded in a different way from the usual analysis of adults. I treated the patient as if he were a child, with special kindness and readiness to help. I fed him, lent him books, money, etc. I took him along on my vacation. I prolonged his sessions if necessary. I did whatever possible to help establish a positive transference. On the other hand, I constantly stressed the asexual character of this relation. Thus, for the first time in his life, in the transference, he came to know a genuine, exclusively affectionate and therefore not dangerous, not destructive, object relation. It probably was this even friendship which helped him to understand that there are object relations which do not destroy the object. This knowledge has probably acted as the central therapeutic factor.

4

A Contribution to the Psychoanalysis of Extreme Submissiveness in Women

(1940)

THE AIM of this contribution is to further our understanding of a morbid development in the character of the woman who is extremely submissive to men and to explain a certain neurotic aspect of her love life. An investigation of this type of disturbance of the relationship to objects may also throw some light on certain properties of immature object relations in general.

In the German language there exists the special expression *Hörigkeit* for which there seems to be no precise English equivalent; the term "extreme submissiveness" will serve. By this term we understand a special dependency of one adult upon another: the impossibility of living without the partner, the willingness to comply with all the partner's wishes thereby sacrificing

Published originally in *The Psychoanalytic Quarterly*, 9:470–480.

all interests of one's own, all independence and self-reliance. I think that such extreme submissiveness is a clear-cut clinical picture which may best be regarded as a perversion. It is found in men as well as in women, but since my clinical material happens to comprise only female cases I will restrict myself to discussing the mechanisms at work in women. It is possible that the mechanisms in men are similar.

Susan, 29 years of age, had been living in such a submissive relationship with a very brilliant but very narcissistic man for nine years. This man was very disturbed sexually and had deep objections to intercourse. It took six years before he finally gave in to Susan's importunate sexual needs, but even after that he was willing to have intercourse only on very infrequent occasions. Life with this man was a perpetual courtship on Susan's part. Notwithstanding the fact that her life had become a long chain of disappointments and rejections, she lived for this man only. Before him Susan had had several intimate friends, but somehow he was the "right" one. She wanted only to be near him, to share his life. She followed him everywhere to the neglect of her vocation, her family, all her former interests.

For all this Susan felt recompensed by the overwhelming happiness which she experienced whenever she succeeded in sleeping with her lover; then she was utterly happy and had the feeling of being completely fused with him. "We become one person," she said. "He is I and I am he."

The overvaluation of sexual intercourse seen in Susan is typical of all similar cases. Another example of this was Mary, 31 years old, married to a narcissistic man who maltreated her and went around with other women. Like Susan, Mary was deeply bound to her husband in an extremely submissive way. She endured all his insults and brutalities only to feel the bliss of having intercourse with him. Describing her feelings during intercourse, she said: "The walls between him and me do not exist any more. I feel what he feels; I even think what he thinks. We are one person, and the only wish I have is to die that very minute."

Intercourse is an experience of extraordinary intensity in these cases of extreme submissiveness in women. Since the feeling of bliss in this *unio mystica* cannot be explained by the orgastic sensation alone, let us try to probe the matter a little deeper.

In the submissive woman the special ecstasy of intercourse must be viewed against the background of anxiety, despair, and helplessness which are experienced when she is separated from the object of her love or when her lover turns away from her. Mary described this in the following way: "I am quite disturbed, as if I were poisoned. It is as if I were in an empty, cold and dark world all by myself. It is absolute solitude." The description given by Susan was somewhat similar: "I feel as though I were in a dark hole, all alone. All other men are dead. I am unable to do anything."

It is worthy of note that the self-esteem of the submissive woman falls to a strikingly low level when she is away from her lover. The man, on the other hand, is overrated; he is considered to be very important, a genius. He is the only man worthy of love.

The submissive woman seems completely to have renounced her own narcissism. It is as if she had projected her narcissism onto the man; she develops a sort of megalomania in regard to him. In the magic of the *unio mystica* she finally regains, through identification, the narcissism which she had renounced.

Susan's history shows this clearly. She was a very ambitious girl with a wild urge toward perfection. She was characteristically compulsive in her work: for instance, she felt that she could never find a composition book of the "right" size in which to copy the most complicated matters of science in the "right" order. If after innumerable struggles she once managed to do so, she would then fall into a state of narcissistic enthusiasm. She began to study philosophy, but finally gave it up as too difficult. A short time afterward she became acquainted with the man who later became her husband. He was a philosopher, and she fell helplessly in love with him. She was quite conscious of the fantasy that she would come to understand philosophy through her love for this man. In her analysis it became quite clear that the perfection which Susan could not achieve through her own efforts, but only through having a man in intercourse, was the penis.

Mary, our other submissive patient, had also fought for masculinity desperately and unsuccessfully. She too found vicarious satisfaction in her husband's greatness. Speaking of her handsome husband, she said: "He is tall, slender, sinewy and muscular. His body is like a large penis!"

As children, both women had imagined that during intercourse the woman would get the penis from the man and keep it. But the presence of this fantasy alone does not clarify the problem of submissiveness. The process of acquiring the desired penis in a magic way through intercourse seems frequently to be the solution of the masculine conflicts of normal girls. The normal girl too has to renounce her masculine desires of puberty and is also partially recompensed by the love of a man. Hence we have to look for factors more specifically determining the development of extremely submissive conduct. The question as to what distinguishes the normal woman from the submissive one is the more important inasmuch as under certain social conditions, for example those prevailing in the nineteenth century, the obedient wife who was submissively dependent upon her husband represented the ideal of society.

A factor more specifically bearing upon the question of submissiveness in certain women is their tendency to fall in love with men who abuse and humiliate them. If we suppose that these humiliations are an inseparable part of their love life, we must look for further signs of masochistic tendencies. These signs are indeed to be found. For one thing, these women consider intercourse an act of violence, or in a more sublime way the act may be experienced as a mystic dissolution of the person which has its climax in death during orgasm. Likewise, the humiliations to which the submissive woman is subjected are obviously a part of the love play: the deeper the despair resulting from abuse or separation from the lover, the greater the happiness of the reunion. There seem to be two parts to the process. That which is destroyed in the first part is restored in the second. The masochistic nature of yielding to the great can also be seen clearly in the masturbation fantasies of childhood. Little Mary dreamed: "A father operates on the penis of a little boy. Then he loves the boy very much." Intercourse in later life is a living out of this fantasy: the woman has first to be castrated and destroyed by the man in order to be loved afterward. In that ecstatic experience we find a unification of contradictory trends and emotions. The ecstasies represent, at the same time, castration and the restitution of the penis as well as death and resurrection.

Before we can fully understand this strange process we must examine another aspect of the behavior of submissive women: their extreme passivity. The submissive woman is helpless if she has to accomplish something unaided and alone. This is not because she lacks ability—all the submissive women I have analyzed were intelligent, distinguished, and highly developed—but because the impulse to act is missing. The submissive woman wants to remain passive far beyond the realm of sexuality. The man has always to take the first step; she wants only to be his executive organ. If the man inspires or orders something she can do it, but independent action has no such pleasure attached to it.

The main symptom for which Susan came to analysis was her incapacity to do anything by herself. During the analysis, she came to understand that every action undertaken by herself was initiated against great resistance, because it showed that she was all alone and without her friend. Mary too was full of complaints about her lack of initiative and her unproductiveness. Only if someone else gave orders was she capable of doing anything. In conversation, she always had to agree with her partner because, as she put it, she did not have brains enough to make independent evaluations. In fact, she found pleasure in this type of intellectual subordination and she built up, in each conversation, a kind of submissiveness in miniature.

The inclination to be passive reveals a very intense sexualization of all of life. Women showing this type of submissiveness continually want attention and love from their men. The mere necessity for independent action represents for them loneliness and lack of love. They only partly learn to renounce continuous gain of pleasure and to adjust themselves to the requirements of reality. Their very childish attitude is clearly crystallized in the fantasy: "I have no penis; I cannot do anything alone; you must continually give me something; you must always do something for me."

Futher analysis of the submissive woman characteristically reveals that her problems arise earlier than the phallic phase. They are rooted in a childish fixation to the mother. From her the child expects protection, tenderness, food—in short, all kinds of attention. This was most clearly seen in the analysis of another submissive woman. Frances, 30 years old, had lost her mother when she was four, after which she was sent from one foster home to another for a year until her father finally provided a new mother by marrying again. The child clung to her new mother desperately and wanted to be cleaned, fed, loved and cared for all the time. In her later life, the same continual demand for attention of all kinds was seen. In masochistically yielding to a very brilliant man, she tried to find fulfillment of these desires through the bliss of an ecstatic union.

In Mary's childhood, this special dependency on the mother played a major role. She did not want to do anything without the help of her mother. She had a daydream of a mighty being who knew exactly what she needed and who fulfilled her every wish without her asking. In later childhood, she hoped to get a penis from her mother. Originally her desires had been anal and oral ones. Those tendencies remained unchanged, crossing each other, overlapping, and extending into her submissive relationship to her husband. Desires that were originally meant for the mother reappear in an ecstatic love relationship to a man.

In describing this ecstatic state we emphasize repeatedly that individuality is dissolved in complete union with the man. We might also understand this union with the great and mighty as a magic fusion with the mother. It is like relapsing to a time in which the ego is about to be formed and when the boundaries between the ego and the outer world were still blurred and only painfully experienced in moments of frustration and tension. Helene Deutsch (1927) believes that the sensation of ecstasy is based upon the restitution of some larger unit in the ego when she describes the ecstatic orgastic experience in terms of the fusion of the ego instincts and superego and, at the same time, with an otherwise hostile, denying outer world.

That the ecstatic experience of orgasm meant a fusion with the mother was substantiated in Mary's analysis. Whenever she was separated from her mother in childhood, Mary feared that her mother had died. She suffered terribly when her mother was dissatisfied or angry with her. On seeing her mother again after an absence or at reconciliation, she felt the same intense happiness she later experienced in her union with a man. She recalled having fallen asleep in her mother's bed with an indescribable feeling of bliss, cuddled up to the warm back of the mother. She used later to fall asleep in the same position after intercourse.

The fear which hung over Mary's childhood that the mother might die we recognize, of course, to be an expression of the repressed hostility directed against that, at times, callous fountainhead of all fulfillment. This hostility was later diverted from the mother and directed toward the husband, but it remained repressed. Thus the extreme infantile ambivalence was not overcome by the later change of object, but merely directed into other forms. The most important transformation was into masochism. The hostility which had been repressed was explosively discharged upon herself during intercourse through identification with the brutal, sadistic man. At these times she would feel intense lust but would experience a sort of split of her personality. At the same time that she was feeling sexual pleasure as a woman, she would also feel like a bystander watching the conquest of a woman. She frequently had the fantasy of being a man and doing the same thing to a young girl. Likewise, some of her masturbation fantasies revealed this coexistence of active and passive attitudes: first, a boy is castrated by his father; then the grandfather performs the same operation upon the father.

The anxiety and despair which Mary experienced when separated from her husband were secondarily erotized to increase the intensity of the later sexual gratification. During analysis she realized that in such a state of despair she really felt hatred and envy toward the man who denied her his greatness, his penis.

In such a state she once bit savagely into her husband's shaving brush, and her subsequent dreams showed clearly that she wanted to bite off his penis. But such an undisguised outburst of rage could occur only when her marriage was about to end in failure. This expression of rage signified a breakdown of the whole mechanism of submissiveness. So long as the marriage was working, her basic hostility was sufficiently neutralized by its secondary erotization; she was able to endure the torture of being alone in order to increase the bliss of the ensuing reconciliation. When the marriage started to go on the rocks, repression failed.

Although a certain overvaluation of the object is characteristic of a normal love relationship, the submissive woman tends to endow her object with a special greatness. Only with such as object is the *unio mystica* possible, the ecstatic intercourse in which all secret wishes are fulfilled, all aggression, all anxiety, and all guilt neutralized.

What happens if this type of woman is thrown into a relationship with an "average" man? Here, in contrast to her behavior with an admired man, her aggression breaks through. This can be illustrated in the case of Frances, cited earlier, whose fixation was determined by her mother's death when she was four. Frances had been bound submissively to an "important" man for 10 years. This liaison came to a sudden end when her lover's child died. A little later Frances began a new sexual relationship but of a very different kind. Her new lover, many years younger than she, was a nice, plain fellow who felt great love and admiration for her. From him she demanded and got economic security. But in this relationship there was nothing of her former devoted yielding. Here she dominated, but she had to struggle with intense feelings of guilt. "I don't love this man," she would muse. "I abuse his young body, his tenderness, his money. If I don't want him I put him in the icebox, so to speak, to have him ready when I need him again." She used the man like a tool. To her he was not a human being but only a penis conveniently at her disposal. She dreamed of satisfying herself with a detached penis.

Susan likewise felt egotistic and guilty when she had a sexual relationship with a man who was not the "right" one. "I do not love him," she felt; "I just abuse him." In this form of sexual relationship the object is not intact; the man does not figure as a human being but only as a means of gratifying an instinct.

This lack of consideration for the object is characteristic of the prostitute. She may be submissive and masochistic in the hands of a bully while she abuses, exploits, and destroys numerous other men. Here there is no identification with the object, no sentiment, no interest in individuality.

The relentless, destroying attitude which the prostitute lives out in her love life, the submissive woman attempts to master by repression. She tried hard to preserve her faith in the greatness and singularity of her man because this overvaluation alone enables her to maintain the underlying hatred in repression. A blind, unqualified glorification of the object insures a lasting relationship to it.

This strained repression, however, is frequently difficult to maintain. Mary, for instance, was always furtively and anxiously evaluating her admired husband to see whether he was really as great, as brilliant, and as beautiful as she had made him out to be. She had continual anxiety that she might discover in him something that was stupid, ugly, ridiculous. To stifle this dread she naturally had to pump hard in order to maintain her object in a perpetual state of inflation. Were this bubble to break, there would emerge the primitive, aggressive, coprophagic, and cannibalistic impulses which in early childhood were predominant in relation to the mother.

The struggle to maintain this balance is characteristic of all object relations in submissive women. There is toward all things a tendency to sham kindliness, sham warmth, sham attachment.

This inclination to destroy, present as a chronic tendency, is not, in this form, characteristic of the early infantile attitude from which it is in fact derived. This impulse dominates the emotional state of the infant only if its feeling of well-being is interrupted by pain and frustration. Then the denying object is wanted intensely, but only then is it at the same time hated and destroyed.

This alternation between unlimited love and the wish to destroy, depending on whether or not immediate wishes were gratified, was observed clearly in the analysis of a schizophrenic patient. At one moment the world was wonderful, its beauty entering his body like a stream of warm milk; in the next instant everything was gray, colorless, hateful. The development of a minor internal tension was sufficient to produce this change: for instance, if he became thirsty and the desired drink did not come to him magically without the necessity of his getting up and getting it. Or if his girl kept him waiting two minutes, his love vanished; there was nothing left but hatred and the wish to destroy.

This patient behaved like a baby in its first month of life. At this stage there is a complete intolerance of tension and frustration. The object is beloved only so long as it fulfills every need. Life is a succession of discrete moments; there is no recollection of any kind. The fact that the object was kind until now is emotionally meaningless. The infant cannot remember nor can it wait or understand that there may be a later gratification. All it can do is rage.

Conformity to the reality principle, emotional continuity, and the minimization of mood swings are achieved in a variety of ways in the course of normal development. In submissive women this is attempted by the narcissistic elevation of the object, by the pleasure gratification of the ecstatic love experience, and finally by the transformation of aggression into masochistic behavior. Instead of the loose, unstable relationships of the early stage there is developed a single, unchangeable, exaggerated fixation to the object.

This solution of an infantile conflict is not the most successful one which could be achieved. The "phallic girl" described by Fenichel (1936), for instance, has worked out a somewhat similar but more stable arrangement. This woman identifies herself with the desired organ of the object by magic incorporation. She is now a part of the man—his penis. The "phallic girl" is not driven to masochism and is not so much threatened by an unstable ambivalence towards the object as is the submissive woman. By incorporating the desired organ of the object she is enabled to live always in a state of satisfied narcissism.

Annie Reich

Summary

A healthy relationship to objects is one where the love of an object can be maintained even if the object be the agent of temporary disappointments or frustrations. This is possible by the development of an ego that is capable of mastering reality. Where there is interference with this development, a perpetuation of early infantile conflicts results. Masochistic submissiveness in women is one way of attempting to solve these conflicts.

5

The Structure of
the Grotesque-Comic
Sublimation

(1949)

THE MOST interesting vicissitude of an instinct is the so-called sublimation. In sublimation the original sexual aim of an instinct is given up and a new desexualized one is assumed. This new aim is genetically related to the original one but is regarded as socially and culturally more valuable. Simultaneously with this desexualization the renunciation of the original incestuous object takes place.

Psychoanalysis always has stressed the importance of this process. However, a number of problems still need further elucidation. It is, furthermore, by no means possible to understand fully the nature of talent. Talent is the entity of preconditions which enable a person to transform the diverted sexual instincts into creative achievements. In persons without this precondition of talent the same conflicts may lead to neurotic symptoms or character deficiencies. We know nothing about the nature of these preconditions, but we can at least un-

Published originally in the *Bulletin of the Menninger Clinic*, 13:160–171. Reprinted with permission from the *Bulletin of the Menninger Clinic.* Copyright 1949 by the Menninger Foundation.

derstand when analyzing sublimations, what kind of transformation has occurred and what dynamic and economic changes have taken place. And we can understand some of the conditions which are responsible for the success or failure of sublimations.

I do not venture to investigate the structure and dynamics of sublimation in general, but I will restrict myself to one very special kind of sublimation—to the analysis of the grotesque-comic. Grotesque-comic productions are particularly labile. Ernst Kris (1938), who has contributed much to the problem of the comic, speaks of the "double-edged character" of the comical (p. 88). The grotesque-comic as a special type of comic is subject to this lability to a particularly large extent.

In the realm of psychology, psychopathology frequently offers the best approach to the most important insights. Thus the analysis of the failure of a grotesque-comic sublimation seems to be a suitable method of investigation. I wish therefore to report a fragment of a case history which throws some light on the nature of an artistic sublimation of this kind and at the same time on the conditions for its success or failure.

A charming young woman—Catherine—has an outstanding talent for grotesque-comic acting. She puts a little make-up on her face and runs her comb twice through her hair; she wraps a rag round her body and makes a funny face—immediately she is transformed into a clown, a prostitute, a funny old spinster, or into the grotesque caricature of a person well-known to her who provokes her derision. Then, extemporaneously, she plays a little scene till her audience roars with laughter. Usually in these sketches she makes use of some little incident that nobody else considers funny. Catherine is capable of seeing something ridiculous in everything and everybody. Her ridicule seems to be infectious to her audience, who all of a sudden begins to see the mocked person through Catherine's eyes and mocks with her. Catherine has terribly sharp eyes. She perceives all the deficiencies, insincerities, and ridiculous aspects of her environment. She has a peculiar faculty of seeing beneath the surface of a human being. She understands all secret vices, weaknesses, and hypocrisies, and is able to portray them by means of a casual word or gesture. These representations are acted caricatures, comic exposures and exaggerations by means of which she unveils the intuitively understood unconscious of others.

From childhood on, Catherine's one great ambition had been to become an actress of comic roles. Although she was undoubtedly talented, she could not achieve this aim; whenever she made an attempt to further her career she was paralyzed by an attack of anxiety and developed a peculiar symptom. Once, for example, she was asked to present herself at a certain theatre which was situated in a district which she knew well. On her way she suddenly lost her sense of direction and wandered for hours, lost and helpless, through the streets. At the same time she felt utterly changed. She was no longer the self-sufficient, charming young woman. She felt like an awkward and miserable girl from a small town who had, for the first time in her life, come to the big city, and who was shy and bewildered and did not dare to open her mouth. She was transformed into a living caricature, into one of the creatures whom she herself loved to impersonate so comically. It was not an artistic performance this time, but an involuntary transformation against which she was helpless. She was, of course, incapable in this state of doing anything for her career.

A similar peculiar transformation also took place on other occasions, for example, when she witnessed another woman trying in vain to get admiration and love by inadequate means, and being exposed. Once Catherine went to see a seamstress to have some work done. The seamstress was a miserable hunchback, living in a dismal apartment. Her pale face showed signs of loneliness and resignation, but a very striking coiffure with curls and pink ribbons indicated her desire to attract attention. Catherine immediately sensed the comedy and tragedy of this life, and suddenly she was identified with the seamstress. She too was a hunchback, and she too envied the patrons who were going to wear the silk nightgowns and negligees during glamorous nights of love. For many hours Catherine lived this strange life, paralyzed with terror and incapable of being herself again. The next day, at a party, Catherine acted the lovelorn seamstress and everybody thought her extremely funny.

However different these two situations are, they have a common element: an attempt to attract and the possibility of its failure. In the first case, Catherine, anticipating her own failure, becomes one of the ridiculous females whose failure she loves to caricature. In the second case, she actually witnesses another woman's failure and has to identify with her. Only long after the event does she succeed in mastering her anxiety in play. But in the most important struggle of her own life, in her attempt to make use of her talent for a career, the anxiety is too great and she finally has to resign herself to failure.

When trying to allure a man the described reaction did not occur. Catherine knew very well how to make men fall in love with her. She played with them without yielding anything. Her greatest pleasure was to make men single her out and to expose their passion for her in public. In that way she turned serious men into ridiculous creatures. Her most successful means of achieving this purpose was to amuse her admirers with comic performances and stories. The butts of these stories were usually other women, potential rivals with whom she felt compelled to identify under certain conditions.

In her childhood Catherine had to compete with a whole group of rivals. She was the middle one of three sisters, who together with the mother sought their father's love. The father was an important man who reigned like a biblical patriarch over this female clan. When only six years old, Catherine played the same role in the family as later in life. She was by far the most intelligent, talented, and charming one of them. She was the family clown, and her funny stories set the family table in an uproar. The essential butts of her performance were always her mother and her sisters, whom she mocked and whose ridiculous traits she impersonated. But as this would have been too shocking, she made use of substitute objects. At that age she was already a master at imitating and caricaturing others. Thus she succeeded in forcing laughter even from her father, who did not like her jokes and disapproved of her behavior. He thought she was frivolous and foolish.

In Catherine's stead her father had wished to have a son who would be his assistant and successor. He expected Catherine to substitute for this son, and she had to live up to this ideal. Thus the father later on denied that her comic acting was of any artistic value and objected to her wish to enter an artistic profession. Art was reserved for the eldest sister who, though lacking in talent, was urged to become a musician. Catherine might have secured her father's consent to become an actress if only she had persuaded him in the right way, for he was very devoted to his children and especially fond of Catherine. But she would not implore him. He had to acknowledge her talent. It appeared to her inferior and cheap to obtain his approval by flattering him and by being affectionate. Moreover, Catherine was full of opposition and resistance. While all the other women admired the father uncritically, she did not believe anything he said and everything had to be proved to her. She observed him with critical eyes; no weakness escaped her attention, and she criticized him publicly. At the same time she suffered terribly because of his rejection, but she was compelled to tell the truth about him and herself and hoped he would love her just as she was. If he objected to her clowning she felt her very nature disapproved of. She would not try to win him, as the others would, by being a good girl. She would not openly attempt to please him. She had only one way of attracting: the grotesque-comic performance—her only conscious wish, to provoke the father to laughter.

Why could she not try to please her father? She felt that she was his favorite child and that she surpassed the mother and both sisters in talent, charm, and personality. But she could not make any real use of her superiority over the rivals when trying to win her father because her superiority feelings were always interrupted by severe attacks of anxiety. All of a sudden she felt ugly and miserable and threatened by various feelings of bodily deficiency. She was unhappy especially about her nose, which she considered too small. This was based on the teasing of a somewhat older playmate who used to say: "Oh, you have no nose at all, you have only a hole!" She reacted exaggeratedly to this mockery. Even years later, when she was grown up, she had some hypochondriacal feelings connected with her nose. She felt deformed by a tiny scar on her nose and had the impression that everyone on the street was looking at her and mocking her.

We understand why Catherine could not attract her father by being an obedient girl. She felt miserable and deformed and she was able to employ but one means of reaching out for him: confession. During analysis, Catherine suddenly remembered the event that made this special compulsion to confess understandable. During the time of her analysis she had to undergo a minor but rather painful genital operation. At the moment of greatest pain she suddenly felt as if she were yielding to an overwhelming and at the same time destructive sexual act. "This is right," she thought. "It has to be like this. I went through this once. I once gave myself to somebody so completely, so exclusively, with such suffering." And then she knew: As a little girl of probably five or six years there had been some sexual play with the same boy who later ridiculed her small nose. In the course of this, the violent boy raped her. She remembered the blood and her tremendous fear that she now was forever ruined and deformed. She remembered how she later investigated her genitals in panic, but now noting the difference between her body and the boy's. She was convinced that her own penis had been destroyed by the painful love experience and that an ugly wound was the result. This experience was repressed, but the feeling of suffering from a secret deficiency distorted her later life. This life was indeed nothing but one great attempt to correct the dreadful consequence of her early sexual experience.

The boy had been only a substitute for her father, who was in fact the center of the child's fantasies. The sexual experience did not remove her from her father; on the contrary, she now longed for him more than ever. She was justified in thinking that her father would withdraw his love from her utterly if he came to know of her sexual crime. Moreover, her sexual mutilation was a real one. How could she possibly be loved anyway? At the same time, though she was only a little girl, she knew now how much a man was in a woman's power when he became sexually aroused. Hence she tried more than ever to seduce her father by exposing herself. She did not expect him to become openly excited sexually, which was of course impossible, but she at least wanted to excite him to laughter. Laughter was a substitute for sexual excitement. Success in that direction meant that her father approved of her disguised sexual activities and in this way rendered unnecessary her fear concerning her genital deformity. Since she could not exhibit something beautiful, she exposed in an only slightly veiled way the castrated, mutilated genitals, but as if she were not exposing herself but the body of somebody else. "Look. Here are the castrated genitals. But they are not mine. They belong to my mother, to my sisters."

Knowing how deformed she was, she feared all the more that her father would prefer not only her mother but also her obedient sisters. Furthermore, she feared her mother's criticism. She constantly felt rejected and unjustly criticized by her. Probably she provoked this disdainful treatment out of her guilty feelings. In any case, jealousy, fear, and not least, disappointed love made her more and more hostile toward her mother. This was an additional reason to attack mother and sisters in her comic performances and to lower them in her father's eyes as castrated creatures. By projecting her own disgrace onto her sisters she not only rehabilitated herself, but at the same time destroyed her rivals.

In her struggle to rid herself of her guilt feelings the tortured child became a fanatic for truth. Not only did she find out that mother and sisters had the same genitals as herself, but she became keenly aware of all their weaknesses and deficiencies which she then portrayed in her caricatures. In time, her faculty for observation increased, her ideas grew more brilliant, her means of expression more abundant: The childish games developed into artistic performance. The better the performance, the more certain the applause, which she needed to get rid of anxiety and guilt. But Catherine's father was not a good audience. He disapproved of her acting and in this way condemned the child's sexual activity. This was disastrous for her further development: Without her father's consent she could not become an actress.

By acting Catherine tried to utilize her infantile instincts in a true sublimation, i.e., to detach these instincts from her incestuous objects and to direct them toward desexualized aims which were culturally more important. Accomplishment and success would have erased the narcissistic injury of childhood. But she failed. Whenever she reached out for professional accomplishment the fatal situation of her childhood repeated itself. It was as if her father saw through her and denied her art any value. Thus the way leading to desexualization of the daughter's relationship to the father that would have enabled her to build up a stable sublimation was blocked. The father's rejection held her in the sphere of the forbidden incestuous relationship and compelled her to endless revenge in the foi m of seduction and exposure of men. Whenever this additional sexual purpose was conscious and permitted, Catherine was in full command of her art. But when profession and achievement alone were involved and sexuality was as forbidden as in childhood, Catherine became helpless and unable to overcome her anxiety by acting.

Let us sum up. What forces drive Catherine to production?

Since early childhood Catherine has never been free of the terrible fear of being deformed. In life she is compelled to hide her defect with great effort. Everything about her has to be perfect. She cannot stand criticism and has to be admired. In her grotesque-comic play she can drop the mask, she can behave as she feels. No more does she have to cover her deficiencies, but she can say: "Love me as I am!" Thus, suddenly, a very large amount of countercathexis becomes superfluous, permitting an intense feeling of pleasure and relaxation. Now she makes fun of her former terror and plays with her deficiencies, thus demonstrating that she is no longer a helpless victim of her fear of castration. This liberation is made possible by the projection of her deficiency. She attributes her deficiencies to her rivals, exposing them in this way to the curse of ridiculousness, and thus discharging her aggressive tendencies. Simultaneously she can permit herself the otherwise forbidden exhibition of the genitals which is accepted now in spite of all deficiencies, and which excites and seduces though only to laughter. This exhibition is of a special type. It is a masochistic one. The early love experiences of the little girl were masochistic. Demonstration of the deficiencies is supposed to evoke sexual interest and in the end to stimulate the repetition of the early sado-masochistic love play. The embarrassing exposure which was originally the introduction of the masochistic experience takes over the entire cathexis of the process and becomes its weakened substitute. Masochistic exhibition takes the place of open masochistic gratification. (Similar ideas were expressed by Reik, 1939.)

But the grotesque-comic play cannot be understood merely as a more or less disguised breaking through of instincts. Here the repressing forces as well as the repressed ones are condensed, just as in the true conversion-hysterical symptom. At the same time the grotesque-comic performance has the meaning of confession, self-humiliation and self-punishment. Thus the requirements of the superego are fulfilled simultaneously. It is evident why Catherine is striving with all her being for this opportunity of expression. So many psychic needs are satisfied by this achievement. So many instincts find discharge, not flooding the ego but subjugated to its mastery. These instincts are deliberately evoked by the ego which makes use of them for the purpose of gaining pleasure. Thus the anxiety, which under ordinary conditions is always the consequence of such a return of the unconscious, is controlled.

But this grand attempt is not successful. The sublimation fails—anxiety breaks through.

This case material permits a rather clear understanding of the conditions which result in success or failure of grotesque-comic sublimation. We may try to make use of the insights we can gather from this case for a more general understanding of the precondition of success of comic sublimation.

The problem of the condition for successful comic production has been the subject of several psychoanalytic investigations. Besides Freud's basic work, *Jokes and Their Relation to the Unconscious* (1905a), I mention only the works of Sachs (1928), Reik (1939), and the very illuminating paper by Ernst Kris (1938) on caricature. In every case the comic effect results from an economizing of psychic energy and from a persistence of the infantile. A sudden breaking through of instincts under conditions which make them acceptable to the spectator's ego, so that countercathexes are unnecessary, is experienced as comic pleasure. Grotesque-comic productions as well as wit are social phenomena. Only the laughter of the hearer makes the originator of the wit burst into laughter too. That means the witticism is a good one. Only the applause of the audience makes the comic performance successful, for only the approval of the audience makes the guilt feelings of the actor superfluous.

Kris (1938) points out an additional element as essential for the comic: What today impresses us as comic was terrifying yesterday. The triumph resulting from mastering the past anxiety helps by repeating the victory and overcoming half-assimilated fear. Thus the function of the comic is to overcome anxiety while at the same time it is based on already mastered anxiety. From this essential peculiarity of the comic arises the double-edged character: the ease with which it passes from pleasurable success to unpleasurable failure.

Our case seems to verify these assumptions. In her comic play, Catherine demonstrates that she does not fear castration any more, but is able to make fun of it and can use it to stress the difference between herself and her rivals to her own advantage.

Some form of disguise to hide the real instinctual aims is a prerequisite for success of any comic production. The grotesque comic is characterized by a special form of disguise, that is, by particular disfigurement and deformation of the object. To understand the specific mechanism that is going on here and at the same time the particular difficulty of achievement and the great probability of failure of these endeavors to produce comic pleasure, it seems to be necessary to consider the particular instincts involved. In our case we find exhibition of devaluated parts of the body, of defects, which serves, via projection, at the same time to unmask the rivals. Confession and self-punishment are combined with aggression against others. This combination of aggression and exhibitionism turned simultaneously toward the actor's own body and against a hated rival are, I assume, typical for all cases of grotesque-comic art whether theatrical or graphic. The synthesis of these contrasting components seems to be the most effective method of weakening and disguising the infantile instincts. The combination of gratifications and punishment seems to be ego-syntonic.

The most important factor of disguise is the mechanism going on in the performing area itself. The aggressive actions are not done to the real object but are expressed on the body of the actor. Kris emphasizes this demonstration of aggression on a substitute object as the most essential element in caricature. The deformation of the picture takes the place of the real degradation of the object. This disfigurement is a substitute for injuring the real object. Kris considers this a residue of old magic practices. The primitive believes in image-magic. For example, by destroying the effigy of a hated adversary, he in fact kills this enemy. Following Kris's assumptions, we discover the derivatives of gesture magic in grotesque-comic acting. What is demonstrated on the actor's own body is intended to happen to the object. The ridiculous deformation of body and soul that Catherine demonstrates in her own person, she wishes to happen to her enemies. In her unconscious she believes in her magic power to transform her competitors in reality.

Similar mechanisms are to be found in the play of children and in primitive customs. The child, for example, makes faces at another child, indicating: "I'll make you look like this!" The second child's reaction of rage proves his understanding of the evil wish. The primitive who seeks to bring rain by urinating on the dry field demonstrates with his own body what he wants the gods to do. For the purpose of artistic representation, such primitive forms of expression are revived. They speak to us immediately; we understand them, since they are familiar to us.

The comic achievements depend, of course, on the spiritual and cultural level of actor and spectator. The film comedy, for instance, the climax of which consists in the throwing of custard pies at one another, may evoke outbursts of laughter from an average movie public, while more refined people may consider the picture boring and coarse. The failure of the comic achievement may occur because the form was too poor or the outward or inward situation of the observer unsuitable, and instead of laughter it provokes boredom, disgust, or even sometimes dread.

Let us stop and review for a moment our insight into the nature of grotesque-comic acting: grotesque-comic performances are acted caricatures. The disfiguration is based on the actor's previous fear of castration which he can utilize now for his aggressive purposes by raising himself high above his rivals and by destroying them by magic means. The success of the performance itself serves as the reassurance that the original castration fear is unnecessary, and as a gratification of exhibitionistic impulses.

It is therefore easy to understand what public disapproval means for the actor. The mastery which the ego has won with great effort over the anxiety collapses. The original anxiety breaks through and the attempt to get rid of guilt feeling in this way fails. The disapproval of the public means not only public exposure but also proof of his guilt. The aggression which he wanted to discard in this way is now nevertheless forbidden and turned against his own person. He confessed but he was not absolved, and the self-accusation was tranformed into an accusation by the outside world. The result is anxiety and a deep depression. Probably often even acclamation from outside is incapable of preventing this reaction from occurring. The forces of the actor's own conscience are too strong and therefore he is overwhelmed with anxiety and guilt. This is why many comic artists in the various branches are ill-humored persons with a tendency toward deep depression.

We were able to observe the failure of the comic performance in Catherine very well. Her mood changed whenever something reminded her of her father and his rejection. What just a moment ago she had enjoyed as a funny play, she experienced suddenly as a tragic reality. She now became in reality ridiculous and deformed and, in her own body, she experienced the pains meant for the recently ridiculed adversaries. It becomes obvious here that the origin of the grotesque-comic performance is a magic one. Now the evil spell turns back against the subject herself. There is no difference in the contents of the presentation, but what was previously performed voluntarily and actively for the purpose of gaining pleasure has now overwhelmed her. She is now passive, helpless, and exposed. What formerly was play, now is serious. What was formerly exhibitionistic pleasure is now nothing but the torture of confession. The childhood situation, her mutilation through her own fault, is repeated. Whatever she tried to master by her artistic attempts has broken through. The comedy has become tragedy again.

The depressive position of comic artists, caricaturists,

and the like seems to indicate that the process observed here of transformation into the attacked and ridiculed object is typical of the case of the breakdown of the comic mechanism. The involuntary transformation of Catherine seems to be therefore more than just a special neurotic symptom in a special neurosis; it seems to be a typical illustration of the process that takes place whenever such a sublimation fails. But this process, as a rule, remains unobserved and unconscious, and only resulting depression and horror is experienced.

This terrible result of failure, the transformation described, is based on the particular combination of instincts we assumed to be essential for all forms of grotesque-comic creation. The turning back of the aggression from the object to the subject takes, so to speak, a prepared course. From the start the aggressive unmasking of the object was linked with the exposure of the artist's own castration. That this particular constellation is in fact, as a rule, to be found in grotesque-comic art of all kind, I should like, if not to prove, at least to state as a probability. It seems to me that whenever someone is talented in caricature or grotesque-comic acting and the like, a tendency to self-exposure creeps in beside the wish to expose others, and that this tendency to exhibit and to confess produces the driving force for creation.

In the performances of clowns we can observe, free from all moral justification, the instinct structure in question in the most provocative and concentrated form. Here the indecent sexual factor is most conspicuous. Here above all the comic verges suddenly on the repulsive. As the justification of "great art" is lacking, the danger of a breakthrough of anxiety is particularly imminent. What does the clown represent? He demonstrates himself as dumb, awkward, disfigured, soiled, beaten, ridiculed. The typical situations of the comic movie stars are, though on a somewhat higher level, almost the same. Even the heart-stirring Chaplin exposes again and again his anxiety, his helplessness, his humiliation, and his flat feet. What may be the motives for this self-humiliation in the clown and this demonstration of misery in the actor? Here, too, the onlooker is seduced to laughter. It seems that the clown who feels castrated and incapable of phallic exhibition wants at least to provoke laughter by means of this exhibition on a pregenital level. But this seems only partly to cover the situation. Here, too, aggression against a third person is shown on his own body. Here, too, the disfigurement of his own body is a magic gesture intended to destroy an adversary. But here the third object is not always known and thus the aggression as a whole can remain undiscovered.

The clown, for instance, imitates and ridicules the rope dancer who some minutes before had evoked admiration and slight horror by his neck-breaking tricks. By awkward falling and faltering, the clown not only demonstrates his own clumsiness, but reveals his wish that the artist should tumble from his rope. He expresses with his body what he wishes to have happen to the more successful hero.

The depressive disposition of most clowns seems to indicate that the attempt to tear down the envied rival, who unconsciously stands for the father, does not remain unpunished. Here too, the funny play turns into terrible reality, that is, instead of triumph, the clown frequently experiences dejection. Here too, the playful self-exposure has a devastating effect on the self-esteem.

It appears as if the grotesque-comic performer would vacillate between melancholic depression and mania. There exists of course a basic difference between the feeling of bliss and gratification, which stems from the success of comic performance, and mania. While the feeling of joy and power in mania is caused by a deep-going ego-regression, in the comic sublimation the ego is really great and powerful. Deliberately, it draws forth the otherwise repressed instinctual impulses from the unconscious and plays with them. If the fateful transformation occurs again, the ego again loses its power, is flooded by the impulses, and its existence is threatened in two different ways. The one is the breakdown of the defense against castration fear; the other is identification with the hated object, a process which has great similarity to that in melancholic depression, though here too some important differences are to be seen. The hated object, though it previously had been repressed by means of the actor's own body, had yet been conceived as an external object and as not identical with the ego. Now it is fused with the ego. In melancholic depression we also find a fusion of ego and object, but a far more complete one. It goes on in an entirely unconscious way, and only careful analysis can discover the introjected object. In the failure of grotesque-comic achievement the procedure of transformation as such is conscious. The difference may be due to the fact that a melancholic depression is a matter of oral introjection based on very deep regression, whereas in grotesque-comic performance the objects are actually imitated, a procedure which, in contrast to the cannibalistic fantasy, is a conscious ego activity. The melancholic renounces his external objects, whereas the world of objects remains intact for the comedian.

The transformation of the comedian is therefore only a passing one, more a feeling he has about himself which does not reach quite the intensity of a delusion. But the diminished self-esteem, the feeling of depression, and the destructive self-criticism are very similar in both cases. In both cases a cruel superego destroys the ego without pity. What is the explanation of this cruelty?

We have stressed the importance of the spectator's approval. The audience takes over the role of the superego. If the world applauds, the comedian's superego is also ready to approve. That means that the comedian remains dependent upon the external world to a very high degree.

Either the superego remained incompletely developed because the father relationship never was really solved, or the superego was reprojected into the environment. In any case, this environment which functions as a superego has to be seduced to the forbidden instinctual activity. This results in a decomposition of the superego which previously had been based on the desexualization of instincts. The father who originally had imposed the prohibition against instinct gratification is being seduced in spite and triumph. (This was what Catherine performed again and again.)

The grotesque-comic play has the same functions that festivals had in the past. As mentioned above, it indeed played and plays an important role in public celebrations and merriments. Prohibited instinctual activities are not only suddenly granted to the common people, but the authorities who gave the laws are de-valuated and publicly indulge in the same transgres-sions. Consequently the grotesque-comic performance is characterized by an extreme sexualization of the re-lationship between actor and public which corresponds to a sexualization of the relationship between ego and superego, i.e., to a decomposition of the superego in the individual.

This dissolution of the superego results in an enor-mous increase of narcissism which is the main charac-teristic of mania. But while in mania this is achieved by a pathologic process, by a regression to infantile states, we find here an active spiteful conquering of the cruel superego that is a real strengthening of the ego. The primitive narcissism had been painfully dis-turbed originally by conflicts with external objects and later on by tensions between ego and superego. Now it is restored by this destruction of the superego. This resurrection of the infantile narcissism is experienced as a feeling of bliss amounting to mania.

If, however, this overcoming of the superego fails, either because the spectator was critical or the super-ego of the actor remained resistant, then the superego gains double power. Now it punishes also for the criminal attempt at rebellion that just has failed. Now the superego regains the whole cruelty of primitive times, thus assuming the same features as in melan-cholic depression.

Success and failure of grotesque-comic achievement correspond in this way with a shifting of power be-tween ego and superego. The struggle with the authority did not come to a final decision but repeats itself again and again.

In successful sublimations, a very strong ego destines the vicissitudes of the instincts. In grotesque-comic sublimations, the strength of the ego is still uncertain. This form of artistic sublimation differs from all other forms of art through its greater closeness to the body and to instincts and anxiety. In all other forms of art the emphasis is shifted away from instinctual pleasure to formal elements to a much larger degree.

This relative primitiveness, this incomplete desexualization, this uncompleted victory of the ego are responsible for the lability of grotesque-comic sublimation.

6

On the Termination of Analysis

(1950)

A STONISHINGLY, the topic of termination of analysis has very rarely been the subject of psychoanalytic investigation. Obviously it represents a great number of theoretical, clinical, and particularly technical problems. Of the many, I should like to take up only a special one: the transference or, more cautiously expressed, one typical transference situation as it exists at the time of the termination of the analysis. Before doing this, however, I should like to turn first to the existing literature. To my knowledge there are only two papers that deal with this subject: "Analysis Terminable and Interminable" (Freud, 1937) and "The Problem of Termination of Analysis" (Ferenczi, 1927). These two papers represent an interesting contrast in their outlook, we might say in their emotional atmosphere. Freud's paper is full of wisdom and scepticism. He is reviewing as if for the last time the therapeutic results of his work. He is pointing out everything that

Published originally in *The International Journal of Psycho-Analysis*, 31:179–183, 1950.

is uncertain; he is revealing whatever he considers the limitations of therapeutic effectiveness. Ferenczi, on the other hand, is full of optimism. He gives us an idea of what he considers a completed analysis. He gives us a wealth of technical advice and clinical details which are pointed out as the preconditions for a completed analysis. Here two aspects are most interesting.

1. The analysis of character traits, of ego behavior patterns which developed as *protective* automatisms in the course of instinct repression and have to be retraced in the analysis to their origin. The rigid crystallization of character has to be dissolved again if a real re-education of the patient is to be achieved. This will lead to infinite inner freedom combined with complete ego control. For this purpose Ferenczi pleads for a thorough analysis of facial expression, postural peculiarities and so on, and proposes the imitation of the patient as a suitable method for bringing these behavior patterns to the attention of the patient and making their analysis possible. Character was here understood for the first time, though not elaborated upon, as a defense which has to be analyzed just like other more obvious forms of resistance.

2. The analysis of hidden distrust against the analyst, the analysis of tendencies to test the analyst's patience and sincerity, and the frequent desire to discover hidden negative countertransference expressions in the analyst. This onslaught the analyst has to be able to meet, to analyze, and to utilize for the analysis. Ferenczi touches on problems which at the time of the publication of his paper were beginning to become more and more the center of discussion: analysis of defenses, character as defense, deeper understanding of

ego functioning, etc., problems which were all based on Freud's new insights into the nature of the ego.

The application of this more thorough technique, Ferenczi indicates, enables the analyst to bring an analysis to full completion. A really fully analyzed case is characterized by extensive new character formation and full overcoming of the castration complex in all its ramifications.

The contrast between this positive outlook and that expressed in Freud's paper, just ten years later, is indeed striking. In praxis, Freud (1937) points out, it is rather obvious what the conditions for termination of the analysis are: the patient has to have lost all his symptoms, inhibitions, anxieties. All his repressions have to be undone. This implies, as is mentioned elsewhere in Freud's writings, that the blank spots caused by infantile amnesia have to be filled out; the childhood history has to be reconstructed. As a means to this end, the transference has to be resolved. The therapeutic result which we desire is expressed best in Freud's (1933) own words: "Where id was, there shall ego be" (p. 80).

These results, of course, we are not always able to achieve. Too violent intensity of instinctual demands or too severe pathology and weakness of the ego frustrate our efforts. Furthermore, our therapeutic aims go beyond achieving ego control only for the present time. We hope to establish a condition that makes relapses impossible. Here Freud (1937) is extremely sceptical. The balance of power between instinct and ego, he stresses, is a very labile one. Any later shift in cathexis may disturb it. Instincts may gain in strength, as happens biologically in puberty or menopause. Reality frustrations may cause recathexis of already relinquished infantile impulses. Illness, age, frustrations, and so on may weaken the ego, and thus preconditions for relapse and new illness arise. Freud discusses at length whether it is possible to prevent such later incidents by "waking sleeping dogs," that is, by analysis of instinctual conflicts which are not actual but only latent ones. He decides that this is not feasible.

It may be that Freud here takes too pessimistic a view. The greater importance which the analysis of the ego has gained during the last few years has sharpened our faculties of observation and understanding. We have learned to discover in peculiarities of behavior patterns, in character traits, and in the detailed analysis of defense mechanisms, the signs not, of course, of really absent, but of latent conflicts. We have learned to unearth indications of latent negative transference, of hidden aggressive trends, which, if not analysed, will endanger the later balance. Does not the analysis of these warrant a greater degree of reassurance against relapse than was assumed before? Or when we consider Freud, are we yielding to the temptation of wishful thinking in attributing our therapeutic failures to not having yet reached the requisite degree of perfection and subtlety, as if, through increased skill and deepened understanding, this were achievable. Do we, together with Ferenczi, harbour a belief which, by the way, is only vaguely implied and never directly expressed in Ferenczi's papers, that an ideal, an absolute state of health can be achieved, that a patient can be so completely analyzed that nothing remains hidden, no traces of neurosis are left, and thus no relapse is possible? Such a concept, of course, would appeal to the narcissistic omnipotence fantasies of the analyst.

Freud certainly is free of such wishful thinking. He enumerates a number of elements which frustrate the therapeutic efforts. He mentions particularly over-intensity of instincts, which is frequently combined with ego weakness. This overintensity of instincts may be constitutional. Beyond the economic factor, one frequently finds here what can be called stickiness of the libido, an unwillingness to give up once cathexed objects, and furthermore the so-called "id resistance" that is a rigidity of libido, an unwillingness to give up old libidinal patterns and to accept more adult substitute gratifications. These three elements are frequently expressed in the form of uncontrollable and unanalyzable transference demands by patients "accessible only to the logic of soup, with dumplings for arguments" (Freud, 1915, p. 167). We are faced here with early and deeply ingrained instinctual patterns which are just not to be modified.

The same rigidity can be found in the realm of the ego, which can be either thoroughly and early distorted by the result of defensive struggles or may even be constitutionally burdened. Freud here envisages the possibility of hereditary transmission of ego behavior. In contrast to Ferenczi's optimistic attitude, Freud (1937) considers castration anxiety, the penis envy of women, and the resistance against submission in men, as something which in certain cases is as unchangeable as "bedrock" (p. 252). Finally he talks of overintense conflicts between ego and superego, of an unconquerable intolerance against one's instincts which may be caused by the diffusion of instincts, by an enormous amount of aggression which is turned against the self and results in a tendency toward conflict.

In the past, it happened again and again that an idea at which Freud hinted in one of his papers became the subject matter of intense investigation and also speculation for many. In "Analysis Terminable and Interminable," Freud (1937) emphasized that the conditions for failure of analysis should be studied more thoroughly. Unfortunately, this has not been done up till now. Indeed, in this paper many questions are touched upon which are still open problems. For instance, the last mentioned precondition for failure, the tendency toward conflict as an expression of internalized aggression or death instinct, represents a concept of the greatest theoretical importance, the discussion of which goes beyond the scope of this paper.

This enumeration of unconquerable difficulties makes explainable many of our therapeutic limitations, which we have learned to accept. We do not hope that, by analysis, we can produce perfect human beings. We are content when we can free a patient from his symptoms and anxieties, when we can make him capable of adult object relations and enable him to function in his work and adjust to his reality. We are happy if we can help him to free old sublimations and to build up new ones. But we do not expect too much in this respect. We consider it as a sign of health if the patient is capable of accepting his own limitations.

Finally, I come to my subject proper. Being more modest in our demands, we do not expect our patients to be able to give up their transference expectations completely, and we take it for granted that a residue of infantile cravings will continue to exist. Even at the end of analysis, some elements of transference are traceable. Here, too, Ferenczi is too optimistic. He believes that the transference can be so completely dissolved that the analysis finally "dies from exhaustion." Neither for the patient nor for the analyst is it necessary "to give notice." When the patient declares his intention to leave the analysis one must always be afraid that by going he wants to keep something neurotic covered. It is not right for the analyst to terminate the analysis, because so long as the patient wants to come he belongs in analysis. In the "ideally completed analysis" the patient severs himself slowly but decidedly from analysis. This process can be described as follows: The patient slowly becomes convinced that in analysis he only preserves new and still fantastic means of satisfaction that do not bring him anything in reality. As soon as he has overcome the mourning over this insight, he looks out for more and more realistic methods of gratification. By holding on to the idea of possible fantasied gratification, he tried to avoid the frustration, in the analytic situation, which is a repetition of the infantile frustration situation that underlay the symptoms. By this insight, a real overcoming of this situation is achieved.

Ferenczi here clearly recognizes the nature of the infantile fantasy which ties the patient to analysis. From my own experience, I can confirm this observation. Even after the transference has been well analyzed and its important infantile sexual elements have been overcome, even after the neurotic symptoms have been given up, the relationship to the analyst is still not a completely mature one. We have to state that the transference is not completely resolved. The analyst is still an overimportant person for the patient, and is still the object of fantasy expectations. As mentioned before, we do not expect to be able to free our patients completely from their infantile fixations. But apart from these individual fantasies, there are certain attitudes typical of all patients. In nearly all cases which I have analyzed, there remained a wish to be loved by the analyst, to keep in contact with him, to build up a friendship. Furthur analysis of these wishes proved them to be derivatives of an early relationship with the parents, mostly diffuse oral pregenital in nature, but aim-inhibited and thus acceptable to the ego. The analyst is still seen as a person endowed with special power, special intelligence and wisdom. In short, to a certain degree, he is still seen as partaking in the omnipotence which the child attributes to the parents. Of course, there are great individual differences. If, for instance, an analysis ends with a free breakthrough of genitality, up till then inhibited, and the establishment of new and important object relations, the transference may indeed be completely decathexed and the analysis may be readily given up. But here one must be a little cautious. Sometimes a patient throws himself into such a relationship as a means of overcoming an unanalyzed disappointment about the loss of the analyst. This is a negative attitude in relation to the termination of analysis, just as we frequently see a negative type of transference as a defense against possible rejections in the course of analysis.

At the termination of the analysis of adolescents, I also have seen great readiness to give up the analyst. In all these cases, a full-blown transference had never developed. Certain secrets were never revealed—the analysis as such had been incomplete. Similar situations are probably found with children.

In any case, I have not frequently seen such an easy giving up of analysis, such as ending of a transference by "natural exhaustion" after really deep analysis. Patient and analyst agree that there is no need for further analysis; nevertheless, the patient has a feeling of loss at the time of the termination which is overcome only slowly in the course of time. It is possible, though, that with my patients there was always this residue of unresolved transference because we hardly ever had "endless time" at our disposal, as Ferenczi postulates as opportune for the ideal situation.

In most cases slight pressure has to be used to overcome a certain "stickiness" of the libido. Only reluctantly does the patient give up the loved object, the analyst whom he had previously charged with so much emotion. Ferenczi is, of course, right when he compares this loss to the original infantile frustration, and undoubtedly the analysis of this repetition situation proves very helpful.

I remember the case of a student who came to me for his training analysis several years after the successful completion of a therapeutic analysis with another analyst, which had lasted three years and had freed the patient from a number of disturbing symptoms and helped him to adjust to various difficult life situations. His description of his reaction to the termination of his first analysis was quite revealing:

> I felt as if I was suddenly left alone in the world. It was like the feeling I had after the death of my

mother [the mother had died during the patient's early adolescence]. I tried with effort to find somebody to love, something to be interested in. For months I longed for the analyst and wished to tell him about whatever happened to me. Then slowly, without noticing how it happened, I forgot about him. About two years later, I happened to meet him at a party and thought he was just a nice elderly gentleman and in no way interesting.

The description the patient gives here is indeed like the description of a period of mourning. It takes time until the libido is withdrawn and new objects can be cathexed. Needless to say, the object which is given up here is an infantile one. One could understand this mourning reaction as a specific transference situation—for instance, in the case mentioned, as a reliving of the death of the mother. But it seems to me that this reaction, though frequently to a slighter degree, is a typical one and is in no way conditioned by the experience of death in childhood. It appears to me as if in the analytic situation as such there are a number of factors which represent not only fantasy repetitions of childhood conditions, but are the expressions of a specific, actually existing relationship. That is to say, the analytic situation as such is an abnormal one, a unique relationship between two persons which necessarily causes the one partner to produce infantile reactions and to hold on to infantile behavior in relation to the other. The analyst has listened for two or three or more years with unending patience and unvarying interest to the patient's most intimate confessions, and helped him through innumerable battles.

Though he has not satisfied the patient's sexual desire, though he has not given the patient the type of love he wanted, he has nevertheless given him something very tangible: his unselfish attention. Through his interest, the analyst has proved to the patient that his inner life is worth being looked at, being heard about. This implies some kind of primitive narcissistic gratification to the patient which, I believe, is the basis for the already described passive-oral attitude of the patient, his hope of further love and his tendency to see the analyst as a powerful parental figure.

We all know that in analysis the patient has to experience frustrations in the transference situation. But the somewhat sublimated passive infantile gratification already mentioned cannot be denied to the patient. The analyst cannot withhold it; it is the basis of our method. Here satisfaction has to be given.

Furthermore, we must not forget that the analyst was hardly ever a real person. Unknown and undescribed, he became the recipient of the patient's fantasies. The lack of reality around the analyst makes it impossible to see him with his foibles and weaknesses as an ordinary human being. He has given help to the patient, and beyond that the afore-mentioned infantile gratification. As correction through reality is impossible, it is no wonder that the patient has a tendency to continue to see the analyst as an aggrandized figure and does not like to give up this gratifying relationship. He may even understand intellectually that further contact would preserve an unhealthy transference situation and condition later acting out. Thus he may understand why there should not be any further social contact with the analyst; but he does not like this.

Thus it appears to me inevitable that the termination of analysis should be felt as a loss, particularly by those patients who are not too happy with their life in reality and for whom it is not too easy to shift readily to other objects the libido invested in the analyst. Nevertheless, in the course of time, after a really thorough analysis, this shift does take place, and slowly the wish to hold on to the infantile relationship to the analyst is relinquished. It seems to me important to understand this sequence as a typical reaction to the analytic situation in order not to be too concerned about it and to be able to determine the suitable time for the termination of analysis. We do not have to be too worried about any lasting negative results of these residues of transference. As in mourning, a spontaneous recovery takes place, we might say a recovery from the abnormal situation of analysis.

With students who have occasion to meet their analyst professionally after termination of analysis this process progresses faster. They have the opportunity to see their analysts in the frame of reality, and the magic omnipotent features of the relationship collapse more readily under these conditions and may be replaced by a mature friendship or a working relationship. The final solution of these last traces of transference can be considered as a final growing up of the patient.

Frequently, as Ferenczi mentions, hidden magic expectations are revealed only as a reaction to the planned termination of analysis—for instance, the tenaciously and secretly kept expectation of the woman patient that analysis in the end will supply her with a penis. To uncover such fantasies, it seems technically advisable to plan the termination of analysis several months ahead of time in order to have the opportunity of thoroughly working through this problem. A fixed date, unless, let us say, a summer interruption or some event in the life of the patient makes it inevitable, is better avoided, in order not to create too much pressure and anxiety. Frequently one experiences a flare-up of symptoms which had been overcome long before, or neurotic elements up to then unknown come to life. Frequently this flare-up can be understood as the effect of the afore-mentioned need to hold on to the analyst who is, so to speak, to be blackmailed into continuing the analysis.

These dependent attitudes as byproducts of the analytic situation as such have impressed various analysts, and some have advocated short analyses as a means to avoid this danger. I cannot agree with this conception. The short analysis leaves so many deeper problems unsolved and untouched that its disadvantage is greater than any gain from it. If I am correctly informed, the Columbia School has recently made this type of dependence the main theme of their transference analysis. With this innovation, as with all other deviations from the classical theory and method, one element is put into the center of the stage in order that other equally important ones may be dropped. If one analyzes solely these vestiges of dependence, one is likely to overlook other important features of transference.

It seems important in this connection to mention briefly certain countertransference attitudes which may complicate the problem. Sometimes analysts have a tendency to terminate analyses too early. Apart from expediency motives, there is frequently a narcissistic need to achieve results quickly which cannot tolerate the slow pace of analytic work. There are others who have a need to end relationships with patients soon before a danger situation in regard to their own badly controlled homosexual urges can arise; others cannot give up a patient and enjoy the dependency situation. These countertransference difficulties, of course, should be eliminated in the analyst's own analysis. But the situation of ending an analysis is seldom one that comes to the attention of the training analyst, as we do not usually see our students so long. Of course, the underlying difficulty should show up in some other fashion.

So far I have mentioned only the termination of a successful analysis. We are, however, not always successful, or at least not completely successful. Frequently, only in the course of analysis does it become obvious how deeply ingrained the anxieties are or how weak the ego, or how over-rigid and overstrong are the instincts. Only in the course of analysis is one faced with the failure of the attempt to solve these conflicts. Patients of this type are usually suffering severely, and a serious attempt to help is justified even if we fail to do so. Frequently we do not fail completely, but we can bring about partial mitigation of symptoms and strengthening of the ego. But the time comes when we have to face the fact that it does not make sense to go on. In these cases, it is my impression that a thorough working through of the reaction to the termination of the analysis as described above is not indicated. It is wisest, in these situations, to wait for a period when the ending of analysis seems to be least painful, when,

On the Termination of Analysis

for instance, suffering has subsided, when certain narcissistic gratifications are available. One could say with justification that this way of ending analysis is not really a psychoanalytic but a psychotherapeutic one. It may be so indeed, but it seems to be the least painful procedure.

7

On Countertransference

(1951)

T HE ACT of understanding the patient's productions
in analysis and the ability to respond to them
skillfully is not based solely on logical conclusions.
Frequently the analyst can observe that insight into
the material comes suddenly as if from somewhere
within his own mind. Suddenly the confusing, incom-
prehensible presentations make sense; suddenly the
disconnected elements become a *Gestalt.* Equally suddenly, the analyst gets inner evidence as to what his
interpretation should be and how it should be given.
This type of understanding impresses one as something
which is experienced almost passively. "It happens." It
is not the result of an active process of thinking, like
the solution of a mathematical problem. It seems obvious that this kind of insight into the patient's problem is achieved via the analyst's own unconscious. It is
as if a partial and short-lived identification with the
patient had taken place. The evidence of what is going
on in the patient's unconscious, then, is based on an
awareness of what is now going on in the analyst's

Published originally in *The International Journal of Psycho-Analysis,*
32:25–31, 1951.

own mind. But this identification has to be a short-lived one. The analyst has to be able to swing back to his outside position in order to be capable of an objective evaluation of what he has just now felt from within.

Anyhow, the tool for understanding is the analyst's own unconscious. When Freud advised that the analyst should listen with free-floating attention, he had exactly this in mind. The material should be absorbed by the analyst's unconscious; there should not be any aim-directed censoring or conscious elimination through the analyst's attempts at rational thinking. This method of listening will guarantee the analyst's ability to remember, in an effortless way, those parts of the patient's previous material which connect with or serve to explain the new elements which are presented.

It is obvious what hazards may arise. If the analyst has some reasons of his own for being preoccupied, for being unable to associate freely, for shrinking back from certain topics, or if he is unable to identify with the patient, or has to identify to such a degree that he cannot put himself outside the patient again—to mention only a few of the possible difficulties—he will be unable to listen in this effortless way, to remember, to understand, to respond correctly.

Furthermore, there are more tasks for the analyst. He has to be the object of the patient's transference. He has to be the screen on to which the patient can project his infantile objects, to whom he can react with infantile emotions and impulses, or with defenses against these. The analyst has to remain neutral in order to make this transference possible. He must not respond to the patient's emotion in kind. He must be

able to tolerate love and aggression, adulation, temptation, seduction, and so on, without being moved, without partiality, prejudice, or disgust. It is, indeed, not an
easy task to be so attuned to another person as the
analyst has to be in order to understand and, at the
same time, to remain uninvolved. Without having
faced his own unconscious, his own ways and means of
solving conflicts, that is, without being analyzed himself, the analyst would not be able to live up to these
difficult requirements.

To be neutral in relation to the patient, to remain
the screen, does not, of course, imply that the analyst
has no relation at all to the patient. We expect him to
be interested in the patient, to have a friendly willingness to help him. He may like or dislike the patient. As
far as these attitudes are conscious, they have not yet
anything to do with countertransference. If these feelings increase in intensity, we can be fairly certain that
the unconscious feelings of the analyst, his own
transferences onto the patient, i.e., countertransferences, are mixed in. Intense dislike is frequently a
reaction to not understanding the patient; or, it may
be based on deeper "real countertransference." Too
great, particularly sexualized, interest in the patient
can most frequently be understood also as a countertransference. We shall come back to this point. (A situation in which the analyst really falls in love with
the patient is infrequent. In such a situation the analysis becomes impossible, and the patient should be sent
to somebody else.)

Countertransference thus comprises the effects of the
analyst's own unconscious needs and conflicts on his
understanding or technique. In such instances the pa-

tient represents for the analyst an object of the past onto whom past feelings and wishes are projected, just as in the patient's transference situation with the analyst. The provoking factor for such reactions may be something in the patient's personality or material, or something in the analytic situation as such. This is countertransference in the proper, more narrow sense.

In a discussion before the psychoanalytic study group in Prague in 1938, between Dr. Otto Fenichel and myself, on the topic of countertransference, which Dr. Fenichel later on used as the basis of a paper entitled "The Implications of the Didactic Analysis," the concept of countertransference was understood in a much wider sense. We included under this heading all expressions of the analyst's use of the analysis for purposes of acting out. We speak of acting out whenever the activity of analyzing has an unconscious meaning for the analyst. Then his response to the patient, frequently his whole handling of the analytic situation, will be motivated by hidden unconscious tendencies. Although the patients in these cases are frequently not real objects onto whom something is transferred but only the tools by means of which some needs of the analyst, such as to allay anxiety or to master guilt-feelings, are gratified, we have used the term countertransference. This seemed to us advisable because this type of behavior is so frequently mixed up and fused with effects of countertransference proper that it becomes too schematic to keep the two groups apart. The simplest cases in the proper sense of countertransference are those which occur suddenly, under specific circumstances, and with specific patients. These are, so to speak, acute manifestations of countertransference. I give you a simple example which was related to me recently:

An analyst was ill, suffering pain, but able to continue work with the help of rather large doses of analgesics. One of his patients chose this time to accuse the analyst of neglecting her, of not giving her enough time, and so on. The complaints were brought forth with the nagging persistence of a demanding oral-aggressive individual. The analyst became violently annoyed with the patient and had great difficulty in restraining the expression of his anger. What had been going on is fairly obvious. The analyst resented the fact that the patient was able to make these aggressive demands for attention while he, the analyst, was in a situation which would have justified similar demands, but he had to control himself. The unexpressed demands then tie up with deeper material which is irrelevant in this connection.

The analyst is here in a special situation in which his mental balance is shaken by illness. In this condition, he cannot tolerate the patient who, as a mirror, reflects his own repressed impulses. The countertransference reaction is based on an identification with the patient. Identifications of this kind belong to the most frequent forms of countertransference.

Another example: A young analyst, not yet finished with his own training, feels irked by one of his patients and feels a desire to get rid of him. Why? The patient has expressed homosexual tendencies which the analyst is not inclined to face within himself. Here again the patient is the mirror that reflects something that is intolerable.

Countertransference phenomena are by no means

always manifestations of defense against the impulse, as in these last examples, but they may be simple impulse derivatives. I remember the case of a colleague who came for a second analysis because he has a tendency to fall in love with young attractive women patients. The analysis revealed that he was not really interested in these women but in identification with them. He wanted to be made love to by the analyst and in this way to gratify the homosexual transference fantasies which had remained unanalyzed in his first analysis.

The sexual interest in the patient which could be called the most simple and direct manifestation of countertransference is here the result of an identification with the patient. This is typical. Most of the so-called "simple" manifestations of that kind are built after that pattern. The patients are not really the objects of deeper drives, but they reflect the impulses of the analyst as if they were fulfilled. But identification is certainly not the only possible danger. At other times, for instance, one is faced with countertransference reactions which are provoked by the specific content of the patient's material. For example, certain material of a patient was understood by an analyst as a representation of the primal scene. Whenever the material was touched upon by the patient, the analyst reacted to it with the defense reaction he had developed in the critical situation in his childhood: he became sleepy and had difficulties in concentrating and remembering.

Sometimes the disturbances are of a more general nature, not dependent on any special situation of the analyst or special material. It is the analytic relationship as such and some special aspects of the relationship to patients which cause the analyst to be disturbed by manifestations of countertransference. For instance, an inclination to accept resistances at face value, a feeling of inability to attack or analyze them, was based, in two cases which I could observe in analysis, on an unconscious identification with the patient, just because he was in the position of a patient. The analyst expressed in that identification a passive masochistic wish (in one case, a homosexual one; in the other case, of a woman analyst, a predominantly masochistic one) to change places with the patient and to be in the passive position. Both were tempted to let themselves be accused and mistreated by the patient. In both cases, to be a patient corresponded to an infantile fantasy.

Such manifestations of countertransference, of course, do not represent isolated episodes but reflect permanent neurotic difficulties of the analyst. Sometimes the countertransference difficulties are only one expression of a general character problem of the analyst. For instance, unconscious aggression may cause the analyst to be overconciliatory, hesitant, and unable to be firm when necessary. Unconscious guilt feelings may express themselves in boredom or therapeutic overeagerness. These attitudes naturally represent serious handicaps for the analyst.

Another example of this kind is a paranoid attitude which makes the analyst concentrate on "motes" in other people's eyes in order not to see the "beams" in his own. This can degenerate into complete projection of his own contents or may remain within the frame of usefulness and enable the analyst to develop an uncanny sense of smell, so to speak, for these particular contents. He does not invent them in his patients but is able to unearth them, even if they exist only in minimal quantities. Obviously the analytic situation is a fertile field for such behavior. The mechanism may originally even have created the interest in analysis. Frequently, though, the analytic situation is not the only battleground for these forces, which extend also to other fields of life. This attitude cannot be considered as a pure countertransference phenomenon in the proper sense any more. It belongs more to the "acting out" group, which I mentioned earlier, and of which I would like to give just one example:

An analyst had the need to prove that he was not afraid of the unconscious nor of his own unconscious drives. This led to a compulsion to "understand" the unconscious intellectually, as if to say, "Oh, I know and understand all that; I am not scared." This caused a tendency to preserve a safe distance from the patient's unconscious by helping to keep up an intellectual isolation, and induced the analyst to overlook the patient's defense mechanisms such as isolation. The aim of this acting out was, of course, to master the analyst's anxiety. Such mechanisms are double-edged. They work only for a certain time and tend to break down when the intensity of anxiety becomes too great. The analyst, being afraid of his breakdown, was frightened by any emotional breakthrough or outburst of anxiety in his patient and avoided anything which could help the patient to reach greater emotional depth. Under such conditions it became important not to identify himself with the patient at all or, at least, only with the resistances, which then were not recognized as such but were taken at their face value, this again seriously interfering with the analyst's tasks.

The bad relationship of the analyst with his own unconscious may lead to constant doubt of the veracity of the expressions of the unconscious. Such doubt is sometimes overcompensated by the extraordinary stress which is placed on any bit of unconscious material that can be recognized. Deep interpretations are then given in a compensatory way, before the patient is ready for them, in order to overcome the analyst's doubts. In other cases I have seen a fear of interpretations.

I shall refrain from giving any other examples for "acting out" in order not to overburden the reader with too many details. But there is one more group that should be mentioned. Here the analyst misuses the analysis to get narcissistic gratifications and assurances for himself. A specific form of this kind might be called the "Midas touch." It is as if whatever the analyst touches were transformed into gold. He is a magic healer. He restores potency and undoes castration. His interpretations are magic gifts. His patients become geniuses just because they are *his* patients. It is obvious what enormous gratification the analyst can get from such an attitude and how dangerous it is. It easily can lead to unrealistic evaluations of the patients, to inability to observe soberly, to therapeutic overambition and hostility against the patient who fails to give his analyst the narcissistic gratification of becoming cured by him. In general, the slow cumbersome process of analysis makes high demands on the analyst's patience and narcissistic equilibrium. It is obvious how detrimental it may become if this equilibrium is shaky, that is, if the analyst depends on his patients for narcissistic supplies.

Related to this are attitudes which one might call pedagogic ones. The analyst feels tempted to fulfill thwarted infantile desires of patients and thus to teach them that the world is not as terrible as they in their childish ways of thinking assume. Thus anxiety is smoothed over; reassurance is given instead of real analysis of the anxiety. The psychotherapeutic past with which most of our students come to analytic training frequently presents us with tendencies of this kind.

I remember the case of a colleague, for instance, who would constantly answer all the questions of a patient relating to the analyst's private affairs. The analyst was unable to let a frustrating situation come to a head, which would lead to the analysis of the childhood situation. Instead, he had to gratify and reassure the patient. It was as if he were saying to the patient: "I am not treating you as you were treated— that is, mistreated—by your parents," which means: "I am not treating you as I was treated by my parents or by my former analyst. I am healing what they damaged." Sometimes pedagogic attitudes like this may stand under the opposite sign: "I shall treat you as I was treated. I will do to you what was done to me." Here something that was originally passively experienced is transformed into something which is actively done to somebody else. This is one of the most effective forms of anxiety mastering.

I shall not continue to enumerate and describe here how the variety of possible disturbances in the activity of analysing is as manifold as the whole psychopathology of neuroses, character disturbances included. In all similar types of behavior in which the activity of analyzing is used in some way for extraneous unconscious purposes, mostly in order to keep up the analyst's inner equilibrium, the patient, as I mentioned before, is not a real object but is only used as a fortuitous tool to solve a conflict situation. Fenichel has coined a specific term to describe this situation: The patient is used as a witness to whom the analyst has to prove, for instance, that he can master the unconscious, or that he has no reason to feel guilty.

Let me stop here and look back. I have given many more examples of the permanent kind than of the acute one. This may be due to the material available to me, which after all was mostly contributed by analysts who came to analysis on account of some difficulty—but I am almost inclined to believe that most countertransference difficulties are indeed of the permanent type. It is obvious that the acute ones are much easier to deal with than the others. Frequently a bit of self-analysis can reveal what is going on and bring about a complete solution of the conflict. The permanent and more generalized forms are consequences of deeply engrained personality difficulties of the analyst for which there is only one solution: thorough analysis. Freud (1937), in his paper "Analysis Terminable and Interminable," advises that the analyst after some years of practice should have some more analysis, even when the difficulties he has to struggle with are not as serious as those described. This is something we really should bear in mind.

The two forms of countertransference manifestations could be compared with incidental hysterical symptoms in contrast to permanent character distortions. The attempt to keep these two types of countertransference clearly separated is of course schematic. As mentioned before, there are transitions from one form to the other.

It would be impossible to attempt to give a complete description and classification of even the most frequent forms of countertransference only. This would amount to a survey of the psychopathology of the analyst. We are most concerned with the effect these psychological mechanisms have on analytic technique. Nearly all the phenomena mentioned will interfere with the analyst's ability to understand, to respond, to handle the patient, to interpret in the right way. On the one hand, the special talent and the pathologic are usually just two sides of the same; a slight shift in cathexis may transform an unconscious mechanism of the analyst from a living out of his own conflicts into a valuable sublimation. On the other hand, what is the preliminary condition for his psychological interest and skill may degenerate into acting out.

It appears to me highly desirable to reach a closer understanding about the conditions under which these unconscious elements do constitute a foundation for adequate or even outstanding functioning and when they serve to interfere with, or at least to complicate, the activity of analyzing. We said before that the unconscious of the analyst is his tool. The readiness and faculty to use his own unconscious in that way obviously must have some deeper motivation in the analyst's psychological make-up.

The analysis of these deeper motives, which are the necessary basis for the analyst's interest, leads us back to the unconscious drives which were sublimated into psychological talent. Sometimes this personal origin of the analyst's interest in his work is clearly discernible even without analysis. I know a number of analysts who, after many years of work, are still fascinated by their being entitled to pry into other people's secrets; that is to say, they are voyeurs; they live out their infantile sexual curiosity. Curiosity is seriously considered by many analysts as an essential prerequisite for analysis, but this curiosity has to be of a special nature. It has to be desexualized. If it were still connected with sexual excitement, this would necessarily interfere with the analyst's functioning. It must be, furthermore, removed from the original objects and has to be used for an interest in understanding their psychology and their structure. In this way the whole process is lifted above the original level of conflict.

I give here a portion of the case material from the analysis of an analyst that throws some light on the psychologic background of such a sublimation. This may permit a somewhat deeper understanding of the structure of such a sublimation. The example I am choosing comes from a person who was capable and successful and had good therapeutic results. The countertransference in his case, in spite of the rather pathological origin, was, one might say, tamed and harnessed for the benefit of the work. I shall limit myself to a few important elements.

One of the special gifts of this analyst was his keenness of observation, his ability to grasp little peculiarities of behavior in his patients and to understand them—correctly—as expressions of an unconscious conflict. He was deeply interested in his work, to the exclusion of extraneous intellectual inclinations. The genesis of his psychological interest could be reconstructed in analysis as follows: Dr. X. from early childhood was again and again an unwilling witness to violent fights between unhappily married parents, which frightened him and brought forth the wish to reconcile them and to undo whatever damage might have been done in their battles, which were misunderstood by the child as sadistic primal scenes. The father, strong and powerful, but intellectually the mother's inferior, was "tearing pieces out of mother," as she complained whenever she wished to ward off his affectionate approaches. This left mother, the boy felt, castrated, sick, complaining, and at the same time, overambitious and demanding compensation for her own deficiencies from her son, who had to become "magnificent" to fill her narcissistic needs. Too frightened to identify with the father in his sadistic activities, the child rather early identified with the mother and felt passive and castrated like her. A mild attack of poliomyelitis during the height of the oedipal period served to engrave the mother identification more deeply. He now began to observe his own body as he had been observed anxiously by his mother who had been looking for signs of the illness. Overstress was now laid on any spark of masculinity, strength, and perfection to contradict the inner awareness of his passivity and his fear of castration. In a partial regression he now became interested in his anal functions, here too following his mother who overanxiously watched his anal productions, willing to give him ample praise when she was satisfied. He now overevaluated himself just as his mother overevaluated him. At that time a peculiar fantasy appeared: He is one with mother as if he and she were one body. He is her most precious part, that is, he is her penis. By being "magnificent" as she wants him to be, his whole body becomes a big penis and in this way he undoes her castration. Both together, they are complete.

This fantasy remained the basis for his tendency to self-observation, which thenceforward continued to exist. In this self-observation he plays two roles. He is identified with the anxious, castrated mother who watches him and at the same time he exhibits himself in order to gratify her. This narcissistic play now becomes a new source of gratification for him. He is proud of his keenness of observation, his intelligence, and knowledge. His thoughts are his mental products, of which he is as proud as of his anal achievements. In this way he is reconstructing what mother has lost. By self-observation he heals her castration in a magic way.

When he was nine, a little brother, the only other sibling, was born. This was a fulfillment of a desire for a child of his own which had already come to the fore in connection with his anal interests. Now he develops a motherly interest in the baby and succeeds in turning away his interest to a large degree from his own body to the baby and later to other outside objects. The self-observation turns into observation of other people, and thus the original play between him and mother is re-enacted by him in projection onto outside objects and becomes unselfish and objective. A necessary preliminary step in the direction of sublimation was made.

Furthermore, another important development can now be noticed. His interest in the little brother becomes a psychological one. He remembers a scene when the little one, not yet two years of age, had a temper tantrum, in his rage biting into the wood of the furniture. The older brother was very concerned about the intensity of emotion in the child and wondered what to do about it. Thus the interest which originally had to do with physical intactness had turned towards emotional experiences.

The psychological interest from now on played an important role in his life. The decision to study medicine and to choose psychoanalysis as his specialty impresses us as a natural development of these interests. Here he can build up a stable sublimation of his peculiar strivings. He can now continue to observe, not himself, but other people. He can unearth their hidden defeats and signs of castration and can use the technique of analysis for healing them. He has a special talent for understanding other people's unconscious and their hidden resistance. In the relationship with the patient, he relives his original interplay with mother. By curing the patient, he himself becomes cured and his mother's castration is undone. The cured patient represents himself as a wonderful phallus that has returned to mother. It is obvious what tremendous narcissistic stress he laid on being a "good analyst." In this new position, as a "magnificent" analyst, he represents his deeper ego ideal as fulfilled; he is a phallic mother. On a higher level, the patient also represents his child, his little brother, whom he wants to understand, in order to educate and help him.

The analytic faculties of this analyst are obviously based on an originally rather pathologic and narcissistic self-interest. That he is interested in a patient is based on a projection of this self-interest; but what he observes remains objective and does not represent a projection of inner experiences and fantasies. This faculty for objective observation has to do with the fact that Dr. X., in spite of the, at some time, unstable boundaries between him and his mother, had had a warm and affectionate relationship with her and was capable of real object-libidinal relations. He sees what is there and not what is within himself, though his motive for seeing and his ability to understand are based primarily upon his preoccupation with the mother's and his own intactness or deficiency. Although deep-down he wants to be a magic healer, he is able to content himself with the slow process of interpreting resistances, removing defenses, and unearthing the unconscious. Thus one can say that though his need to understand is the result of his highly pathological mother fixation, he has succeeded in sublimating these infantile needs into true psychological interest. That he wishes to understand and to heal is motivated by the past. What he understands and how he tries to heal is based on objective reality. This is essential, as it represents the difference between acting out and a true sublimation.

I am aware that in presenting this bit of case material I am not being fully successful in really shedding light on the finer prerequisites of this accomplishment. The problem of why a sublimation is successful or not depends to a large degree on economic factors, and these are beyond the scope of this discussion. This is a problem, by the way, which is by no means specific for this type of sublimation.

The wish to heal and the psychological interest could be traced in this material to specific infantile set-ups. I do not feel entitled to assume that the wish to heal is typically based on a similar conflict situation. A further investigation of the origin of the interest in psychology and healing in a more general way would be a challenging problem.

What is of interest for us here is the similarity and the difference of the well-functioning sublimation and the aforementioned types of acting out. Here as well as there, deep personal needs are fulfilled. But while in this sublimation the fulfillment is achieved *via* the route of desexualized psychological insight, this transformation has not taken place in the pathological forms of countertransference.

The double-edged character of such a sublimation is obvious. The intensity of interest, the special faculty of understanding, lead to a high quality of work, but any disturbance of psychic equilibrium may bring about a breakdown of the sublimation and the satisfaction of personal needs may become overimportant so that the objectivity in the relationship to the patient becomes disturbed.

What I would like to stress is that in this case of undisturbed functioning the psychological interest obviously is based on a very complicated "countertransference," which is desexualized and sublimated in character, while in the pathological examples the conflict persisted in its original form and the analytic situation was used either for living out the underlying impulses or defending against them, or for proving that no damage has occurred in consequence of them.

We might come to the following conclusion: Countertransference is a necessary prerequisite of analysis. If it does not exist, the necessary talent and interest are lacking. But it has to remain shadowy and in the background. This can be compared to the role that attachment to the mother plays in the normal object choice of the adult man. Loving was learned with the mother. Certain traits in the adult object may lead back to her, but normally the object can be seen in its real character and responded to as such. A neurotic person takes the object absolutely for his mother or suffers because she is not his mother.

In the normally functioning analyst we find traces of the original unconscious meaning of analyzing, while the neurotic one still misunderstands analysis under the influence of his unconscious fantasies and reacts accordingly.

8

The Discussion of 1912
on Masturbation
and Our Present-Day Views

(1951)

IN 1912, a Discussion on Masturbation was held at the Vienna Psychoanalytic Society. It was subsequently published in book form (1912; see also Freud, 1912a). At that time, it was already well understood that to talk about masturbation was almost identical with talking about sexuality in general. Thus Victor Tausk, in his discussion, offered the following formulation: "The conflicts around masturbation . . . are *in nuce* the conflicts around sexuality as such."

The problems of masturbation are as interesting today as they were in 1912. Lampl-de Groot (1950) published a paper on masturbation, also taking the 1912 Discussion as its point of departure and comprising what might be described as an outline of the development of infantile sexuality.

The diversity of the problems which can be discussed from this starting point is enormous. I shall have to limit myself to a very brief report on a few

Published originally in *The Psychoanalytic Study of the Child*, 6:80–94. New York: International Universities Press, 1951.

highlights of the 1912 Discussion, pointing out the differences between the ideas expressed then and those prevailing now, 39 years later, and stressing a few additional problems which seem especially important to me.

As pointed out by Federn (1928) in his review of the 1912 Discussion, at that time ego psychology had not yet been introduced into analysis, the Oedipus complex had just been accepted as a universal human fate, and the role of castration anxiety as the core of neurotic anxiety was not yet fully understood. Indeed, only two of the authors who participated in the Discussion—Ferenczi and Sachs—connected the anxiety which arises around masturbation with castration anxiety, and this relationship was perceived there for the first time in analytic literature.

As the opinions that were voiced then do not quite conform to our present-day conceptions, it seems worthwhile to point out the differences. On the other hand, the great wealth of ideas first presented on that occasion now forms part of our everyday analytic understanding. Many basic clinical conceptions of later periods can be found therein in an embryonic form.

Most striking, for our present-day thinking, is the stress laid by many of the discussants—with Freud as their leader—upon the harmfulness of masturbation. It was Freud's original conception, which he had already developed in the eighteen-nineties, that masturbation as an incomplete sexual discharge caused physiological damage to the sexual apparatus and led to neurasthenia, which comprised the symptoms of headache, constipation, and fatigue, based upon the so-called spinal irritation. On the other hand, damming up of libido in frustrated excitement, too long-lasting abstinence, coitus interruptus or reservatus, would cause anxiety neurosis. Both syndromes were classified as actual neurosis, a term hardly used today. They were understood to be the physiological results of a disturbed sexual economy. The exact nature of the physiological factor was—and has remained—unclear.

I feel that at this point I should say a few words about our present position on actual neurosis, although to a certain extent this goes beyond the topic of masturbation.

Freud's conception of the scope of actual neurosis, as it was first formed in the eighteen-nineties and still persisted in 1912, was certainly much broader than ours today. In his early paper, "On the Grounds for Detaching a Particular Syndrome from Neurasthenia under the Description 'Anxiety Neurosis'" (1894), we find a great number of clinical phenomena listed as symptoms of actual neurosis, which today we do not hesitate to classify among the psychoneurotic symptoms, such as agoraphobia, pavor nocturnus, anticipation of death and calamity with regard to members of the family, etc. Furthermore, we know of many cases which at first glance seem to fit completely into the syndrome of neurasthenia, featuring a disturbed sexual regime and symptoms of anxiety, insomnia, cardiac pressure, constipation, etc., but which under careful analysis prove to have a much more complicated structure. We frequently succeed in analyzing these symptoms and in reducing them to an underlying conflict. Often we can relate them to the castration anxiety which is mobilized by the ego in its state of danger.

Annie Reich

Federn (1928) reported that when the topic of actual neurosis was rediscovered in 1928 in a private circle in Vienna, Freud remarked that actual neuroses and psychoneuroses were of different origin, and that those who would explain the actual-neurotic symptoms on a solely psychogenic basis, as well as those who would exclusively stress the factor of physiological sexual frustration in regard to cause and curability of the neurosis, were simplifying complicating facts.

Although Freud's new theory of anxiety, which was published more than a decade after that discussion, shifted the accent to the role of the ego in the genesis of anxiety, he did not abandon the concept of the two-fold origin of neurosis. In "Inhibitions, Symptoms and Anxiety," Freud (1926) was no longer interested in the nature of physiological factors. He stressed that the state of dammed-up libido may become a traumatic one; in it, the ego is helpless either to control the demand—for instance, by psychic modification—or to provide discharge. The ego reacts to the traumatic situation with anxiety. This anxiety, however, is not voluntarily produced by the ego as a signal, but is a sign that the ego is, for the time being, out of commission and overwhelmed by involuntary physiological discharges. These discharges can be regarded as either the physiological side of the affect of anxiety or as actual-neurotic symptoms.

Neurotic symptoms thus can be provoked in two ways. In a danger situation the ego may give an anxiety signal, which stirs up defenses and leads to the formation of psychoneurotic symptoms; or a traumatic situation may arise which brings about automatic discharges, i.e., actual-neurotic phenomena. The inability to provide discharge is frequently, as we all know, caused by psychic conflicts. It also often results from an ego regression which deprives the ego of adult methods of handling the demands of the id.

Thus we recognize that we are faced with complicated interactions between ego and libido, between psychic conflict and primitive traumatic reaction. Without giving up the original idea of the twofold origin of neurosis, we have therefore come to a more integrated and, at the same time, a more complex conception. It should be mentioned here that Fenichel, more than any other author, demonstrated again and again how Freud's original conception has to be integrated into the later, structural theory of personality.

The interaction between actual neurosis and psychoneurosis was always realized by Freud. He held that any psychoneurosis was based upon an underlying, actual-neurotic symptom. In 1912 he formulated the problem as follows: "The psychogenetic symptom has an actual-neurotic core, like the grain of sand which is the stimulating agent for the formation of a pearl."

This, of course, can be most easily understood in cases with conversion-hysteric symptoms. Hartmann, in a discussion before The New York Psychoanalytic Society in November, 1950, formulated that the ego, in a psychogenic conflict, makes use of slight symptoms of dammed-up libido to find tangible expression for infantile anxiety contents.

Under the influence of Freud's conception of neurasthenia as resulting from masturbation, the Discussion of 1912 was to a large extent overshadowed by the idea of the harmfulness of masturbation, although Freud himself, and others, felt that this was not a scientifically justifiable starting point. In his concluding remarks to the Discussion, Freud grouped the ways in which masturbation might be injurious under three headings, viz.:

a. That of *organic damage*, through a mechanism as yet unknown, wherein the factors of excessive indulgence and inadequate gratification . . . may play a role.
b. The establishment of *psychic patterns*, inasmuch as a great need may be gratified without having to strive for an alteration of the external world. However, where the pattern is responded to by a strong reaction formation, this may lay the foundation for the most valuable characterological gains.
c. By providing an occasion for the *fixation of infantile sexual aims* and arrestment in psychic infantilism, thereby creating the disposition to neurosis. . . .

As far as point "a" is concerned, Freud pointed out that the question as to when masturbation is injurious is identical with the problem as to when sexual activity as such becomes pathogenic. He felt that it was of help here to distinguish between the direct noxious influences (actual-neurotic), and the indirect ones which result from the resistance of the ego against this sexual activity.

It is obvious that from our present-day point of view we do not see masturbation-neurasthenia as a direct and simple sequence. Freud himself, as far as I know, after 1912 mentioned masturbation as a direct cause of actual neurosis only once, in the *Introductory Lectures on Psychoanalysis* (1915–1917), at that time no longer giving weight to the distinction between neurasthenia and anxiety neurosis. Otherwise, he spoke more generally of a disturbed sexual regime which causes actual-neurotic symptoms.

In the 1912 Discussion much attention was devoted to the description of and distinction between masturbation in infants, children, adolescents, and adults. The concern about the harmfulness of masturbation related mainly to pubertal and adult masturbation. Tausk formulated most clearly that it depends upon the stage of the libidinal level whether masturbation can be considered an adequate method of gratification or not. Masturbation is an autoerotic method of sexual gratification. When a certain maturation of object-libidinal strivings is reached, masturbation cannot supply adequate gratification. Thus it would appear a satisfactory method in infancy and childhood, less so in puberty, and no longer so in adulthood. The continuation of masturbation beyond the phases to which it is adequate is caused, as Tausk pointed out, by society, which on the one hand wishes the adolescent to become a man, which expecting him at the same time to remain a child sexually. This point of view still prevails today. We believe, as was variously stated in the Discussion, that infantile and childhood masturbation is "normal," that is to say, ubiquitous. In boys, the nonexistence of masturbation during adolescence is usually a sign of serious illness, as was also observed in 1912. Reappearance of masturbation in the course of analysis is frequently an indication of the lifting of repressions and a forerunner of therapeutic improvement. On the other hand, masturbation in adults, apart from periods of transition or special sexual deprivation, must be considered a symptom. Fenichel (1945) stated this very clearly in *The Psychoanalytic Theory of Neurosis:*

> Masturbation as such does not produce neurosis. It has been proven clinically, however, that . . . masturbation that increases sexual tension but is not capable of discharging it adequately results in actual-neurotic symptoms.
>
> Masturbation is certainly pathological . . . whenever it is preferred by adult persons to intercourse . . . [p. 76].

Not all of the discussants in 1912 would have agreed with this point of view. One of them, the most radical, Stekel, claimed that masturbation is a necessary and universal form of sexual gratification and that every human being masturbates or has masturbated. This is indeed true; but no particular distinction was made whether the past or the present tense should be used, which seems an unacceptable simplification. Stekel believed that disturbances in connection with masturbation were due to guilt feelings caused by the attitude of the environment. This, again, is a simplification. He contended that masturbation was the only possible outlet for individuals fixated to perverse fantasies, that with the help of masturbation a discharge could be found, and that in this way perversions could be avoided. He gave an example of a patient who masturbated with the fantasy that he was cutting off his father's head and that the ejaculate represented the stream of blood spurting out of his father's body. How, Stekel argued, could such a fantasy have been gratified in reality? With the aid of masturbation, this man was able to keep his balance. Stekel did not understand that such a fantasy is a serious neurotic symptom, and that in such a case it does not make any difference whether masturbation takes place or not; severe guilt feelings will ensue in any event. Stekel's later development toward "wild analysis" had already begun there.

In general, the importance of the accompanying infantile and incestuous fantasies and of the ensuing guilt feelings was well understood by all of the authors. They saw clearly how an endless struggle against masturbation then follows, which may lead to various neurotic symptoms. Most of them agreed that conflict and guilt feeling interfere with the gratifying effect of masturbation, and that it was only unsatisfactory masturbation which became injurious. This insight, of course, still holds today. We believe that one can observe a vicious cycle here. Guilt feelings cause masturbation to be unsatisfactory. The inadequate gratifications may lead to continued tension, disturbance of sleep, etc., which in turn serve as so-called rational reasons for increased guilt feeling, in form of the conviction that masturbation is harmful. Attempts are made to desist from masturbating; these are futile, as unsatisfied desire continues to exist. The failure to conquer the impulse leads, again, to renewed guilt feelings. The final result of these conflicts usually is the development of neurotic symptoms.

In 1912, there was a general opinion that the origin and intensity of the guilt feelings could not be ascribed to the attitude of the environment alone and were not fully explainable. Only one of the authors connected the guilt feeling with the internalized figure of the father, thus anticipating Freud's concept of the superego. This was Victor Tausk, whose contribution appears in many respects the most brilliant. We still agree with his formulation, and would say that the guilt feelings are caused by the underlying oedipal fastasies. They are the expression of the conflict between the superego and infantile sexuality.

Until now we have talked about those difficulties which arise through the reaction of the ego to masturbation. A number of the discussants in 1912 were concerned with the direct, physiological effect of masturbation. A few concentrated particularly on the physiological harmfulness which they believed to be caused by the accumulation of "sex toxins." Others however, especially Ferenczi and Federn, introduced a new point of view which was to prove fruitful in later years, as it focused attention on details of sexual behavior and special forms of sexual disturbance and thus sharpened our clinical understanding. These two authors pointed to the consequences of disturbed sexual rhythm and of disturbed sexual excitement. Ferenczi believed that the forepleasure of looking, fondling, kissing, and so on, brings about a sexual charge of the whole body. As this forepleasure is missing in the case of masturbation, the backflow of sexual excitement, which should take place after the act, becomes impossible. Thus there results a damming-up of libido, which is experienced by the patient as a short-lasting neurasthenia (*Eintagsneurasthenie*). The phenomenon described by Ferenczi is well known to us. We are inclined to see it rather as a guilt reaction than as a purely physiological consequence. Federn pointed out the pathogenic importance of lack of gratification in masturbation, emphasizing that a particular inability to tolerate the tension of frustration is a sign of a neurotic disposition—a point of view which we certainly share today. He further spoke of the disturbed rhythm and the disturbed orgastic discharge curve. It is the insufficient discharge which interrupts the otherwise automatic self-regulation of sexuality and of the sequence of sexual urge, sexual act, orgasm, and placid interval. This disturbance is responsible for "excessive" masturbation. Since gratification can never be achieved, masturbation has to be repeated over and over again. It is this excessive masturbation which is pathogenic. This opinion, which was shared by most of the discussants, was taken up again by Nunberg in his *Principles of Psychoanalysis* (1932). Nunberg believes that the lack of gratification, which leads to excessive masturbation, is caused by the damming up of libido as a result of the fact that in masturbation no real objects are cathected, but only fantasy objects.

Generally speaking, we all agree that insufficient gratification, whatever its cause, frequently is the motivating factor in excessive masturbation. But something else should be pointed out here. Excessive masturbation often resembles a compulsive symptom. While seemingly it is merely the expression of desire for sexual discharge, it has, at the same time, an important defensive function—most frequently, the warding-off of anxiety. It is often structured like a diphasic symptom. For example, a little girl masturbates with the fantasy of producing a penis which is supposed to enable her to outshine her mother and attract her father's admiration. The act is followed by guilt feelings and by the fear of having damaged her genitals forever. Only a new act will dispel her fears, by again producing the illusion that she is in possession of a penis, that the terrible consequences of the previous act have not taken place, and that she is in a position to gratify her incestuous fantasies. As in a chain reaction, one act of masturbation necessitates the next. In these cases, pregenital contents, often with strong sadistic coloration, are also frequently discharged by genital means. This obviously must remain unsatisfactory. Self-destructive tendencies are also important in this connection. Originally the fear existed that masturbation would lead to the destruction of the genitals, and a desperate struggle against it set in. The struggle being unsuccessful, a need for punishment arose; and then, the sinful activity as such, the dangerous masturbatory act, had to be undertaken again and again, no longer for purposes of pleasure, but as an instrument of punishment by a relentless—and corrupt—superego.

Thus, apart from lack of gratification and from possible physical consequences, excessive masturbation is in itself a rather serious symptom. But even without being excessive, masturbation may leave decisive pathological traces in the personality. This brings us to the other two points of Freud's summary, which I would like to discuss together.

It was pointed out repeatedly in the Discussion how object choice and object finding become more difficult through masturbation. Masturbation requires no effort; no attempt to find a mate need be made, no aggression mobilized to overcome difficulties. Normal aggressiveness and normal adjustments to reality are retarded.

Idealized fantasy images are preserved, to which no object in reality can live up, and which are but the lightly disguised incestuous objects. The step from fantasy objects to reality objects is not made, and reality in general need not be fully accepted. Infantile fixations need not be relinquished. In this way, too, masturbation resembles a vicious circle: Inhibitions prevent turning to real objects. On the other hand, masturbation is a hotbed for infantilism; a gliding into more and more infantile fantasies is made easier by it. Sadger stressed that masturbation is based upon a reversal of original longings for passive gratification, received from the mother's care during childhood, which, in identification with the mother, the masturbating adolescent later administers to himself. From here, the step to homosexuality is easy. Tausk showed that the same outcome can result from a prolonged concentration of autoerotic interest on the own genitals. He described how, in the course of masturbation, the genitals may become personalized. It is then as though the masturbating person had fallen in love with his own genitals. This pathological increase of primitive narcissism is, of course, highly injurious to any object choice. It may, as already mentioned, lead to exclusive interest in the genitals of a person of the same sex; or it may lead to exclusive interest in the female genitals as such, with complete incapacity to develop more integrated, affectionate relationships to women as persons. Tausk here anticipated his own later brilliant paper on the "Influencing Machine," in which he was to draw attention to the role of the narcissistically cathected, own genitals in schizophrenia (Tausk, 1919).

The pivotal importance of infantile masturbation and of the struggle against it, for the whole later development, was given due weight in the Discussion, particularly by Federn and Tausk. The latter pointed out that, after the repression of genital contents, there occurs a regression of the fantasies to pregenitality. The sexual theories of little children, which often show a strongly pregenital coloration, are such modified masturbation fantasies. Federn, however, emphasized that sometimes the persistence of genital masturbation preserves the child from regression to pregenital and sadistic strivings, and prevents the development of serious pathology. Here Federn implied the importance of preserving the genital level of development. Tausk described how, after the repression of genital masturbation, extragenital and sadomasochistic practices are substituted for the pleasure thus renounced. Sometimes, this may represent the starting point for later perversions, or masturbation substitutes such as nail biting, tearing of hangnails, rhythmical knocking, enuresis, etc., may continue to persist. Masturbation substitutes were also mentioned at other points in the Discussion. It was Tausk who shed light on their genesis. These substitutes are frequently the only traces of masturbation that can be found in the latency period. Often they show the same compulsive character as masturbation. In many cases the substitute masturbation is displaced away from the body and acted out with inanimate objects, e.g., biting of pencils, rolling of bread pellets between the fingers, etc. Such substitute activities lead, with but little transition, into compulsive symptoms.

Today we know that in later years, most often in

puberty, there may be a return from the pregenital activity of fantasy back to genital masturbation. But these apparently genital activities are frequently found to be still accompanied by unconscious, pregenital fantasies. Peculiarities of the method of masturbation often reveal the pregenital core of the activity. The ego reaction of guilt is often intensified in these cases, as it consists of a fusion of the fear of punishment for genital activity (castration anxiety) with earlier, archaic anxieties. For example, in a woman patient, masturbation was accompanied by "cleansing" of the genitals, i.e., by removal of genital discharge or residue of menstrual blood, which was looked at and smelled as a substitute for putting it in the mouth. The underlying anal and oral fantasy is obvious.

In this context, it should be mentioned that, besides the pregenital strivings, otherwise relinquished homosexual tendencies also reappear in puberty and become equally recognizable through analysis of the method of masturbation. For instance, men with unconscious homosexual fantasies when masturbating sometimes hide the penis between the thighs. Clitoris masturbation in girls is frequently based upon a fantasy of having a penis. A young woman, for example, who was capable of good sexual relations with men which led to full vaginal orgasm, at the same time practiced clitoral masturbation with the fantasy: "Here I have something which the man cannot take away like his penis."

The regression to pregenitality is regarded today as one of the most important occurrences in childhood development. Usually the repression of genital contents is accompanied by a severe struggle against childhood masturbation and is a manifestation of the breakdown of the Oedipus complex. The later configuration of neurosis and character structure is largely determined by the particular developments which take place at that stage. In any event, this emphasis upon pregenital regression, in the papers of 1912, strikes us as one of the many instances where important elements of our present knowledge were for the first time conceived on that occasion.

The problem of character had, by 1912, only been approached by Freud (1908) in his paper about anal character; it was certainly not yet the center of interest. In the Discussion in that year, various attempts were made to relate character structure to the struggle against masturbation in puberty. Sadger and Rank spoke of the character of the "onanist," as though this were a particular, neurotic syndrome. They pointed out very specific reactions which develop in the course of the fight against masturbation, showing how habitual mendacity is often a consequence of the need to lie about masturbation and how, on the other hand, the reaction formation against such lying leads to confession compulsion and compulsive honesty. Rank went further by speaking, in this connection, of certain character traits which we usually attribute to the compulsive character, such as collecting compulsion, washing compulsion, penuriousness based on the need to save the ejaculate, etc. This same tie-up between masturbation conflicts and compulsive traits was also made by Hitschmann. Moreover, Rank mentioned the displacement of the struggle against masturbation to the oral zone in the form of compulsive starving or muteness. For the first time, as far as I know, masturbation thus was recognized as a starting point of certain oral disturbances as well as of compulsion neurosis. Even though the deeper connections—i.e., pregenital regression as a defense against genital temptation—were not clarified, again this represented a very important first step.

Although our present-day understanding of character problems, which is based upon our greater knowledge of the ego, the defense mechanisms, and the superego, by far surpasses that displayed in the Discussion of 1912, those first outlines proved to be fundamental. There, for the first time, character structure was understood as being conditioned by the reaction formation of the ego in the fight against masturbation. Today we are inclined to see the results of masturbation conflicts not only in the specific forms described in 1912, but we have learned to recognize a great variety of clinical pictures as traceable to this cause.

The struggle against masturbation does not always end in a victory against it for which the ego pays, so to speak, with self-distortion. Not infrequently, the impulse to masturbate finds an outlet in roundabout ways. That this is the case in symptom formation, is obvious. I should like here to mention two types of "life figuration" which result from a "breakthrough" of masturbation, under special conditions, in the form of acting out in life.

The first type of acting out of masturbation conflicts can be perceived in the so-called "masked" masturbation (*larvierte Onanie*), which consists of activities which are accompanied by sexual excitement, but where the sexual character of the feelings as well as of the activity are not recognized. There is a similarity to the aforementioned masturbation substitutes which represent a displacement of sexual activities to other parts of the body, without any noticeable sexual excitement. However, in masked masturbation, sexual excitement persists, but is not recognized as such. We speak of masked masturbation, for instance, in referring to the masturbation of girls which is done by thigh pressure without use of the hands, and without any awareness of the sexual character of the sensations and of what is going on. This lack of awareness does not prevent the development of guilt feelings, which then are usually connected with a secondary reason.

There are other cases in which the sexual excitement becomes connected with completely nonsexual activities. There is no awareness of the sexual character of the excitement and therefore, of course, of the masturbatory meaning of the activity. Displacement of masturbation to nonsexual activities already implies that masturbation has spread over into life. An example of such a displacement of masturbatory excitement may, for instance, be seen in gambling. Often physical activities which involve a certain risk of danger, such as flying or reckless driving, lend themselves well to such a purpose. Children's violent games, like jumping down from high places, wild running, etc., may have a similar basis. Many of these activities involve the possibility of ending in catastrophe. The child may wind up by hurting himself; the reckless driver, by smashing his car; the gambler, by losing everything. In analysis one can recognize the sexual excitement, which was unnoticed before, and understand the catastrophe as a mixture of punishment and disguised orgasm.

There are cases in which the whole life configuration seems to be determined by an endless sequence of masturbatory excitement and masturbatory guilt. As an illustration, I would like to give a brief clinical example.

A woman patient had spent her life in an unending sequence of contradictory moods. For a time, she would be exhilarated, active, vivacious, outgoing, and intensely engaged in some kind of interesting activity. This would be followed by a mood of depression with feelings of unworthiness and of being destroyed. In these moods she was passive, silent, could not do anything, and felt "stuck." Some time later, the sequence would repeat itself. In the analysis, it was possible to connect these mood swings in the patient's adult life with similar ones during the latency period. At that time open masturbation, having resulted in too intense anxiety, had been given up, and other activities had been sexualized instead. There was, for instance, a game of jumping into a sandbox and urinating into it. This was done in a state of high excitement, but was followed by guilt and disgust. Here the sexual character of the game is still evident. Other games, however, were outwardly nonsexual, like sailing little boats in a basin of water, riding on a large toy elephant, or sneaking into the attic to look through the rummage there. All these games were undertaken by the child in the same state of excitement, with a feeling that she was doing something wonderful— the little boat was an ocean liner, the elephant a real one, the attic filled with untold mysteries—but they all ended in terrible letdown: The boat and the elephant were just toys, the attic merely full of dirt and rubbish. This letdown expressed both the fact that the masked masturbation failed to lead to any really gratifying discharge, and the fact that the guilt feeling related to the repressed original fantasy. Without realizing it, the patient was constantly alternating between masturbatory sexual stimulation and punishment for it.

It seems that repetitive mood swings which overshadow a person's entire life are frequently of such origin. Simmel (1930) has pointed out that drug addiction sometimes has the same structure. Repetitive temper tantrums in children also belong in this category. But frequently the specific content of the mood swing or temper tantrum relates to the content of the masturbation fantasy.

This brings us to the second type of acting out of masturbation conflicts, the analysis of which seems to me the most important contribution made in the last decade to problems involving masturbation. The contribution I refer to concerns one specific, possible outcome of the masturbation struggle. This particular mechanism was repeatedly described by Anna Freud in discussions and seminars; but the single mention of it which appeared in print is found in a rather inconspicuous place, a paper on "Certain Types and Stages of Social Maladjustment" (1948). There a mechanism significant in the general pathology of neurosis is discussed only from the point of view of a special pathology and in its application to delinquency.

Anna Freud first speaks of the child's double struggle against masturbation. On the one hand, this struggle is directed against the physical activity which, when avoided by the child, frequently leads to masturbation substitutes; on the other hand, it is aimed at the content of the fantasy, which may become completely unconscious. Sometimes, when the bodily outlet is entirely blocked, the fantasy is displaced into the realm of ego activities and acted out in dealings with the outside world. These ego activities thereby become distorted, sexualized, and maladjusted. That masturbation fantasies re-emerge in the form of symptoms is, of course, an old part of our analytic knowledge. What is new is the insight that behavior patterns are derivatives of masturbation fantasies. It is frequently very difficult to discern this acting out of unconscious masturbation fantasies which are completely isolated from sexual activity in life. Again, a very brief clinical example may serve to illustrate this. A woman patient with definite masochistic character traits had always desired a child. Twice during her marriage she permitted her husband, who was an obstetrician, to perform abortions upon her, ostensibly motivated by the claim that he was too old to raise children. Though suffering bitterly, the patient felt that she had no right to burden him with unwanted responsibilities. In her analysis she remembered a masturbation fantasy of her childhood; she imagined that a child was growing in her belly. This child had developed without the aid of another object; it just grew in her, like a tumor. It obviously represented a phallus. A surgeon—i.e., a father figure—was cutting the baby out of her body. This operation represented a masochistic union with the father, for whom she sacrificed her masculinity in this way, and at the same time a delivery. The abortions in adulthood constituted a living out of this fantasy. This acting out was not understood by the patient as being motivated by anything but reality-syntonic reasons; it did not have the value of a symptom for her.

Similarly, all kinds of peculiarities which are well

integrated into the personality can frequently be understood as the representations of a masturbation fantasy completely isolated from conscious sexuality.

After this digression into aspects of the masturbation problem which were not touched upon in the Discussion, I should like to return once more to the papers of 1912. I hope I have succeeded in conveying an idea of the richness and, one might say, the pioneer spirit of the ideas developed at that time. Nevertheless, on reading the Discussion, one frequently gains an impression that it was time-conditioned, in the sense of the German word *zeitgebunden*. That is to say, these papers are, to a certain degree, influenced by the moral values of the time. The repeated advice found there, for instance, that children should be helped to avoid excessive masturbation by means of a bland diet, hard beds, and plenty of exercise; or the recommendation that only a minimum of affection should be given in the handling of small children in order to avoid overstimulation which might lead to masturbation—such views reveal the influence of the general, social condemnation of masturbation which prevailed at that time. The last-mentioned recommendation may be found side by side with awareness of the importance of experiencing stimuli in early childhood as necessary for normal sexual development. It is also impossible to avoid interpretation of the deeper reasons for this condemnation. As Nunberg (1932) put it in his *Principles of Psychoanalysis:* "The exaggeration of the danger resulting from masturbation seems to have the same basis as the denial of infantile sexuality, namely, one's own sexual repression" (p. 181). Even though the discussants were the first to understand the importance of infantile sexuality, they were not completely free of emotions about it. A great and general change in the social attitude toward problems of this kind has taken place since 1912. For us, who are but the heirs of the heroic champions of psychoanalysis of that hard time, it is easy to smile at some of their ideas now, almost 40 years later. Psychoanalysis undoubtedly contributed to the change in sexual mores; at the same time, it did not remain entirely uninfluenced by the prevailing sexual morality.

This is demonstrated, for instance, by the completely different tone to be found in the issue of the *Zeitschrift für psychoanalytische Pädagogik* which I mentioned before (see Federn, 1928). By 1928 the pendulum had swung to the other side. The main problem then was, only, how to free the adolescent from his masturbation guilt feelings. The very important insights concerning the implications of masturbation with respect to character and sexual development, which had been gained through the first Discussion, were forgotten by then. At that time, masturbation appeared as a panacea. Of course the 1928 Discussion was published in a popular periodical; but even allowing for this, and notwithstanding the over-rigid concepts I have mentioned, the one of 1912 surpassed it by far in depth and scope.

I would like to add that much of this too superficial attitude toward masturbation is currently prevalent in this country. A few weeks ago, Grete Bibring reported on the White House Conference on Mental Hygiene. To the amazement of all the other participants, she—as a psychoanalyst—was the only one who did not fight with flying banners for masturbation, but pointed out its disadvantages for the mental hygiene of the adolescent. This is merely one example to show that here, too, the pendulum has swung out in the other direction and is caught there at the present time.

9

Narcissistic Object Choice in Women

(1953)

F REUD'S (1914) paper "On Narcissism" has a special place within the frame of his work: it is the
forerunner of ego psychology. A number of problems
which later are dealt with from the point of view of
ego psychology are treated here on the basis of the libido theory.

Freud distinguishes the choice of objects resembling
the feeding mother or the protecting father, the
so-called anaclitic type, from the choice of objects
which resemble the own self: the narcissistic type. In
the above-cited paper, he gives four possibilities. A person may love: (1) what he is himself; (2) what he
once was; (3) what he would like to be; (4) someone
who was a part of himself.

Narcissism means the cathexis of the own self with
libido. I use the term "self," because the state of primary narcissism exists only prior to any ego differentia-

Published originally in *Journal of the American Psychoanalytic Association*, 1:22–44, 1953.

tion, a point made by Hartmann (1950). What we call secondary narcissism is the later return of object cathexis to the own person.

Freud (1914) says that the instinctual aim in narcissism is to be loved. Most pregenital sexual aims are of this nature. Objects, at that level, are "selfishly" used for one's own gratification; their interests cannot yet be considered. Pregenital behavior, incidentally, shows similar traits in both sexes. Whether we define such behavior as fixated on pregenital levels of object relations or as narcissistic is a question of terminology.

The separation between self and object world develops gradually. In early phases of object relations, objects exist only temporarily and are dropped after gratification has occurred, or destroyed in violent rage when they withhold gratification. Objects are experienced as part of the own body; inside and outside are constantly fused. Thus we should use the term "narcissistic" in concentrating on certain conditions: (1) when body cathexis predominates and the own body is treated like a love object; (2) when a fixation has occurred on a level on which the differentiation between ego and object is very diffuse, and primary identifications prevail instead of object love; (3) when infantile ideas of, or longing for, omnipotence were either not outgrown or regressively revived, and problems of regulation of self-esteem are predominant. Such conditions are characterized by a state of narcissistic want and are usually caused by a narcissistic injury.

When Freud (1914) states that women are generally more narcissistic than men, it seems as though he were largely thinking of a fixation at early levels of object relations. At these early levels, passive attitudes are more frequently found than an active reaching out for an object. He states that, in contrast to men, whose love is of the anaclitic type characterized by overvaluation of the love object, the predominant sexual aim of women is to be loved. This, Freud stresses, applies particularly to the "truest type" of woman, who is primarily preoccupied with her physical beauty. By very reason of her narcissism this type of woman is most attractive to men, because narcissistic self-admiration is enchanting to those who themselves had to give up this gratification long ago in the course of their development. The narcissistic interest in the own self should, by the way, be distinguished from the physiologically passive sexual aims of female sexuality which frequently are connected with love of the anaclitic type.

Our increased knowledge about the preoedipal development of children has taught us that this passive-narcissistic attitude—even in those women who really belong to the type defined by Freud—by no means represents a primary fixation on that infantile level. Freud (1931) and others (Brunswick, 1940; Lampl-de Groot, 1933) have described how, after the original oral and anal passivity, the little girl goes through a period of active—pregenital as well as phallic—attitudes in relation to the mother. This active period is brought to an abrupt end by the trauma of the discovery of the difference of the sexes. One of the possible solutions of the ensuing conflicts is *regression* into the aforementioned pregenital, "narcissistic" passivity or demandingness. In many cases, on the other hand, the phallic level is never relinquished and the fantasy of possessing a penis persists. Numerous women continue to have masculine longings which find expression in many ways, frequently in the form of inferiority feelings and of specific, unrealizable ambitions and ideals. A solution to such conflicts is sometimes reached through a specific choice of a love object representing what these girls originally wanted to be, and which they can love on this basis. An object that is different from the self, but which has qualities they once desired for themselves, indeed represents a narcissistic object choice. About this type, Freud (1914) wrote:

> The sexual ideal [i.e., the idealized sex object] may enter into an interesting auxiliary relation to the ego ideal. It may be used for substitutive satisfaction where narcissistic satisfaction encounters real hindrances. In that case a person will love in conformity with the narcissistic type of object-choice, will love what he once and no longer is, or else what possesses the excellences which he never had at all . . . what possesses the excellence which the ego lacks for making it an ideal, is loved [p. 101].

Narcissistic object choice of this kind is intended to undo a narcissistic trauma of castration, to undo a state of narcissistic want. The fact that such an object choice is a narcissistic one does not yet make it pathologic. There are flowing transitions, here as everywhere, from the normal to the pathologic.

Normal cases of this kind are well known. There are

many women who replaced their original wish for a penis by developing male character traits and interests. If these character traits later on prove incompatible with their femininity, it becomes a good solution if they can love the same traits in a male object. In this way they can form a durable and stable relationship with men with whose achievements, standards, etc., they identify. These women thus love men who represent their own, externalized, former ego identifications.

Other women, particularly those who were unable to sublimate their masculine wishes, retain constant, unrealizable masculine ambitions. Their identifications did not effect any change in the ego, but remained restricted to the ego ideal.[1] It is obvious that any conspicuous pathology of the identifications and particularly any pathology of these special layers of identifications, of the ego ideal, will contribute to the pathology of the narcissistic object choice and object relation.

Frequently the object represents a composite of both these forms of identifications. Object choices based upon the externalization of the second type lead more often to pathology than do object choices based upon the first.

Among the many interesting clinical entities representing pathological forms of narcissistic object choice, I shall concentrate on two particular ones, the discussion of which is the subject of this paper.

The first group is that of women who are in a particular relation of dependent subservience (in German,

---

[1] I am deliberately using this term, which appeared in Freud's earlier papers (1921), instead of the later term "superego." I shall explain presently why I make this distinction.

Hörigkeit) to one man,[2] whom they consider great and admirable and without whom they cannot live. The second group consists of women who have short-lived, dependent infatuations during which they completely take over the man's personality, only to drop him again after a short time and to "deify" another object. The rapid changes of personality and love objects and, indeed, all emotions of these girls have a spurious character.[3] The two types impress one as complete opposites; however, there are certain similarities. In both of them the pathology is caused by the underlying pathological identifications which have been externalized.

Extreme Submissiveness in Women

Often these women are deeply attached to one man, who to them is outstanding and great. Usually, some masculine characteristic is stressed: either the man's physical strength, attractiveness, sex appeal, or his power, importance, intelligence, creativeness, and so on. The woman feels that she cannot live without this partner; in order to maintain the relationship, she is willing to bear anything and, masochistically, to make all kinds of sacrifices.

Such women suffer from intense inferiority feelings. They are overcritical of themselves, and the admired qualities of the partner represent what they felt unable to attain for themselves in childhood and adolescence

[2] Cf. "A Contribution to the Psychoanalysis of Extreme Submissiveness in Women" (*this volume*).

[3] This type was described in an excellent paper by Helene Deutsch (1942), who called it the "as if" personality.

when only masculine values were of importance to them. The predominance of male identifications is evidenced by the frequency, in such cases, of early daydreams with an all-male cast. The daydreamer herself appears as a boy, often without being conscious of her own identification with the hero. Girls are considered too uninteresting and ugly to be used at all for fantasy purposes. One such patient's daydreams, for instance, dealt exclusively with a sadomasochistic relationship of a son with a grandiose father, the patient alternately identifying with both these fantasy objects.

Later on the sexual partner becomes the representative of the grandiose component of these masculine ambitions. It is very striking that in many of these cases the partner's body as a whole has to have phallic features. "He has to be tall, lean and sinewy." "His body has to look like that of a Greek athlete." Or: "He has to be strong, upright, and broad-shouldered." These traits are equally predominant in the daydream heroes of adolescence. The patient whose sadomasochistic daydreams I mentioned above became aware in analysis that during intercourse she felt as though she were the man with the phalluslike body making love to herself, the girl.

The narcissistic gain of such an identification is obvious. It results in a feeling of oneness, of being one body with the grandiose sex partner, a feeling which is the complete opposite of the aforementioned overstrong feeling of ugliness and inferiority that predominated when this girl evaluated her personality by herself. It is obvious that a separation from such a partner is intolerable; it leads to a feeling of complete castration and has to be prevented by all means.

In several cases of this type which I analyzed, these magic methods of restoring self-esteem could be particularly observed in the feeling of ecstacy accompanying orgasm. In this state it was as though the woman's individuality had ceased to exist: she felt herself flow together with the man (see Helene Deutsch, 1927). This *unio mystica* can be compared to what Freud calls the "oceanic feeling"—the flowing together of self and world, of self and primary object. It has to do with a temporary relinquishment of the separating boundaries between ego and id and ego ideal. A unity with the ego ideal, which equals the unrealizable longing to be like an admired early object, is thus reached for these passing moments. It was obvious that the sex partner represented the personification of such a very phallic ego ideal. Grandiose masculinity was gained through the ecstatic intercourse.

In the analysis, the phallic object with whom this mystic identification occurred could be traced back to the father. We are dealing here with an ego ideal of the paternal type. In these instances, as mentioned above, the phallic features of the ideal were conspicuous; they completely overshadowed any individual traits of the father as a person. One might say that this type of ego ideal is characterized by regressive, primitive traits: (1) by its grandiosity; (2) identification with an organ; (3) the tendency to undo inferiority feelings via flowing together with a stronger object, that is, via regression to a very primitive form of object relation, going back to a time in which ego boundaries were not yet stable and whatever appeared to be pleasurable and strong in the outside world could easily be experienced as belonging to the self.

As is not surprising in persons with such regressive traits, in a number of cases analysis showed that the fantasy of becoming one with a grandiose love partner was related to the original homosexual object, the mother, primitive attachments to whom had never been relinquished. The undisguised phallic character of the later fantasy represented a subsequent addition, as a reaction to the disappointment at the lack of a penis in the mother.

The masochistic subservience is the outcome of the woman's need to hold on to the object at any cost. This situation, however, is complicated by a number of factors. It is obvious that girls with a particular, narcissistic structure—i.e., with particular, grandiose ego ideals—are necessarily in a difficult position. No object really can live up to the grandiosity of the narcissistic demand. They must, so to speak, inflate the partner in order that he might meet their standard. Whatever contradicts the fantasy now has to be denied, and a great deal of countercathexis becomes necessary to hold on to the inflated image of the love object. This state of affairs is further complicated by the necessity to keep in check aggressive tendencies against the man who is, after all, in possession of the masculinity that the woman originally desired. Even greater over-inflation of the love object is needed to counterbalance this aggression. This underlying ambivalence causes such women furtively to watch and evaluate the partner. There is constant doubt whether the man is really as wonderful as he is supposed to be. The warded-off aggression frequently is transformed into the aforementioned masochistic behavior.

Relationships of this kind impress the superficial

observer as specially "real" forms of love. Only analysis reveals their infantile, narcissistic character. Not infrequently, women who need this type of relationship have otherwise well-integrated personalities. They maintain a critical self-evaluation and accurate reality testing. Infantile megalomanic longings shine through only in their attitude toward love objects, but do not otherwise appear in their personality structure. Greatness, so to speak, is completely ceded to the partner; union with him is their only way of establishing a feeling of this kind.

At this point a few remarks should be added about the ego ideal and its relation to the regulation of self-esteem. The formation of the ego ideal has from its very beginning to do with the keeping up of self-esteem. As his sense of reality grows, the child, recognizing his own weakness, endows his parents with the omnipotence he has had to forego. From this time on, desires set in to become like the glorified parent. The deep longing to become like the parent creates a constant inner demand upon the child's ego: an ego ideal is formed. In cases of insufficient acceptance of reality, the differentiation between ego and ego ideal may remain diffuse, and under certain conditions *magic identification* with the glorified parent—megalomanic feelings—may replace the *wish* to be like him.

Such ego ideals should be distinguished from the concept of the superego. The superego represents a taking over of the parental do's and don't's. In spite of childish misunderstandings, the formation of the superego is based upon acceptance of reality; in fact, it represents the most powerful attempt to adjust to reality. The ego ideal, on the other hand, is based upon the desire to cling in some form or another to a denial of the ego's as well as of the parent's limitations and to regain infantile omnipotence by identifying with the idealized parent.

Nunberg (1932) differentiates in a similar way between ego ideal and superego. He believes that the ego ideal is formed earlier and is based upon identifications with the mother, prompted by love for her, whereas the later fear of the father leads to formation of the superego. Nunberg also stresses the greater closeness of the superego to instinct mastery and reality adjustment —a conception I can confirm completely, while I feel that the respective role played by father or mother in the formation of the ego ideal is dependent, in each instance, on their particular characteristics. One can describe the ego ideal as the earlier structure, as the precursor of the superego. I would like to add two points:

1. In such cases ideas about the parental magnificence sometimes are completely fused with desires for a particular organ of the object, upon which the entire cathexis is concentrated. This is originally the breast or, somewhat later, the paternal phallus. In the phallic phase, a great deal of libidinal-narcissistic cathexis is concentrated on the penis and may spread over the whole body. It is at this period that the fantasy of the whole body being a phallus originates. I may mention here that Lewin (1933) has described this fantasy as being always based on oral incorporation. Body narcissism of particular intensity appears invariably combined with this fantasy. Its purpose of combating castration anxiety is obvious. This condition probably represents the basis of the fact that the ego ideal of particularly narcissistic persons with deep

fixation and insufficient faculty of desexualization *is to
be the paternal phallus.* This may be compared to a
stage in which the ego did not perceive the object as a
whole, and identification was limited to the imitation
of gesture. Here, instead of identification with the
quality of the object, there predominates the wish to be
identified with an organ of the object. It is obvious
how far such an ego ideal is removed from any possibility of realization. Clinical material bearing on this
point has been given above.

2. Not infrequently the ego ideal is tinged with features of grandiosity, since it is based upon wishes to
identify with a parent who is seen in a very infantile
way.

In normal development these ideals gradually are
modified. With the growing acceptance of reality the
image of the parent becomes more and more realistic,
superego elements gain in importance and become
fused with the ideal, and—most important—ego capacities are developed for the translation of inner demands
into organized activities. Persistence of intensely narcissistic ego ideals obviously represents serious pathology. The formation of such ideals is a regular process
of development; normally, however, they do not endure in their infantile form. Persistence of a megalomanic ego ideal is not caused by one isolated traumatic
incident but by general weakness of the ego, immaturity of the superego, and early disturbances of object
relations. This latter factor is usually the most conspicuous. It is as though early disturbances had prevented the libido from attaching itself to objects, so
that too much cathexis remains with the ego ideal. An
over-grandiose ego ideal—combined, as it not infre-

quently is, with inadequate talents and insufficient ego strength—leads to intolerable inner conflicts and feelings of insufficiency. The reattachment of this ideal to an outside object and the reunion with it via sexual union, as in the cases of subservient women, thus represents an undoing of a feeling of narcissistic want, which coincides with the undoing of castration.

Let us now proceed to the second type of pathology of narcissistic object choice to be discussed here.

Transitory Pseudo Infatuations: "As If" Types

In contrast to the submissive-dependent woman who often clings to one object throughout life, the other type I have mentioned shows a similar overvaluation of the object, with signs of deep dependency, merely for a limited time. These women "fall in love" with men whom they "deify" and without whom they consider life unbearable. They take over the man's personality, interests, and values completely; it is as if they had no judgment of their own, no ego of their own. But suddenly, after a short time, the thus elevated object is dethroned again. He is regarded as valueless, inferior, and dropped like a hot potato; and at the same time, the identification with him is relinquished. Often this dropping of one object coincides with turning to a new one who is now elevated instead, only to be exchanged, in turn, for yet another after some time. However, the devaluation of any object is accompanied by a feeling of degradation of the own personality, which can be overcome only through the idealization and acquisition of a new object.

In such cases it seems as though the intensity of the

feelings were spurious and unreal. In her very interesting paper, dealing with the "as if" personality, Helene Deutsch (1942) describes a number of cases characterized by precisely this type of behavior. In her cases, as well as in those I myself have observed, the "as if" pattern emerged in relation to objects as well as to causes or thoughts. The patients spuriously fell in and out of love in the course of a few days. Similarly, whenever they were under someone's influence, they would, for a short time, be enthusiastically religious, or fanatically communistic, etc. The "as if" behavior of these persons was based upon a failure to develop real object relations during childhood, due to unfavorable family situations. They were incapable of loving anybody and only could relate to external objects via a primitive form of identification. Of course, such relations have no continuity. Each identification is followed by another, and all relationships and emotions are spurious and impermanent. Helene Deutsch points out that the rapid sequence of identifications may be understood as a method to appease external objects by becoming like them. She also stresses the deficient faculty of sublimation, ego weakness, and lacking internalization of the superego. Furthermore, it appears that the rapidly changing identifications have the function of undoing narcissistic injuries. In a magic way, narcissistic compensation is gained and, simultaneously, a substitute for the lacking object relations.

Again, as in the cases of subservient women, we find here an exaggerated, grandiose ego ideal which is unrealizable. Precisely because there is always an early disturbance of object relations and libido could not be invested in a normal way, the narcissistic structure, the ego ideal, is overcathected. But there is an essential difference between the two types. Submissive women of the first group need men with definite qualities that have had a high value for these girls since early childhood and represent well internalized identifications. By contrast, the women of the "as if" type show a lack of discrimination in the choice of objects. Some of them can glorify anything and are ready to identify themselves with anyone happening to enter their sphere of life. In the case of others, their admiration is tied to one condition: the man's worth must be recognized by other people. The content of his qualities is irrelevant. These identifications are not really internalized; they are superficial imitations. Only the endeavor to achieve greatness in this way is relevant.

In two of my own patients, I could observe that they attempted, time and again, to attain narcissistic gratification without the help of objects, but that the failure of these endeavors caused them to turn to objects in the manner described. The necessity of restoring the impaired self-esteem via the detour of narcissistic object choice, instead of being able to produce megalomanic feelings without the aid of outside objects, is an indication that acceptance of reality has been achieved to a certain degree.

None of the "as if" patients among my cases presented quite as complete a lack of object relation as some described by Helene Deutsch; but all of them were characterized by a deep distortion of the relationship to the mother, caused by outstandingly narcissistic traits of the mother's personality.

In one of these cases, the mother completely dominated the family and created in them the conviction that she was the most beautiful, elegant, efficient, and all-around most wonderful person in the world. She was predominantly concerned with the impression she made on people. The relationship between this woman and her child was governed by her constant, critical evaluation of the latter's appearance and superficial behavior, which led the girl to develop intense feelings of insufficiency connected with her masturbation guilt. The child was continually used by the mother for exhibitionistic purposes, and was from an early age taught to behave in such a way that she would be admired by whatever public she happened to encounter. She was sent to a drama school at the age of three, so that she might learn the art of charming people. Later, it became particularly important for her to find out what people appreciated in order to "become" what she thought they wanted her to be. External tokens sufficed to make her feel changed. This girl, a European of Czechoslovak nationality, would feel herself to be "an American glamor girl," for instance, when she wore a sweater like one she had seen pictured in an American magazine; or she would be a "sophisticated demimondaine" when she visited a night club. It is characteristic that there was no consistent content in these "ideals." They changed like feminine fashions and were influenced by anything that happened to come along.

With such methods she achieved, from time to time, what must be described as narcissistic fulfillment. She would feel grandiose because she was what her public wanted her to be and would admire. This happened, for example, when she had a minor success as an actress. The euphoria that accompanied the episode was characterized by intense excitement experienced over the entire body surface and a sensation of standing out, erect, with her whole body. Obviously she felt like a phallus with her whole body.

But such feelings never lasted long; they were always followed by periods of anxiety and deep feelings of inferiority. It was as though her reality testing returned. Her awareness of her lack of a penis could not, at length, be overcome by such magic means. Instead, she then turned to other methods: she now had to find a man whom she could admire. By winning this object she would participate in his achievements, whatever they were. With one, an Englishman, she felt that she had now incorporated British aristocratic culture; with another, a physicist, she felt like an expert scientist. These infatuations, however, were short-lived; the objects soon lost their glamor, and to be loved by them was meaningless. The patient turned away from them and was depressed until she could find a new victim.

One seems able, in this case, to observe the pattern of the narcissistic object choice *in statu nascendi*. It was obviously a second choice. What she primarily desired was the achievement of phallic grandiosity of her own. It was only after she had failed in this endeavor that she was forced to turn to identification with a man. In the analysis, her need for phallic grandiosity could be traced back first to her father, but finally to her mother.

Masturbation fantasies between the ages of four and five were remembered. The content of these was that she was urinating while sitting naked on a merry-go-round horse, and many people watched her. In this fantasy she had changed places with a phallic mother (the horse, urination) whom she imagined engaged in some exhibitionistic, sexual activity. Now she herself was the performer—the mother and the mother's audience (the father) had to watch her. In puberty, she had fantasies that were the model of her later life configuration: she was herself in an endless series of love adventures with different types of men, going from lover to lover, completely changing her own personality in accord with the imagined characteristics of the men. These fantasies accompanied mutual masturbation with her older sister to whom, as a substitute for the mother, they were being told. She was, in fact, showing her sexual excitement—i.e., her erection—to the mother, thereby negating her feeling of castration which had become overwhelming in consequence of the masturbation. The merry-go-round in childhood, the lovers in adolescence, and the men in her later life, all represented the same: a glorified phallus through which she was outdoing her mother. She was becoming the (for the patient, unquestionably phallic) mother and doing away with the mother at the same time, a kind of ambivalence which is inherent in the nature of identification.

It has been stressed repeatedly that the identifications seen in this type of patient are highly pathologic. It has been said that they consist of superficial imitations instead of deeply internalized transformations of the personality. Identifications of this type are characteristic for an early stage of development.

Identifications are older than object love. They form the first bridge from the self to the world. Via identification, the strange and therefore disturbing outside objects are assimilated ("digested") and thereby made pleasurable. One of the mechanics of this primary taking into the self consists in imitating the out-side object. The oral incorporation takes place at the same time, or shortly before. Imitation is an ego activity, oral incorporation a libidinal process. The interrelation between the two procedures is none too clear. I shall concentrate here on the first-mentioned form: primary identification via imitation.

This magic method—the imitative gesture, as Berta Bornstein calls it (personal communication)—can be considered a prestage of identification. This primitive identification can take place with many objects and not only with "loved" ones. Whatever is impressive at the moment is imitated. This implies that such initial identifications are transitory at first. It is only by manifold and long exposure that any lasting identification comes about. Stable relationships to beloved objects greatly facilitate such development. New skills, interests, and patterns of behavior are developed. For a time the little boy *was* father when he put on his father's coat and played at driving the car. Normally, this stage is gradually outgrown. The child not only makes noises, but learns to talk; he not only holds a newspaper, like his father, but learns to read. Thus he learns to master reality and acquires a capacity for sound reality testing. These now stable identifications are, so to speak, the building materials from which the ego is made.

In the course of development, differentiation takes place between identification and love. Objects different from the self can be loved without the need to take over their qualities; and, on the other hand, identifications, with objects as whole persons, real ego transformations, are achieved. A great many of these identifications are based on the desexualization—or, as

Hartmann (1952) puts it, the neutralization—of libido, thus leading to real sublimations which are not reversible even under unfavorable conditions. On the other hand, a fixation at a level of immature ego identifications, of transitory imitations, of playing at being something instead of really becoming it, amounts to serious pathology. A regression to this state can, for instance, be seen in schizophrenics to whom imitation of gestures stands for being something. I remember a schizophrenic patient, for example, who believed he was Cary Grant because his smile was like that of the movie star. These fleeting pseudo identifications can, however, also be found in nonpsychotic individuals. It is obvious that if such a pathological identification becomes the basis of a narcissistic object choice, serious consequences must result.

The transitory identifications of the patient described before were caused by the mother's own narcissistic disturbance which made it impossible for the child to develop any feeling of depth in relation to the mother, but kept her on the level of imitation. Since the mother only demanded superficial imitation from her and presented such behavior as an example, the patient could not outgrow this stage.

A small episode may serve to demonstrate on what infantile libidinous level these superficial identifications take place. The patient once went to rent an apartment, and immediately became impressed with the very loud and talkative landlady. After a short while, she began to talk and behave like this woman. This lasted until a girl friend of hers came along, who after a few minutes took her away, telling her that the landlady was psychotic. The patient became frightened by her indiscriminate readiness to identify, and said: "This is as if I had eaten something poisonous. Whenever my mother gave me something to eat, I ate it, and I never knew what it tasted like. My taking over of other people's personalities is just like that. I do not know what I am taking over. I am ready to consider wonderful anything that is offered to me."

Her attempts at idealization became fused with unsublimated sexual fantasies. This is understandable too. Here the patient likewise identified herself with the mother, whose unconscious phallic wishes she intuitively understood. Considering the mother's character, it is obvious why the ego ideal of this patient—to become like the mother, whom she conceived as being in possession of a phallus—presented such features of grandiosity.

I believe that this case shows clearly what is meant by the term ego ideal: an identification with the early, glorified maternal object. This identification leads only partly to ego configuration. The mother's exhibitionistic behavior becomes the predominant pattern of the patient's personality. But to become completely like the mother remains an unattainable ideal: something she wishes to be, but can be only in moments of temporary manic triumph or via her identification with a man.

In the course of the analysis, it became clear at what point and under what circumstances she had to drop a lover and exchange him for another man. This change was always caused by the feeling that she had failed to impress her mother with the grandiosity of the love object. In fact, any criticism expressed by another person about her heterosexual object would cause her to devaluate the man. This girl had evidently not succeeded in forming an independent superego of her own. She remained dependent on the maternal judgment, and this forced her to adjust her own values completely to those of the environment. To be dependent on the environment was precisely what her mother had taught her. To impress the mother was her only really deeply felt impulse.

A breakdown of the narcissistic overvaluation of love objects is always caused, in such cases, by some negative judgment about the object on the part of a third person. This implies an incomplete stage of superego development. In the normal process, the superego develops but slowly. For a long time, identification with the parental demand occurs only in the presence of the love object. After the breakdown of the oedipus complex, complete internalization is achieved. Full independence of values from the environment represents the highest maturation of the superego. It was Freud's opinion that many women have greater difficulty than men in reaching this point, since their oedipal attachment does not end as abruptly as that of boys; often it continues for a long time and, with it, dependence on the parental values.

It is not unusual for this type of moral dependence later to be transferred from the parent to the husband who, as one might say, then takes the place of the superego and has to decide what is right and wrong. We are dealing here not with projection of the superego but with an infantile personality that had never succeeded in forming an adult, independent superego. Such a woman's dependence on the man has to be understood as an immature relationship of a weak ego to an object that is seen as strong and powerful, as the parent was seen by the infant. It is a symptom of insufficient superego development.

This immaturity of the superego may find expression not in dependence on the judgment of one object, but in a diffuse dependence on "other people's opinions." In women, closer investigation frequently reveals a dependence on the judgment of various homosexual objects; i.e., in many cases the dependence on the maternal judgment has never been displaced to men. However, this situation, as well as dependence on men, must be distinguished from the projection of a well circumscribed and often overstrict superego onto the love objects. Projection of the superego does not seem to be more characteristic of either sex. Some persons with intense, inner guilt conflicts try to solve their internal tensions by reprojecting the critical superego onto external objects whose benevolence and forgiveness are now sought for. Sometimes in such cases one finds that a real, psychotic loss of object relationship had taken place at some point, and that the projection of the superego is an attempt at restitution. This mechanism must be strictly distinguished from those which we wish to investigate here.

Just like the superficiality of the identifications on the imitation level, the dependence on outside judgment facilitates the abandoning of objects. This does not yet explain, however, why with the relinquishment of such a relationship the former object so often suddenly evokes disgust or hatred instead of admiration, nor why this process is connected with such a sudden drop in self-esteem.

Sudden changes of mood and of self-esteem, from

the feeling of grandiosity to that of nothingness, are characteristic of an *infantile ego.* Such vacillations of mood appear regularly in early phases. They represent the shift from gratification = omnipotence to hunger = extreme feeling of powerlessness. At that stage, no degrees of self-assurance exist. Shadings of good and bad, great and small, require a greater acceptance of reality, an ability to stand tension, to wait for gratification, to judge and think without being overwhelmed by desires and emotion. Just as tolerance toward others is a late and complicated achievement, tolerance and objective appraisal in relation to the own self are, likewise, a late acquisition of maturity.

Normally these extreme vacillations are stabilized through some gratification coming from the objects. We know, furthermore, that by identification with the powerful parent the child restores his narcissistic balance in a magic way. These narcissistic desires to take the place of the parent coincide, normally with a positive attachment to the object. But if there is no consistency of relationship to the object, or if objects are really lacking, or if aggressive feeling or a particular ambivalence prevails, then this negative, devaluating attitude will destroy the object as well as the ego ideal which is formed in his pattern. The tiniest frustration, or any devaluation of the object by a third party, will not only undermine the child's own self-esteem (i.e., his feeling of power), but unleash relentless hostility against the object and against any ideal of the object which the child is trying to establish in himself. Then the vacillation of mood does not stop before the object that represents the externalized, narcissistic ideal. The ego ideal-object is loved, elevated, imitated for a short while, but after the slightest disappointment it is immediately hated, destroyed, abandoned. Whereas, when an object is loved and admired, its splendor falls via narcissistic identification upon the ego, here the aggression against the object—the "shadow of the object," as Freud (1917) formulated it in "Mourning and Melancholia"—falls upon the ego. However, in contrast to what happens in melancholic depression, the identification on the imitation level can be stopped at will. The shadow can be cast off at once, most easily by turning to a new object and starting a new relationship; the mood of dejection, too, is only *transitory*. Another case, of which I shall only give a short fragment here, illustrates this origin of the vacillation of self-esteem rather clearly.

The patient was a young woman, very pretty and very narcissistic; she said of herself that her body was like that of the Venus de Milo. She was flirtatious and seductive and had many suitors, whom she would at first admire but drop after a short time. She was equally inconsistent in her other interests. During the time of the analysis she was a singer for a while, then specialized in "child development," then became a writer of short stories, all these activities being pursued with intense pseudo enthusiasm and dropped at the slightest criticism. She was constantly vacillating between intense feelings of being wonderful and special, and of being ugly, deformed, and terrible. In one of these depressions, which had to do with her intense masturbation guilt, she had made a serious attempt at suicide. She continually fell in love with men whom she endowed with greatness and in union with whom, for a time, she felt great and wonderful herself. The intensity of her "love" invariably collapsed once she had conquered the man. Then she felt that people would laugh at her and think her a fool ever to have become involved with him. Her appreciation of the man thus was completely dependent on outside judgment. In the first, happy stage of the relationship her association with the man would uplift and aggrandize her. He then became devalued; whereupon she, herself, would be torn down by him and destroyed. In the course of the analysis, she expressed it openly. In the positive stage, the lover as a whole had phallic qualities, and she saw him in her dreams as a phallus which she could bring to erection. In the negative phase, she "had made a hole into the lover," and he was like her own castrated genitals.

Under the surface of these phallic fantasies it became evident that the taking over of the object's greatness or deficiency processed on an oral basis. Her husband, whom she now despised, "made her sick." Precisely under these conditions, she had fellatio fantasies to which she reacted with intense disgust. Then, in a fantasy, she suddenly saw him, first as a penis representing the whole body; but then the image changed and became a nipple from which milk was coming. To this she associated a time immediately following the birth of her brother, when she was four. At that period the mother had sent the child out of the rather well-to-do Jewish environment into a Catholic convent. The little girl felt strange, deserted, and depressed. She had experienced such loneliness many times before on being left by the mother, who was a career woman. She was frightened of the nuns and felt terribly unhappy that the little sibling could stay at home. She could not stand the food given to her in the convent, became ill, and had the thought: "My mother, by sending me here, makes me sick."

This is the same thought which rose up whenever she felt disgusted with one of her heterosexual love objects. Her desire was to idealize the love object and, by loving him, to become like him. But at that moment she would become overwhelmed by negative feelings against him, which originated in her deep ambivalence toward the mother. Her love for her mother had become intermixed with tremendous, aggressive impulses. She has wanted to get the breast, like the little brother. On week ends she could witness his breast feeding. But this breast, which was denied to her in such drastic fashion, became something to be hated; she wanted to destroy it, to tear it to bits. Thus, any wish for the mother was superseded by the feeling: "She makes me sick; I am not incorporating something wonderful but something poisonous."

The mother, the mother's breast—later superseded by the paternal phallus—represented the core of the ego ideal—largely unsublimated—which she aspired to in order to undo the intense, narcissistic injuries, particularly feelings of being deserted and castrated, that she had experienced. The heterosexual love object represented this ideal; but her aggression against the original, homosexual, love object made her devalue the ideal and destroy the partner. However, she was so fused with the object, which after all she had elevated into her own ego ideal, that by destroying it she destroyed herself.

The fragility of object relations that becomes manifest in such mechanisms leads us to classify the "as if" conditions among the borderline states. Anna Freud (1936) believes them to be initial phases of psychosis. In *The Ego and the Mechanisms of Defense,* she shows that "as if" conditions are quite frequent during puberty. She thinks that fear of the overwhelming intensity of instinctual drives in that period causes the adolescent to withdraw libidinal cathexis from the object world, which leads to narcissistic, psychotic, or near-psychotic withdrawal. The pseudo relations on a primitive identification level are attempts at restitution. When the storm of puberty has abated in violence, and the instinctual danger decreases, the object-libidinal world can be recathected and the narcissistic pattern relinquished. It may also be the initial phase of an incipient psychosis.

The cases I myself have observed, as well as those described by Helene Deutsch, showed disturbances of object relations that preceded puberty and did not give the impression of resulting from defensive mechanisms. These patients had never reached a level of mature object relations. Moreover, their "as if" condition was neither a transitory symptom nor the beginning of a psychosis. It is likely that the acute outbreak of such a symptom is of more dangerous character than its continuous persistence.

Let us return to the two particular types I have described. Both use narcissistic object choice to master injury to self-esteem, to overcome their feeling of *castration.* Both function on a level of infantile ego mechanisms, although there is a difference in degree. Both, despite their conspicuous preoccupation with the phallus, are *predominantly homosexually* fixated, which is understandable, since they are both fixated at early levels.

The described phenomena do not constitute all the existing varieties of narcissistic object choice in woman; however, they may be considered particularly important. The various forms of narcissistic disturbances need further investigation.

Summary

1. The ego ideal, in contrast to the superego, is based upon a narcissistic identification with the parent, who is seen in an infantile, glorified way. Persistence of particular, grandiose ego ideals has to do with disturbances of object relations and ego development.

2. Unsublimated sexual features of the ideal, expressed in the fantasy of becoming the paternal (or, sometimes, maternal) phallus, represent a special, regressive trait.

3. Fixation on the level of imitative gesture leads to a lack of internalization in the ego ideal and constitutes the basis for the "as if" personality.

4. The impact of narcissistic injuries, such as, in women, the becoming aware of the difference between the sexes, may lead to a regressive revival of primitive, narcissistic ego ideals.

5. The externalization of such an ego ideal and its fusion with a love object represent a form of narcissistic object choice in women.

6. The degree of pathology of the narcissistic object choice depends on the normalcy or pathology of the ego ideal.

7. Need for identification, not infrequently in the form of ecstatic-orgastic flowing together with the

idealized object, can become the basis for a subservient relationship of a woman to a man.

8. The masochistic element in such subservience is frequently based on the overcompensation of aggressive feelings against the man.

9. Idealization and identification with the idealized object may represent the only available form of substitution for the lacking ability to form object relations.

10. A greater degree of disturbance of the ego ideal frequently goes hand in hand with an insufficiently developed superego and leads to dependence upon "public opinion" or specific third persons.

11. Sudden, aggressive demolition of idealized figures, combined with depressive lowering of self-esteem, is based upon a predominance of aggression against the objects on whom the ego ideal is built.

10

Early Identifications as Archaic Elements in the Superego

(1954)

Iɴ ᴀ ᴘᴀᴘᴇʀ on "Narcissistic Object Choice in Women" (this Volume), I have tried to show that it appears useful to distinguish between the superego, as the later and more reality-syntonic structure, and the ego ideal as the earlier, more narcissistic one.

Briefly, I outlined the distinction between identifications with parental figures seen in a glorified light, which are based on the child's longing to share or take over the parental greatness in order to undo his own feeling of weakness, and identifications resulting from the breakdown of the oedipus complex. The former represent the ego ideal; the later, the superego. Or one would say: the ego ideal expresses what one desires to be; the superego, what one ought to be. In this paper I shall attempt to elaborate further on this concept and to clarify it with the help of some clinical material.

Published originally in *Journal of the American Psychoanalytic Association*, 2:218-238, 1954.

Freud's original concept of the ego ideal goes beyond what is usually understood by superego in psychoanalytic literature. Most frequently, superego is equated with conscience. In "On Narcissism," Freud (1914) says that man creates ideals for himself in order to restore the lost narcissism of childhood. By internalizing the parental demands and living up to them, the narcissistic hurt caused by the critical attitudes of the parents is being undone and narcissism restored. However, the original, wider concept of the ego ideal leaves room to include other, more direct ways of correcting painful feelings of inadequacy and weakness, which will be discussed later. It should be mentioned, first, that Freud's idea of the superego is not identical with conscience either.

The superego is a complex structure. Most conspicuous, of course, is usually the identification with the moral side of the parental personality, which is used for repression of oedipal strivings. It can be a positive identification (you should do as your father—your mother—did) as well as a negative one (you must not do—or not do everything—your father did). But identifications can as well represent a substitute for the (oedipal) love objects that have to be relinquished, as for objects of aggression which are eliminated by putting oneself in their place. Thus, character traits of the parental figures are taken over which are no longer connected with the task of instinct mastery.

The choice of identification used for the formation of the superego is determined, as Freud (1923) stressed in *The Ego and the Id,* by the degree of bisexuality present and also by the pregenital history. The instinct-restraining identifications, in their task of restricting incestuous genitality, become fused with earlier ones directed against pregenital indulgence. The afore-mentioned later identifications with parental figures, which substitute for the parents as objects of love or aggression, become fused with more primitive, earlier identifications that occur usually during pregenital and preoedipal periods, often at a stage of considerable ego immaturity. Normally, a modification of the earlier, more primitive identifications takes place through their fusion with the later ones.

It is self-evident that the superego identifications retain, thoughout life, their special form of differentiated structures within the ego. We are used to thinking of earlier identifications as ego identifications, i.e., as identifications which are completely integrated into the ego, and which do not lead to a differentiation within the ego. It is the aim of this paper to show that even early identifications do not always result in such complete integration. Early identifications with parental qualities which are envied and admired may take place in order to undo a narcissistic hurt. They may be represented by a longing to be like the idealized parent and may lead not at all, or only to a certain degree, to personality transformation in the desired sense. These longings must be described as ego ideals. The ego is measured against them, and self-esteem depends on the distance between them and the ego, just as, later, on the distance between ego and superego. It depends upon the level of ego development reached by a person whether or not this measuring between ego and ego ideal will result in attempts to achieve realization of these ideals. On a primitive level of ego development, such ideals may express themselves predominantly via imaginary wish fulfillment: as narcissistic fantasies.

This is the more primitive method, referred to before, of restoring injured narcissism.

Narcissistic fantasies in which one sees oneself big, powerful, a genius, etc., vary in their degree of *Ichzugehörigkeit* (belonging to the ego). Sometimes they represent only a pleasurable pastime; they may, for example, be an element of masturbation fantasies that is taken up during periods of sexual excitement. But frequently they are an essential, permanent element of the personality, against which the ego is measured. Only in this case can one consider them ego ideals.

The origin of accentuated narcissistic ideals appears to be twofold.

1. Sudden threats to narcissistic intactness necessitate the formation of a narcissistic ego ideal. Particularly strong castration anxiety causes the main part of the libido to be withdrawn from love objects and to become concentrated upon the ego. This leads to the formation of grandiose ideals which indicate what one would want to be like. In such cases the ideals are frequently characterized by phallic features; moreover, it is as though only the most overwhelming grandiosity were enough to ensure phallic intactness. For this purpose, early identifications with grandiosely seen parents often are revived.

2. Early identifications can also persist throughout childhood. Such identifications take place at a time when the infantile ego is weak and when fusion with the strong parental object, or a magic taking over of its strength, occurs for the purpose of undoing the feeling of insufficiency in the child. The primitive identifications of that early period are of a peculiar, "superficial" nature; i.e., they are transient and changing. The child

simply imitates whatever attracts his attention momentarily in the object. Such imitations express, in a primitive way, the child's fantasy that he *is the object* or, later, that he is like the object. A definite wish to be like the object presupposes a realization of the own self and the object as distinct and different entities. Normally these passing identifications develop slowly into permanent ones, into real assimilation of the object's qualities. This is a sign of growing ego maturity. On the other hand, this assimilation of the qualities of the identification object can only be partial. In many respects the child cannot be fully like the adults. There normally develops a faculty for self-evaluation and reality appreciation, which enables the child to recognize certain aspects of the parental images as something he has not yet reached but wishes to become. Here we see a type of ego ideal—we might call it the normal one—which will lead to attempts gradually to bring about a realization of these aims, as soon as the individual's growing strength and capacities will permit it. This presupposes that the parental image becomes divested of its unrealistic, grandiose, infantile aspects and is reduced to human proportions. A clinging to the original scope of the image indicates a fixation on or regression to an early level of ego development; i.e., mature reality testing has not been fully reached or has been partly given up. Via identification with the aggrandized object, omnipotence can be attained for the own self. The overvaluation of the object thus serves as a detour to obtain otherwise unreachable magnificence for the own ego.

In more pathological cases, however, the primitive form of identification is not outgrown. Instead of solid identifications being formed, imitatives ones persist or, at best, there develops the wish to be like the object, with awareness that this stage is not yet reached. But in contrast to the aforementioned normal development, there is not even an impulse to translate these fantasies into reality. The ability to achieve these goals in reality is lacking, as frequently there is no capacity to stand tension, to wait and bring about gratifications via effort and concentration. Gratification of desires must be instantaneous and can only be obtained through wish-fulfilling magic. In addition, a clinging to the unmodified, infantile, grandiose parental images is prevalent in such cases.

Under such conditions the narcissistic fantasy remains a permanent, important part of the personality. These ego ideals thus are unattainable; either they are unrealizable *per se*, because they are too grandiose and set too high a goal, or the step from fantasy to reality cannot be taken. Either situation results in a permanent state of unsatisfied narcissism, i.e., in an intense feeling of inferiority and, not infrequently, states of depression of varying intensity. Or, if the ego level is a more primitive one, reality testing may be partly relinquished and a condition may prevail which might be described as a state of partial and temporary megalomania. Such persons feel as if they really were whatever their narcissistic ideal may be, and this despite not having lost contact with reality. To give an example: A patient who on account of his infantile ego and neurotic difficulties did not succeed professionally, would spend hours practicing an "important" signature like that of a banker. Although well aware of all his failures in reality, when penning his signature, he felt gratified, as if he were the president of a bank.

It is this condition of partial and temporary megalomania, on the basis of a pathologic ego ideal, which is the topic of this paper.

Frequently, narcissistic ego ideals become conspicuous only in puberty. It appears that under the increased pressure of conflicts at puberty, the aforementioned withdrawal of libido from objects dangerous to the ego takes place, in order to undo the heightened danger of castration as a consequence of pubertal masturbation. Narcissistic ideals of the described compensatory, grandiose, phallic character are now developed or regressively revived. This implies that object-libidinal strivings are regressively replaced by identifications of the above-mentioned early infantile kind.

The ego ideals of puberty, though, are normally a mixture of such early identifications and various superego elements. The persistence of narcissistic ideals in their original form points to the presence of more or less severe pathology. However, traces of the narcissistic identifications can be discerned in the normal superego.

Among these residues of earlier identifications—these "archaic" elements, as I would like to call them—I shall concentrate upon the positive, grandiose elements only. The instability of early images—the sudden transformation of a "good" object into a "bad" object, with all the serious consequences such a change involves for early identification and narcissistic equilibrium—thus is omitted here deliberately. It should be stressed, furthermore, that evidently ego ideal and superego are most often fused, overlaid and intertwined to such a degree that the differentiation between the two structures becomes rather theoretical. On the other hand, it appears that any attempt to come to an understanding of narcissistic nonpsychotic states necessitates the concept of the ego ideal.

While a prevalence of narcissistic ego ideals leads to such serious pathology that it cannot be overlooked, milder cases frequently remain unnoticed. The admixture of unmodified narcissistic "ego ideal" elements into the superego often is expressed by a feeling of full identity with the ideal, without sufficient ego transformation and real achievement. Such feelings are not too easy to grasp in analysis. When they can be reached, they impress one as a slight confusion about the own self. It is as if a narcissistic fantasy about the self had become fulfilled, as if the narcissistic aims were reached, and the distinction between fantasy and reality could not be made in certain circumscribed areas. Any objectivity toward the own self is lacking. Frequently, however, these feelings are well covered and do not find any conspicuous expression. Also, such feelings may be transitory, may be the immediate response to a specific situation—e.g., to the danger of a breakthrough of incestuous impulses—and thus may represent regression to early identification as a defense.

I shall try to substantiate this conception of archaic superego elements with clinical material from two different cases. The first of these illustrates how, under the impact of the castration complex, early narcissistic identifications are regressively revived and included into an otherwise normal superego. In the second one, the particular childhood history makes an abnormal development of identifications self-evident and clearly demonstrates the causes for the formation and persistence of a pathological ego ideal.

Case 1

The first case is that of a bright and talented young man who came for treatment because of phobic and conversion-hysteric symptoms. In the analysis, his symptomatology was revealed as the expression of pathologic identifications which were an outcome of the oedipal conflicts of childhood. The most important conversion symptoms consisted in hysterical sinusitis and colitis, combined with a great deal of hypochondriacal concern about illness. Moreover, the patient was afraid of collapsing as he walked on the street —particularly when walking through the "canyon-like" streets of Manhattan—of falling out of windows, getting stuck in the subway, etc. The fear of illness led to his mother, who was always hypochondriacally concerned about her own health. She never left the house without "smelling salts," because she might collapse in the street. The father—an outstanding man, intelligent and capable—was a busy obstetrician whose office was located in the family home. From early childhood on, the boy had seen many pregnant women. He knew his father operated on them; he had heard them scream in his father's hospital. He understood the medical activities of the father as being sexual and sadistic. The father cut and hurt the women; but it was he, also, who made the babies for them. The father, therefore, was seen as being promiscuously sexual. Thus the boy concluded (not without sound psychological insight) that the mother's illnesses were likewise a reaction to his father's "brutality." On the other hand, to be sick, to be fat, to be pregnant, was caused by eating something bad and being constipated. Pregnancy and illness thus also had a pregenital origin. This he inferred from the behavior of the mother, who was forever warning about unwholesome food and was mostly interested in feeding and purging her children, alternating these attentions between the patient and his two older sisters. The patient's concern about illness represented a pregnancy fantasy which was expressed as "being stuffed up with pus at both ends." This same pregnancy fantasy was also expressed in his extreme obesity, a condition lasting from his fifth year until the age of 17, when he was in college and cured himself of this affliction by means of self-prescribed, drastic therapy: he lived on crackers and apples for three months.

The onset of the obesity (i.e., of his feminine identification) coincided with the breakdown of his oedipal strivings, comparable to a very conspicuous announcement of what had happened. It is necessary here to give a brief account of his oedipal history. The child's relationship to his mother, who was affectionate and protective, appeared to have been a very positive one, with predominant oral strivings centering around fantasies of eating and being eaten by the love object. There were memories of very early fear (at the age of two) of falling into a well in a courtyard in the country, of falling into a subway excavation, which led in a straight line to later sexual anxieties. When as a young married man, awakening from sleep, he wanted to have intercourse with his wife, he had the terrifying image of falling into an abyss. The aforementioned phobic symptoms, referring to the canyonlike streets of Manhattan and to falling out of a window, also belong here.

He remembered a slightly later incident. While

spending the summer with his mother on a farm in the absence of his father, when he was three, he entered the dining room ahead of the others and consumed an entire dish of crullers which was intended for the whole party. Crullers, he assured me, were some kind of cakes fried in fat that looked exactly like female genitals. (Having two older sisters with whom he was bathed in one tub, he had had ample opportunities to make his observations.) He became violently ill following this feat and thereafter retained an eating disturbance, keeping away from everything that was greasy, mushy, without definite structure, such as stew, liver, kidneys, etc. He also developed disgust with regard to "oriental," i.e., Jewish, women (the patient is Jewish) because they were "like dipped in oil." Various anxieties about becoming sick from bad food persisted from then on. These anxieties, pregenital as far as the underlying strivings were concerned, were also strictly preoedipal. They took place between himself and his mother; the father did not yet appear to be a rival. These anxieties did not cause the child to give up the mother as an object, but to proceed, at least partly, to a new sexual level.

At the age of four, again alone with his mother and sisters, he spent a summer at the seashore. He now became interested in seeing them exposed; the mother's curves became very attractive. At night he shared a big bed with the mother. While she slept, he pressed his body against hers and finally crept under the blanket and touched her pubic region with his lips; or, possibly, this was the content of masturbation fantasies. Play with his genitals appeared at that time. After his return to the city, the father was seen for the first time as a rival. The boy not only became aware of the father's medical-sadistic activities and terribly anxious about them, but also, sharing the parental bedroom, he now noticed love scenes between the parents at night. In the analysis, he remembered his rage against the father, his wish to do away with him, to walk over to the mother's bed himself. (His later "fear of walking" had one of its roots here.) During the day he was still completely alone with the mother, his sisters being at school. Helping her with the housework, he had the fantasy that while allegedly engaged in innocent occupations they would indulge in love play as on the seashore. Such fantasies also accompanied masturbation. He believed he remembered having been caught masturbating by the father and shrinking in panic—probably a screen memory representing an anxiety dream. One terrifying experience, however, brought his fantasy and his masturbation to a traumatic ending. When he was five, both he and his older sister were taken to the father's hospital for tonsillectomies and were operated upon in the actual delivery room. He remembers his terror when the ether mask was brought to his face. After this operation, he was convinced he was castrated and no longer a boy. His masturbation and undisguised fantasies about the mother stopped. Instead, he began to please her in a more infantile way. He started to overeat and soon became obese. He gave up his aggressive genitality and regressed into recently relinquished orality. But he also now became identified with the sickly mother and the pregnant patients, the only possible sexual position being the feminine one in relation to the father.

At this point features of a strong paternal superego

developed, which will be described later. These enabled him to enter a rather normal latency period, characterized by good functioning in school and the development of rich intellectual sublimations.

With the resumption of masturbation in adolescence, the hypochondria, the guilt feeling, the sexual and, by this time, also social inhibition grew and interfered more and more with his life until, finally confronted with the demands of adult sexuality and adult masculine mastery of life, he broke down. He was a brilliant student, but after being graduated *summa cum laude* from a top-level university, he became overwhelmed by a feeling of hopeless inferiority and worthlessness. For a period of several years, instead of entering a profession or otherwise preparing a life for himself, he "loafed" on the living-room couch in the parental home, reading voraciously and masturbating abundantly. When he finally began to work, in a field connected with creative artistic production, he could do it only under a very special condition: he had to work anonymously, hardly making a living, acting as a ghost writer for various well-known and recognized friends who gathered laurels and money via his secret production. It was only after a number of years of analysis that he could come into his own.

The meaning of this behavior became clear in analysis. As a boy, he had been intensely interested in his father's profession, full of curiosity, reading the father's medical journals at an incredibly early age, obviously eager to step into his shoes and to outdo him. That in his early childhood the father's medical activities were understood as completely sexualized, has already been indicated. But when urged by his family to study medicine, he could not do it; instead, he chose the sideline of the father who, as a hobby, interested himself in the arts and acted as a patron to a group of struggling artists. Reduced to following this sidetrack, the patient developed considerable talents and made extremely high demands on himself with regard to the level and perfection of his production. However, even this substitute had to be pursued furtively; he had to leave the rewards to a father figure. It was as if he could identify with the father in his brilliance, but success was reserved for the father. He was able to identify with him in relation to effort, but not in relation to gratification.

After he began to work, his sex life, which thus far had been restricted to masturbation, also underwent an extension, although not without disturbances. He now could approach girls, but only under special conditions. That is to say, when they were in need of comfort, help, love, he was able to please them—even with his penis. He would then be their rescuer and support; he made love purely "altruistically." His erective potency was good. It was very important to give the woman an orgasm, but he himself had no sensations whatsoever. To quote his own description of the situation, he had to be a "knight on a white horse, who used his lance only to protect helpless women." Here again, as we can see, he is identified with his father, but in a negative way. The father, in the child's view, had lacerated women with his penis-scalpel.

This by no means complete description of the patient's symptomatology and behavior permits us some insight into his personality and superego structure.

The superego of the patient was a complex structure. Predominant was an identification with a strict and punishing father who did not tolerate the son's sexual or aggressive transgressions. From the fifth year on and until the analysis, there existed intense guilt feelings which came to a peak during the period of "loafing." He felt that he was "a monster," "a goilem," "had a rotten core," "was in constant danger of a breakdown of moral values." This last phrase, of course, was an adult way of expressing his concern that warded-off (incestuous) sexual impulses might break through. The "rotten core" came from having eaten something bad, which expressed a sexual wish and the guilt reaction against it, clad in pregenital language. The "goilem" and the "monster" represented the danger of breaking out with uncontrolled, sadistic, sexual impulses. At the same time they indicated a feeling of already having been punished for incestuous crime by castration, and of being found out.

This identification with the strict father expressed itself in his high moral standards. The negative side of his father identification has been mentioned already: Where real gratifications are involved, he was forced to resign. Sexuality, success, and money are reserved for the father. While the father was sadistic, the patient was good. Thereby he not only warded off the forbidden identification with the sexual father, but he also outdid him. He expected to be preferred by the mother—by women—for his goodness, in competition with the father. But at the same time the knight on the white horse, who used his lance only for healing purposes, is by no means a completely masculine figure. He also wanted to act as a protective, loving mother equipped with magic powers, who, when the child has hurt himself, kisses and blows the pain away. The second meaning of this feature of the ideal had become richer in content and detail in the course of time. Already in adolescence, there were fantasies about having a house of his own, furnished in the most exquisite taste, in which he, as a bachelor, received guests for elaborate meals cooked by himself. He wished to surpass the mother's more simple tastes in her own field. To be the one who gives and feeds in the most refined way became most desirable. From the direct oral field, this fantasy expanded to many others. He wanted to be the one who guided and advised everybody else. He succeeded in creating a large circle of friends. His efforts on their behalf grew into a 24-hour job. He tried to become their "therapist," to give them money, to advise them in love affairs, to provide jobs, find apartments, arrange trips, procure unobtainable theater tickets, offer the most important ideas for their creative work, and so on. Here again, as in his work as a ghost writer unknown to the world, he was the creator of other people's fame and happiness. With this behavior, he lived up to an ideal of an omniscient, all-powerful, all-giving mother. Thus the negative father identification coincided with this very special form of mother identification. He was identifying here with the loving, protecting mother whose main interest in life was the family's food, health, and happiness. Although the father was the physician, it was she who doctored the children when they were sick, who was the helper, while the father was seen as the sadist. This image of the mother contrasted sharply with the one underlying the patient's hysterical symptoms in which he identified with the sexual mother, i.e., with a suffering, mistreated, sick, and pregnant one.

The image of the protecting and giving mother originated before he became involved in his oedipal, sadomasochistic fantasies. Oral and anal patterns, feeding and giving, seemed to predominate. In the foreground was the relationship to the child, for whom she could do anything. In view of the long history of oral strivings toward the mother, this pregenital coloration of the early image was not surprising.

Most striking in this ideal were the megalomanic traits. The patient felt himself to be omniscient and omnipotent—in the interest of others. Whatever anxieties and feelings of inferiority plagued him, via this identification, they were undone. His behavior and character pattern had been formed according to this ideal. Though to a large extent able to live up to the inner demand, he obviously was not really in a position to accomplish all of these fine tasks. Very gratified for a time to be a member of a large organization that placed all kinds of technical and other facilities at his disposal (e.g., a private telephone line with Washington, etc.), he felt the powers of this organization to be his own. However, this feeling of being all-powerful was not confined to such realistic situations. Separated from the support of the organization, he soon developed the same feeling of omnipotence which now surpassed by far his real possibilities of accomplishment.

On the other hand, the conditions for the development of this feeling could be studied during periods of utter helplessness that occurred after separation from his mother. For instance, when after years of clinging to the mother he finally married and moved away from the family home, he felt angry with the mother and the analyst because they did not help to furnish his new home, to find domestic help, to locate a cleaner and a laundry. It was as though without the mother he could neither feed himself nor keep himself clean. Shortly thereafter, he again took over. His home became the center of his circle, and he felt once more as though he were running a private social agency. The process is obvious: After the loss of the object, which was seen in a predominantly pregenital light, he identified with it, and with this identification the helplessness changed into grandiosity.

In this grandiosity—and this is really my point in presenting this lengthy case history—the otherwise very well-developed faculty of the patient for reality testing and self-evaluation gave way. We are here faced with the narcissistic core of the superego; here his infantile feeling of omnipotence was preserved or, better still, revived. However, and we shall also find this to be true in the second case I intend to describe, a certain fluidity of the megalomanic feeling was present. What at times was an inner conviction of his own greatness, became at other times an inner demand, and the differentiation between ego and ego ideal was re-established. Thus the megalomanic feeling was transitory. It was contradicted here not only by the ego, that is by the reappearing sense of reality, but by other parts of his superego which, for instance, caused him to see himself as a "goilem."

Such conflicts within the superego are by no means unusual. It has been mentioned before that the superego is composed of various elements of identifications. Normally, a fusion takes place between these various elements. The failure completely to achieve such a fusion facilitates the changes between megalomanic and deeply self-critical moods.

One could ask here why this identification is considered an ego ideal. Indeed, to a large degree we are dealing with an ego identification. He actually behaved toward his friends as his mother behaved toward him when he was a young child. To this identification, however, an element was added which was not reality-syntonic, namely, the omnipotence which is ascribed to the mother. This early image of the all-powerful, pregenital and preoedipal mother was used to counteract the terrifying later image of the sick, suffering, pregnant mother with whom, as his symptoms proved, he was also identified. Thus, when he could no longer feel as a man, he could at least identify with the powerful mother of early childhood and thereby counterbalance his identification with the castrated one. To serve this defensive need, the mother was idealized and very early images of her were used for the purpose.

These very early images of the mother appear to belong to periods of ego immaturity in which clear reality testing and an objective awareness of what the mother really was or did were not yet possible. Furthermore, the child could not yet differentiate clearly between himself and the object. Frustrations may easily be undone by giving up the awareness of separation from an object and becoming again one with the object. The patient, in his longing to identify with the idealized mother, could not realistically become like her, i.e., become identified with her in his ego and become as grandiose as he saw her. This must remain a narcissistic desire, an ego ideal. The faculty to evaluate himself realistically and to know that he wanted to be like this ideal, but that he could not be like it, could easily be abandoned. Magically, he could become one with this ideal. He was prone to regress temporarily into those phases where the mere wish already stood for fulfillment. Such periods became noticeable in his behavior when he indulged in bragging and exaggeration about his power and accomplishments. On the other hand, this regressive, megalomanic pattern appeared only as an admixture to his otherwise reality-syntonic mother identification. It appears that the traces of megalomania in the normal superego are based on the regressive revival of the mechanism of flowing together with an idealized object. It is likely that the clinging to such an ego ideal is mostly motivated by defensive needs.

The fluidity of the differentiation between ego and ideal, the easy revival of the mechanism of undoing the separation between self and powerful object, the loss of ability to distinguish wish from fulfillment, the temporary disintegration of reality testing, are the decisive characteristics of these primitive structures which I would prefer to call narcissistic "ego ideals" in contrast to the normal superego. When in pathologic states, as for instance in manic triumph, a dissolution of the superego occurs, we may speak of a regression of the superego into more primitive ego ideals.

This fluidity of ego differentiations is regularly found in so-called "narcissistic personalities." Undoing of the differentiation becomes the basis for exorbitant self-esteem; its reappearance leads to the outbreak of "narcissistic anxieties," like fear of being inferior, over-concern with other people's thoughts about oneself, etc.

The faculty for regressive undoing of ego differentiation is based upon fixation at early levels of ego development. The patient I have just described, although reaching the genital level, was characterized by a definite fixation on an oral level. He was able to achieve a far-reaching desexualization of his pregenital trends, resulting in a well sublimated form of character structure. The ability regressively to revive former ego states was the only residual ego weakness stemming from his early fixation on an oral level characterized by not yet stabilized ego boundaries.

The pathology of the ego ideals becomes more conspicuous in cases where the disturbance of ego development is greater. Not only the megalomanic aspects of the ideal are pronounced, but frequently the ideals show bluntly unsublimated sexual features. Thus the discrepancy between reality and ideal content is widened. The most frequent form of such unsublimated ideals is to be found in the wish to become, or in the feeling of being, a penis. Here an identification has taken place—again characterized by fluid frontiers between ego and ego ideal—with a glorified parental phallus. Such an identification is a very primitive one. A part of the parental body, the sight or touch of which causes excitement, is acquired, so to speak, by becoming it. Lewin (1933) believes that this fantasy is always based on oral incorporation. Greenacre (1947), if I understand it correctly, indicates in her paper, "Vision, Headache and the Halo," that premature exposure to the sight of an erection may lead to idealization of, and identification with, the phallus.

Such a primitive identification precedes the ability to integrate into a person various impressions emanating from the object. It is based on awareness of a *concrete* thing, the organ. Ability to identify with qualities of the object apparently presupposes a greater differentiation of perception, greater complexity of response, in short, a higher level of ego development. Such an identification is almost an id response and not yet an ego mechanism; its pleasurable, sexual character is conspicuous. Here no sublimation of blunt, sexual features was possible. Identifications on this primitive level obviously can take place via infantile methods, i.e., via wish-fulfilling fantasy. If they persist in their original form, they cannot lead to any real ego transformation but must remain isolated structures (ego ideals).

Preconditions for the persistence of these primitive identifications are disturbances of the development of the ego as well as of object relations. Thus some particular sexualization of the relationship between parent and child—early seduction, for instance—may express itself in this way. Most frequently such ideals are regressively used for the purpose of warding off castration anxiety. In the service of these defensive needs, identification with the glorified phallus may acquire moral values. It may be used, for example, in the struggle against masturbation. A fusion may take place of this ideal and identifications with instinct-restricting figures of later times. For example, I remember a patient who, during adolescence, in a desperate struggle against masochistic homosexual impulses, wanted to feel and felt his whole body become stiff and hard like the statue of George Washington. Needless to say, in such cases the afore-described grandiosity is also present.

I shall outline, very briefly, a fragment from a history which will demonstrate this fusion as well as the genesis of the pathologic ego ideal. It will also illustrate the further complication, resulting, in such cases, from a combination of these primitive ego ideals with superego elements of particular cruelty.

Case 2

The patient was a young woman of good intellectual endowment who had achieved a promising career as a teacher. She came to analysis because of various anxieties of the narcissistic type and masochistic behavior. Under the anxious and self-effacing surface, feelings of grandiosity soon became evident. She felt that she was a genius, that she would "suddenly reveal herself and stand out like an obelisk," that whoever knew her looked up to her. Whatever she did was experienced as an extraordinary achievement for which other people would admire her. She felt sure people would envy her for whatever she had. These megalomanic feelings were transitory, however. Frequently, she felt unwanted, deprived, guilty about being selfish and greedy; thus she wavered between her feelings of grandiosity and an awareness that she was not as grandiose as she wanted to be. At such a time the grandiosity was an ideal against which she measured her ego, while at other times she could not distinguish between wish and reality.

An only child, born a few months after her father's sudden death, she grew up with her mother and the maternal grandparents. A short time before her father's death, the mother's only brother, a very attractive and gifted young man, had also died of a sudden illness. The father had no siblings; thus, she was the only remaining offspring of the family. Her young mother refused to marry again and devoted herself exclusively to the child, on whom she showered her whole pent-up love and affection. The child was treated as the most precious and wonderful thing in the world; that is to say, her own narcissism was overstimulated. From early childhood on, there was the demand that she substitute for the dead father and uncle. There was early awareness of the existence of the phallus, as the grandfather had exposed himself before her. The child's sexual theories were, of course, influenced by the complicated family situation. Moreover, there was a predominant oral fixation. She imagined that the mother had devoured the father in the sexual act, which was equated with having castrated him through biting off the penis. She (the patient) was the father's penis—or the dead father or uncle come back. The intellectual and other outstanding qualities of the deceased father and uncle became fused for the child with the overwhelming impression of the grandfather's genitalia, and with her fantasies about the paternal phallus, at a time when her libidinal level was still an oral one and the state of her ego development correspondingly primitive. In her fantasy, she offered herself to the family as a love object to replace those they had lost. This was a highly gratifying sexual fantasy, but at the same time she felt that the family demanded from her the replacement of the dead son and husband. Thus the moral and the sexual aspects became hopelessly confused. In contrast to the normal course of superego development, symbolic sexual gratification and narcissistic self-aggrandizement became the content of a moral demand.

The admiration which mother and grandparents lavished on the child increased the little girl's narcissism and directed her interest to an enormous degree upon her own body, thus serving as a narcissistic seduction. Hence the development of ego controls became almost unnecessary and greatly retarded. Acceptance of unpleasant reality was refused for a long time and a readiness preserved to undo any kind of frustration by fantasy wish fulfillment. The persistence of the identification with the glorified phallus demonstrates that she never fully succeeded in overcoming infantile methods of self-esteem regulation.

Any desexualization of the fantasy became impossible. No stable identification with nonsexual qualities of the objects could be attained, since the child was, after all, trying to identify with objects that existed in her fantasy only. The normal impact of reality on this fantasy object, which would have helped to achieve some degree of desexualization and also to reduce to normal size the figure of the father that was seen in such supernatural dimensions, was absent in this case—hence the unsublimated phallic character of the ego ideal and its megalomanic scope. She wanted to be a phallus with her whole body ("standing out like a tremendous obelisk"), which was equal to being a creative genius of monumental proportions, admired by everyone around her.

These fantasies, however, were contradicted by her awareness of being a girl. The lack of a penis was experienced as a terrific trauma which caused her to cling even more tenaciously to this overcathected identification with the father-phallus as such. Thus oral-sadistic impulses were regressively intensified. On the other hand, fear of loss of the mother's love led her to develop strong reaction formations. Finally, this ruthless, pregenital aggressiveness was turned against the self as a relentless superego. This became combined with the megalomanic, phallic identification. The end product was a poorly integrated mixture which resulted in the oscillations of self-esteem described above.

This particular pathology of the superego can be considered typical. When early identifications with unsublimated sexual behavior have taken place and sexual characteristics as such remain an ego ideal, a fixation on or regression to primitive, aggressive, pregenital levels is frequent, which leads to a persistence of particular, cruel superego forerunners. This combination of opposite factors—of megalomanic, sexualized ideals and of particular, sadistic superego elements—must lead to a type of superego which cannot possibly be lived up to in reality. The described vacillations of self-esteem, which result from an instability of the ego structure, from a wavering between transitory megalomanic illusions about the self and the regained capacity to distinguish between fantasy and reality, become considerably increased by the admixture of cruel, primitive superego elements. Therefore, megalomanic states will alternate with periods of intense self-devaluation, which may indicate a pathology of the borderline type.

Summary

The revival or persistence of an early identification within the structure of the later superego imbues the personality with characteristics of the ego level on which the identification was originally formed, such as unstable ego boundaries, confusion between ego and object, between wish and reality. In more regressed cases, the picture is complicated by an admixture of sadistic superego forerunners as well as of crudely sexual ideals. Such superegos are marked by inadequate integration which expresses itself in continual vacillations of self-esteem. In our not too precise analytic language, we frequently speak of such persons as narcissistic.

Finally, it should be stressed that a narcissistic type of this kind was already described very early in the psychoanalytic literature, long before the publication of Freud's papers on ego psychology. I am referring here to an essay by Jones (1913), "The God Complex," in which the narcissistic personality is conceived as the result of identification with a father figure that is seen in an infantile light.

11

A Special Variation
of Technique

(1958)

In RECENT years, the pathology of the ego and superego has increasingly become the center of psychoanalytic interest. There exists as yet no systematic
classification of the forms of ego pathology and character disturbances; hence there cannot be any systematic
description of variations in technique or of parameters,
to use Eissler's term (1953, p. 110f.; see also 1958),
necessitated by this pathology.

Methods of giving initial support to a weak ego, so
as to strengthen it for the task of facing instinctual
conflicts, have been most frequently discussed. For
example, it has been described how the violence of
anxiety in these cases often necessitates all sorts of
supportive measures, such as "nurturing" some positive
transference by giving the patient the feeling that the
analyst is always there for him and can be called in a
situation of panic. Sometimes his relation to the analyst

Published originally in *The International Journal of Psycho-Analysis*,
39:230–234, 1958.

may become the first really reliable object relation in the patient's life, a contingency which of course entails the danger that it may seriously interfere with the possibility of the transference ever being analyzed.

I shall concentrate on a special variation of technique dealing predominantly with a particular form of superego pathology in a certain group of patients who can be defined as impulse-ridden characters or acting-out hysterias. The ego disturbance in these cases appears to be a secondary effect of the defective superego. Such patients are a helpless prey to uncontrollable outbursts of libidinal and/or aggressive impulses, which cause violent anxiety and guilt reactions. Between these powerful drives and a relentless superego the ego seems weak, almost nonexistent, so to speak; but it may manifest itself very forcefully in negative ways, i.e., as inhibitor of normally ego-syntonic, important gratifications and activities. Such an ego is of little help to the analysis. Repetitive acting out occurs outside and within the analysis, cannot be stopped, and threatens to make the treatment impossible.

In cases of this kind, the analyst frequently finds himself in the same role as the child analyst who has to observe the conflict going on outside the analysis, between child and parents or siblings. It appears that this undesirable situation also has a positive aspect, because the violence of the conflict is so intense as to make analytic work impossible. The analyst remains outside for a time—and is not completely the butt of unsatisfiable libidinal demands and aggressive impulses, until slowly, with the progress of the analysis, a shift of cathexis and the establishment of a genuine transference can be achieved.

Within the analysis, these patients try, via their acting out and the ensuing guilt-ridden anxiety, to force the analyst into the role of a primitive superego against which an endless and tumultuous war of ambivalence is being waged. The superego is insufficiently internalized and is constantly reprojected. It is as though no real love objects and no integrated ego existed, but only externalized superego figures, as though the pathological superego, like a parasite, had usurped the place of all other psychic structures.

The roots of this pathology are found in a premature, overstrict enforcement of superego demands, while simultaneously the normal development of object relations was severely interfered with by a too-extensive and too-early repression of libidinal as well as aggressive strivings, under the impact of too-forbidding early objects. The disintegration of the pathological superego, which is necessary in order to achieve restructuring of the personality and establishment of normal object relations, should be brought about by careful analysis of the dependent and highly ambivalent relations to these early objects. But the violence of the acting out makes this impossible. To break this impasse, it proves useful to take sides with the patient, in a rather unanalytic way, against the object—demasking and dethroning it, so to speak. It is this active intervention, this stepping out of his natural role by the analyst, which I would like to describe. It is, I believe, a variation of classical technique that is often necessary in cases of this kind.

I shall give some fragments of the material from a long analysis of such a case, to illustrate the structure of the pathological superego as well as the ways and means by which its virulence finally was abated.

The patient, Abigail, a strikingly elegant and attractive, although not beautiful woman, was in her forties when she came to analysis. She presented a curious mixture of very upper-class social graciousness, impeccable manners, and uncontrolled aggressive outbursts. She suffered from alcoholism and addiction to barbiturates which were taken during the day, so that the patient spent most of her day in bed. In the evening, before her husband returned home, she would get up, longing for his affection and companionship. At this point, in order to dispel tension and be able to be gay, she would begin to drink. Invariably, she felt the husband's response to be inadequate. She felt "misunderstood and left alone," and sooner or later she would have a temper tantrum, attacking him physically and provoking him to such a degree that he also would resort to violence.

By and by, it became clear that the barbiturates were taken to permit withdrawal into sleep, which was needed to allay the unbearable anxiety Abigail experienced when left to her own devices. When she was alone, it was as though she were not a real person. There was nothing she wanted to do; it was as though she were paralyzed in all her ego functions. She was like a little girl needing to ask every few minutes, "Mother, what shall I do?" Indeed, it turned out that as long as there had been somebody telling her what to do, Abigail had been much better. There had been no temper tantrums, hardly any drinking, no sleep addiction. All these symptoms started to appear a few years before she came for analysis, following her marriage to a man of wealth and social standing who was 25 years her senior.

Abigail stemmed from a socially prominent family; there was more prestige than money. She had lost her father at the age of 15. In order not to be financially dependent on her mother, the complicated relationship with whom will be described later, she did the most revolutionary thing in her life: instead of having a "coming-out party," she insisted upon getting a college education and training as a social worker. Being a person of high intelligence and sensitivity, Abigail was able to function very well under the pressure of school and job. She worked until the age of forty, when her mother died. Only then was she able to marry. The husband clearly was a parent figure. Before they were married, he had been her boss with whom she had had a thrilling flirtation. After marriage, she was completely frigid and reacted to his sexual advances with only anxiety and disgust.

Now Abigail lived under conditions of which she had always dreamed. She finally had a husband and a lovely house, although owing to a hysterectomy she could have no children. She was wealthy and did not have to work any more, but could do whatever she pleased. Yet, there was nothing that she felt she wanted to do. It transpired that empty boredom had already been predominant in her early childhood. As far as she remembered, she had been unable to do anything on her own. She had started very late to walk and talk. She could not play by herself; neither could she play with other children. When brought together with them, Abigail would stand in a corner, in despair, not knowing what to do or how to talk with them. Clad in a lovely white lace dress, she spent many hours just sitting motionless in the parlor, in a chair much too big for her, while her mother entertained lady friends. Much later, it emerged that this was exactly how her mother had wanted her to behave. Her near-paralyzed state was thus the expression of obedience to the mother, whose demands she had taken over so completely that it was as though she had no impulses of her own. Therefore, she constantly needed to be told what to do. When, in later childhood, she found herself in a situation where she had to make a decision, she was able to do so only by "consulting" her stomach. If she thought of an alternative that was really not pleasing to her, she would feel somatic discomfort within her body; in this way she knew what she wanted.

The same pattern was repeated in the analysis. She wanted me to tell her what to say; free association remained impossible for a long time. More and more, she saw me in the role of an imaginary companion who would constantly accompany her and advise her what to do. It was as though the analyst represented a personified superego.

In the presence of her husband, on the other hand, Abigail was overcome with vehement emotion, longing, and rage. She was then completely unreasonable in her demands; the docility and good manners would fall away, and in rebellious defiance she would give rein to her violent outbursts.

The superego problems led back to the mother. To describe the latter, as she emerged in the analysis, one could best characterize her as being "a lady" in the truest Victorian sense. Most important for her were good behavior and the opinion of other people. Life was narrowed down to a pleasantness of voice and manner. Any expression of emotion, of deeper feelings, any activity beyond the scope of church, charity, and good society, was considered to be not "ladylike." Any unrestricted play that might be accompanied by noise, by dirtying of clothes and hands, any abandon, any spontaneous expression of affection, was unacceptable. Whatever was connected with sex in any way could not mentioned and should not be seen. Pregnant women were shameless if they went out in public. One of the patient's terrifying, originally repressed memories was of once having, as a very little girl, put her hand into a box in the dark cellar and, to her horror, touched a litter of newborn kittens that had been hidden away from her; of course, no explanation had been offered her.

Another example was an incident which Abigail remembered late in the analysis, under extreme anxiety. When she was about five years old, she was riding with her mother in a horse-drawn carriage when her mother suddenly seized the child's head and pushed her face into her lap. The horse, without any consideration for the ladies, had lifted his tail and followed his natural urge. Little girls just could not look at such disgusting things as a horse's anal productions. The mother's attitude with regard to anal training followed this pattern. The patient was trained at an incredibly early age and had to be always spic and span. It was most important that the child produce every morning at a regular hour, lest she become ill with appendicitis. On the other hand, any interest in anything not perfectly clean—by looking, touching, smelling—was completely out of the question.

The mother's inability to accept bodily contact

extended to Abigail even when she was still a baby. She could not tolerate the child snuggling up to her or, as a toddler, clinging to her hand in the street. Even endearing words were considered vulgar.

Most important for the patient's pathological development was the relationship between her parents. They slept in separate bedrooms, the mother having banished the father from her bed. Abigail, an only child, owed her existence to a night spent in a hotel, on the way to a vacation spot, when the father had been too stingy to take two rooms. The latter, a judge in the juvenile court and a kindly man who could tear himself apart for a juvenile delinquent, met his wife only at the dinner table and then took revenge upon her by behaving in the rudest manner he could devise. He would eat in a disgusting fashion, spit in a wide curve into the floral centerpiece, and break into violent outbursts of temper against the mother, who through all this would remain silent, gentle, well-behaved, and saintly. The parents would not talk to each other. For the little girl, the father was almost a complete stranger; as he was so unacceptable to her mother, she dared not love him. During endless dinner hours, the child would just sit there, silent and motionless, unable to eat or speak.

The mother, never raising her voice, always gentle, had achieved an almost total repression of instinctual forces in the child, including all wishes for affection. This was combined with a complete lack of interest in, or direct disapproval of, any timid attempts at sublimation, most of which were condemned as "not ladylike." The result was a grave interference not only with the child's libidinal vicissitudes and object relations, but also with her ego development. Abigail's inability to function independently gave the impression of a serious intellectual defect.

Later, in adolescence, by a great effort of will, the patient consciously forced herself to behave "as if" she were outgoing, cheerful, charming. This artificial, gracious behavior proved very helpful: she became "popular." But it was based on continuous effort. She had to sense what people wanted and to behave, not as she really felt (which she did not know), but as she thought others wanted her to be. She had many friends now, but could tolerate them only for a short time. To be with them demanded a tremendous effort on her part. Thus, after a short while, she could not bear her friends any more and wished only to get rid of them again.

After moving to college and away from her mother's presence, she became able to do all kinds of things that were anathema in the mother's eyes. She flirted around, acquired many admirers, and permitted them to neck and pet with her, only to disappoint them when they became in any way serious.

The patient thus behaved, indeed, like the classical "as if" case described by Helene Deutsch (1942). She had no real object relations. Her friends represented merely temporary superego figures. Trying to divine their commands, she found it impossible to live up to this relentless task. The superego demands were not only excessive, but were not really integrated into the personality; they were experienced as coming from outside objects, and her tremendous ambivalence against these superego objects prevented any real relationship with them.

After her marriage, the tenuous balance of this "as if" existence proved insufficient. The husband clearly represented the mother—and the maternal superego. He became too much of a temptation for Abigail. Everything she had warded off all her life now broke through; she became childishly demanding. The husband was expected to continually shower her with love and affection (which had been so severely denied by her mother). He was supposed to share all kinds of things with her (which, as we understood much later, were derivatives of infantile activities, genital as well as pregenital). She succeeded in experiencing his behavior as an endless repetition of maternal condemnations of her unconscious strivings, to which she reacted with uncontrollable temper tantrums facilitated by the effects of alcohol. These outbursts alternated with desperate anxiety and clinging to a superego figure.

While acting out thus in her marriage, she was unable to carry these emotional storms into the analytic hour and to face what she felt, or associate to it. She could not lie on the couch because she had to watch my facial expression, "to find out what I wanted her to say." Whatever childhood material emerged was offered because she knew this was expected of her. In the absence of an integrated ego with whom to form an alliance, the patient's deadlock between impulse and guilt could not be broken until I finally resorted to the aforementioned very active form of intervention, which is my reason for presenting this lengthy case history. This method can be described as a frontal attack on the original superego model, i.e., as a systematic devaluation of the idealized mother.

From bits of material about the mother that were

reported here, it might appear as though an analysis and solution of the patient's relationship with her mother would have come about by itself and led naturally to a disintegration of the pathological superego. But this was not so. The mother had actually imposed herself on the child as an absolute ideal. This ideal, like a malignancy, usurped the place of an independent ego as well as of any genuine love object and had to be undermined before either could be restored. The patient felt so overwhelmed by guilt as to be incapable of critical judgement. The mother was seen as a saint, and her opinions as moral law. Hence it was only with my active help in demasking the mother that this patient could develop something completely new: tolerance and understanding of her libidinal and, eventually, also of her aggressive impulses. Only then could a mass of repressed material be recalled and finally experienced as belonging to the past; only then did the patient become an integrated person. Only then could she become aware of what she felt and wanted. In this way a diminution of her emotional violence could be achieved, and the acting out was then controllable.

What I did, concretely, was to put together for the patient the fragments of information I had about her mother and, so to speak, to analyze the mother for her. I went even further and expressed value judgements with regard to the mother.

I could show her that mother was no saint indeed. Mother was not kind. Mother had not been able to give love to anyone. Mother had driven her husband as well as her only child close to breakdown and had brought endless misery into their lives. Mother wanted the girl to behave like a grown-up when it so suited her, but treated her as a baby when this was what happened to suit her. Mother herself, in fact, was a very neurotic person, which caused her not only to frustrate the father so completely, but also to frustrate Abigail as an infant in her most natural demand for closeness. Mother's neurosis made her utterly narrow, self-centered, and selfish.

Slowly the patient became able to see the mother clearly, and many confirmatory memories emerged. The most impressive of these was the following. As a small child, she had run into a glass door; her face was badly cut and had to be bandaged for weeks. Her mother's main concern was: "What will people think of you!" Thus the mother became divested of her halo, and as a result the patient succeeded in breaking through her defenses.

Of the wealth of repressed material that became available after the mother's demotion, not more than a hint can be given here. In the beginning, this material centered exclusively on the mother and consisted in an intense, pregenital type of longing for love and for sexual activities "shared" with the mother. Gradually it emerged that, because of the utter frustration of her need to touch, to see, and to understand, curiosity had played a tremendous role in the child's fantasy life. While sitting motionless and apparently doing nothing, she was filled with wishes to put her fingers into all holes, all body openings, to tear everything apart, the mother's clothing, the mother's body. Thus she finally progressed to the father and her inability to understand the difference between the sexes.

The complete blocking of any outlet into active play and the unusual amount of pregenital frustration had led to an inability to bind and modify aggression. It was not surprising, therefore, to find a particularly sadistic coloration of fantasies. She finally remembered how, again while sitting still and doing nothing, she had been simply boiling with rage and hatred, wanting to tear her mother into shreds. The dinner hours would be filled with a repetitive fantasy: she imagined the big oak chest behind the mother's chair, in the dining room, falling on the mother and smashing her. All these fantasies were extremely frightening to the child because her only love object would be destroyed, and she would be left all alone.

The thorough analysis of these conflicts enabled us finally to unearth the repressed love for her father, and brought to light a wealth of material referring to childhood masturbation and feminine sexual wishes. The way in which this patient was eventually able to analyze, and the very gratifying therapeutic results, convinced me that despite her apparent borderline pathology she was, after all, a hysteric who had, already in childhood, reached a genital, heterosexual level from which she had then so impressively regressed.

Impulse-ridden characters not infrequently belong to this group of acting-out hysterics. It seems to me that in cases of this type, which are characterized by an intolerant but insufficiently internalized superego and by oscillation between breakthrough and guilt, such active attack upon the superego pathology is often very helpful. On the other hand, closer scrutiny of this method shows that its use involves something more, which is not a part of classical technique either. When the disintegration of a pathological superego is undertaken in this way, value judgements of the analyst, expressions of his understanding, tolerance, and different moral attitude, which usually have no place in the analytic process, come to the fore. To a certain extent, the analyst offers himself as and becomes a new object of identification to the patient. Evidently this is permissible only if it is combined with a careful analysis of the conflict. Were the "technical device" to predominate, we should be educators and not analysts.

12

A Character Formation
Representing the Integration
of Unusual Conflict
Solutions into the Ego Structures

(1958)

T HESE NOTES represent some material from the analysis of an obsessional character which lends itself well, I believe, to illustrate the complex interaction between the many factors that have a bearing upon character development. It points up the interaction between the drives and the ego, environmental influences, peculiarities of the object relations, and the role of the superego, which finally result in the complicated structure of the human personality. However, my presentation will neglect the constitutional element because I am unable to shed specific light on it, although it may have been present in this case. In general, it is likely, for instance, that such factors influence the choice of particular conflict solution, speed of development and particular structure of the

Published originally in *The Psychoanalytic Study of the Child*, 13:309–323. New York: International Universities Press.

ego. A preponderance of particular drives, etc., may to a large extent be constitutionally conditioned; but it also may be the result of identification with important childhood objects characterized by the same instinctual strivings. Thus, in my case, there was a prevalence of sadomasochistic drives and conflicts in both parents as well as in the patient. It is impossible to determine whether the constitutional element or the impact of the parental influences represents the decisive factor. There may frequently be an interaction of both determinants.

The example I have chosen concerns a man who, by himself and his environment, was considered "normal"—a rather meaningless concept, reflecting sociocultural value connotations. But he was unencumbered by circumscribed symptoms and was capable of functioning well enough with regard to work, sexual performance, adjustment to love objects and to society in general. Only the deeper scrutiny of analysis disclosed peculiarities in his behavior, due to a prevalence of inhibition and reaction formation that blocked a more productive and gratifying use of his energies.

His history, as will be shown, reveals an abundance of traumatic situations, difficult conflicts, and a preponderance of regressed pregenital and sadomasochistic strivings. Conditions for the formation of good object relations and healthy identifications were far from favorable. Nevertheless, the all-over result of this complicated development was an amazingly positive, one might say ego-syntonic, one. Important sublimations were formed; libidinal strivings found acceptable forms of expression; lasting object relationships were established.

It is my feeling that, in general, we do not really or fully understand what makes such a successful character development under difficult circumstances possible. To my knowledge, there is not much in psychoanalytic literature that is concerned with special study of the prerequisites and conditions of favorable character development. To understand these conditions in a special situation may contribute toward a more general understanding of the problem.

Roger V. was in his forties, a successful psychologist in an academic position, happily married, and the father of three nice teen-age boys. He was a man of above-average endowment, keen intelligence, and a particularly astute faculty of psychological observation. He was well established in his field, although not as outstanding as he would have wished to be, loved by his family, well liked by his friends. His behavior was a tiny bit stiff, his way of talking a shade circumstantial. He was utterly reliable, a solid citizen, the "Rock of Gibraltar" in his group. He was a little overconscientious, too well-intentioned—maybe one could best describe it as too "virtuous." He came to analysis because he felt, with justification, that he was not living up to his potentialities, that he should have been more productive in his work.

In the analysis, the reasons for this insufficient productivity became clear. Roger lived too much in doing his "duty"; he was too much concerned with other people's welfare. He not only had to strive during his long working hours to be "helpful" to others (students, colleagues, etc.), but when he came home he had to devote himself completely to his family, had to have time for the special needs and wishes of each, listen to every worry and concern of his wife, supervise the boys' homework, try to "help" them to "cope with their problems." On top of all this, he had to spend an inordinate amount of time on household chores, walking the dog, doing small repairs, etc. In more ways than one, he was also strictly a "do-it-yourself" man, as will be shown later. It was important to be able to do everything by himself, without having to call in outside help. His behavior had accustomed his wife and children to rely on him and to be much more dependent on his manifold assistance than was good for them.

The most disconcerting of Roger's self-imposed duties, however, was to concern himself with his parents and to see or at least telephone them very frequently. He had to make constant and futile, but very burdensome, attempts to "straighten them out." His mother was a masochistically complaining, aggressive, demanding, depressed person, forever in strife with her husband, whom she accused of being inconsiderate and brutal. They were continually involved in bickering and scenes. The father was a masculine, active, but rather primitive, crude, and not very bright man. Lacking in understanding, he provoked the mother by inconsiderate behavior, in reaction to which she would masochistically egg him on to further attacks. The father was mostly interested in the financial success of his business, but was not unkind to Roger.

Since early years Roger had endeavored to "make his parents happy" by showing them how to be happy, how to live in a more reasonable way. Already as a young child, he was his parents' mainstay; he was treated as though he were the parent and they the children who were entitled to receive his constant support. Only in a financial way had the father, a successful engineer, been of help when Roger was younger. The mother, a little more sophisticated, was proud of her son and ambitious for him, but for her own purposes. Always dissatisfied with her lot, unhappy in her marriage, feeling damaged and deprived, she sought to use him as an antidote against her narcissistic injuries. At the same time, she wanted him to remain tied to her and was jealous of his accomplishments.

As mentioned before, Roger's complaints were justified. That his excessive "kindness" and concern for others took up too much of his time was obvious. But beyond this, something else interfered with the full concentration on his own work. There was a twofold motive for this inhibition. To work for himself appeared inordinately selfish. He had to shrink back from the success to which he aspired, and which would put him in the limelight. Such exhibition was intolerable to him because it implied standing out above others, a victory that would cruelly wound his rivals. Here the warded-off, competitive hostility clearly shone through his self-sacrificing kindness. The second reason was his feeling that real success and a full life in the world of his scientific interests would destroy the bond between him and his parents, not only by reducing the time he devoted to them, but by bringing into focus the disparity between his life and theirs, between his accomplishments and their crude primitivity. Thus he would lose these most important objects of his childhood, a prospect that filled him with "deep sadness." He preferred to maintain his compulsive "goodness."

His position as friend and helper of the parents was

the pattern after which virtually all his other relationships were modeled. He tried to help everybody to behave reasonably, thereby giving "nourishment" and "strength" to others. The deeper meaning of this wish and of the compulsion to imbue mankind with reason will be discussed later. The same pattern was evident in his sexual behavior to his wife. There was no conspicuous disturbance of functioning, but a complete focus on gratifying his partner, entirely subordinating his needs to her wishes, which interfered with his full pleasure and abandonment.

Freud said that a person's sexual life serves as a pattern for his life in general. In the course of Roger's analysis it emerged that his muting of sexual pleasure, as a consequence of reactive overconcern for the partner, was in fact paralleled by interferences of similar kind casting a certain pall on his interests, his object relations, indeed on all contacts with reality. He recognized that he was always in a state of watchfulness with regard to himself. He could not just let himself go when talking, lest some "nonsense" might emerge. Nothing could be done with full spontaneity because he constantly had to "control" himself lest some unacceptable, selfish, aggressive, infantile sexual strivings might break through.

Besides this reactive behavior, there was a difficulty of a different kind. Bent though he was on being helpful to people, he always felt some abstractedness while with them; he was never quite present. During his analysis, he learned to understand that what distracted him in such situations was a continual preoccupation with fantasies which absorbed a large part of his libidinal interest.

Thus there were, one might say, two sides to the coin: a stream of "subterranean" fantasies, so to speak —not completely repressed, but kept in a state of isolation—and the more conscious efforts to keep the danger in check. This can be described as typical obsessional behavior pattern. As a result, Roger lived in a lasting state of inner loneliness and isolation, which represented the antithesis to the deepest aims of his fantasies.

On the surface, the content of this fantasy world was "pure" and "innocent" enough. It was precisely a yearning to escape from such isolation. He longed for closeness with his love objects, for a closeness that would reach the utmost degree. He dreamed of some kind of fusion with another being, some kind of mystic communion. This almost religious daydream proved to be multi-layered. It contained elements from all instinctual levels, and in all of them danger was inherent that had to be warded off. The final form in which it appeared, of a melting together with the beloved object, related to earliest oral aims which had been regressively revived; hence it was closest to Roger's conscious awareness. The oral fantasies served to ward off later and even less acceptable desires. He would stress that he had to think of the "communion with his beloved ones" in terms of "taking in," "feeding," "melting," because anything else was more objectionable.

These "melting-together" fantasies were based on pleasant memories about his relationship with his mother, on sensations of being taken care of when sick, of being bathed in warm water by her until a relatively advanced age. Impressions of heat and cold were highly sexualized and experienced as a completely pleasurable, passive dissolving with or within the mother. But even this passive, nondestructive relationship with the mother could not be enjoyed for a greater length of time. She had been an anxious person, inclined to be overconcerned about any illness of the boy, and her anxiety about her own intactness had thus been transmitted to him. He felt that she liked to keep him a baby and, by infantilizing him, interfered with his growing up. She insisted that he could not do anything on his own, get dressed, tie his shoe laces, go anywhere, etc. She wanted to make him helpless and keep him close, like a part of her body. But he could not trust his mother; there was a feeling that in this helpless state she would hurt him. She was wont to ridicule him for being sick so much, which was felt by her as an injury and a special burden to herself. A particular memory stood out of being hungry after play, when he was very little, and wanting something to eat; his mother kept him waiting for his meal, and he fainted. Somehow the sensation of blacking out reflected the negative, highly unpleasant form of giving up his identity, of dissolving into the mother due to being starved by her. The mother thus was experienced as cruel and murderous. It became obvious that, on the deepest level, his fantasy of fusion with the mother meant mutual devouring—to be eaten up by the mother.

The reaction against this unacceptible passive surrender was strengthened by the fact that the oral wishes overlaid later, even more unacceptable, anal and phallic ones. The anxieties appropriate to these levels were fused with the oral dangers. Hence the oral escape proved of no avail.

His regressive trend into orality was rooted in count-
less traumatic experiences of witnessing the continual
sadomasochistic play between the parents. Various
primal-scene observations were interpreted by the boy
as rape and violence. Believing his father's sexual approaches to be responsible for his mother's constant
complaints about her suffering and for her accusations
that "pieces" were being brutally "torn out" of her, he
thought that she was left bleeding, injured, and defective forever. The observations stirred up intense excitement and the wish to participate in the savage sexual
experience alternately as the active and the passive
partner; yet the child would shrink back in horror
from playing the role of the cruel castrator. He was
aware, furthermore, that the parental love play had
something to do with the production of babies, which
likewise meant cruel injury to the mother. In her vehement complaints, she would accuse both father *and* son
for having done this terrible thing to her, so that by
Roger's birth she was damaged forever.

Moreover, the primal-scene experiences probably
occurred at a very early age when the pregenital
phases, still far from being outgrown, were easily subject to regressive revival. In these very regressed fantasies about the parental sexual activities, everything was
confused. Male and female role could no longer be distinguished. Either partner could act as aggressor or victim. In violent, tumultuous fights, either partner would
tear the other to pieces and incorporate him in any
one of various ways—via the genital, anus or mouth,
via hands, or legs, or skin. As the result of this gruesome conjugation, after having gone through some
kind of digestive union, the baby would emerge via

any of the body openings. Phallus, feces, and baby were confused in these fantasies. Mouth, anus, genitals merged into one cloaca. Anal, oral, and genital sadistic concepts flowed together. The whole body, the penis, the scybalum, were being digested, to be ejected again anally or orally.

The "union" with his beloved—which in beautiful and pure, near-religious disguise remained the center of his fantasy life—thus represented a terrible, complete annihilation of the love object. I shall discuss later in what form the longing for this experience could be preserved and made innocuous.

The fantasy of mutual devouring was so horrifying that it had to vanish from the boy's conscious thought. Its slightly less regressed derivatives, however, remained conscious and filled him with anxiety. He had a fantasy, for instance, in which sexual union with the mother took the form of falling into her vagina as into a bottomless cavern; here his concern about the mother's lack of penis was obviously merged with his fear of being devoured. Because of the deep confusion about phallic and anal wishes, he had the feeling that his mother treated his penis as she treated his anal productions, as something objectionable and disgusting. The final outcome of his by now phallic-oedipal wishes consisted in fantasies of uniting with the mother in a violent love play, of "tearing pieces" out of her with his phallus, which represented an aggressive tool for the purpose of producing babies. Forced to withdraw from the active-sadistic role, in which like the father he was the cruel castrator, he visualized himself as being *invaded* or *penetrated* by the mother, a fantasy that was also related to frequent enemas administered by her.

It is likely, although this was not fully clarified by the analysis, that the fantasy about passive penetration by the mother covered an even more terrifying one with regard to the father. In any event, the danger of passivity left important traces in his character structure, which will be discussed later.

The passive fantasy was extremely frightening, since it left him in the position of the castrated mother. To avoid this terrible danger, he resorted regressively to another, again active, form of anality which was to prove greatly significant. The phallic-sadistic elements of the fantasy were given up, and a shift of libidinal interest occurred from the dangerous love object to the self. The child fantasied that he was giving birth anally to many babies by cutting or tearing a long column of feces into many small pieces with his anus, at will. The anus had become a female organ: a big, black hole—a cloaca—like the cavern into which he had feared to fall. In addition, it also represented a mouth equipped with sharp teeth. In this fantasy, however, he was strong, active, *creative*, and quite on his own, completely independent of the dangerous love object. Thus, a new feature emerged here which was to become very important in his later makeup: for the first time, he was a "do-it-yourself" person.

Furthermore, this represented a partial narcissistic withdrawal. He could love and fertilize himself in manifold, not only anal, ways. Thus he could establish a "union with himself," avoiding danger and annihilation. This narcissistic withdrawal, however, was not the only method by which Roger tried to cope with the phallic-sadistic strivings which, in their active as well as their passive variety, were completely unacceptable.

It seems that a toning down from sadistic to exhibitionistic wishes took place, which made it possible to preserve the phallic drives in a predominantly exhibitionistic form: exhibition as wooing of the mother and competition with the father. But this, too, was felt to be extremely destructive and had to be modified.

Soon the child's exhibitionistic wishes became divested of their directly phallic quality. Phallic activity appeared only in an already regressed, passive form. There were early games with the mother, in which she would fondle his naked body while he lay on a pillow, waiting to be dressed. He remembered her caressing hands, and how he would stretch his whole body with pleasure. In this memory and in the resulting fantasies, the erect phallus was replaced by the whole, stretched-out body being passively caressed; violence, penetration, invasion, tearing, etc., were carefully excluded.

As I just mentioned, exhibitionistic fantasies were apparently the most acceptable ones at the height of infantile sexuality. The thorough inhibition of aggressive-phallic urges, combined with the need for compensatory undoing of castration anxiety, restricted the boy to what might be called a "phallic passivity." To be looked at and admired, without actively doing anything, were the most permissible aims at this time. They were to remain important throughout life, and we shall come back to the imprint thus left on his character structure.

The most significant immediate consequence of this phallic passivity was the absence of any open genital masturbatory activity in childhood; masturbation equivalents in the form of tongue-sucking and hair-twiddling took its place. But more striking—to anticipate the later history—is the fact that there was no open masturbation in puberty; he merely would indulge in prolonged fantasies, without any manual manipulation. (Masturbation started only after the age of nineteen, when adult sexual experiences with girls had already taken place.) An important incident contributed to this pattern. When he was fourteen, at the height of pubertal development, his mother had to undergo an operation. It stirred up all the old memories about her being injured and castrated, which strengthened the defensive forces so that the step into masturbatory activity was made impossible. Indeed, the repression of active sexual drives was so thorough as to forestall any intense struggle against the temptation to masturbate. After that time, he detached himself from his family to some degree, becoming interested in school and intellectual achievements. The addiction to fantasies took the place of masturbation.

But let us return to Roger's childhood. Attempts to break through his passivity seemed to have received a decisive blow by an event, at the age of six, which seriously impeded the budding tendency toward identification with the active-aggressive father and hence the development in the direction of an active masculine sexuality and character structure. At that time, the mother threatened to leave her husband and to take Roger with her, a threat to which the boy reacted with profound fright. Fully aware by then of his mother's helpless and neurotic behavior, he saw his father as a brutal, but strong person without whom they would both be lost. His mother was offering him the chance, so to speak, to step into the father's shoes. Yet he felt so frightened, weak, and in danger of starving, that he had to forego his wish to play an active role with her, but had to cling to the father who alone could sustain them both. His castration anxiety thus was clad in oral terms: both he and the mother were weak and "defective," needing "strength and nourishment" from the father.

The impact of this traumatic episode effected a final turning away from the original instinctual aims; and a rigid superego was established whose most preeminent demand was *not* to be like the aggressive, sexual parents. Important defenses were mobilized, among which powerful reaction formations stood out.

When Roger later learned from other boys about sexual intercourse, he found it revolting. It meant "invading other people's privacy," "violating their dignity." From then on, he had to control himself in order to make sure that he would not indulge in any "savage, infantile, sexual orgies." What had to be warded off most severely were the active-aggressive, phallic urges. He escaped from them into the already well-prepatterned, passive position, which, however, was equally unbearable.

But this was not all. At that period, he started his attempts to re-educate his parents, to reconcile them and induce them to live without violence and strife. Obviously he tried to extend his own reaction formations to them, to wean them away from sexuality too. He became moralistic, and at the same time mature beyond his age. Looking back on himself later, he was to remark: "I was already an old man as a child." He become his parents' support: he gave them "strength and nourishment." A reversal thus had set in. What he originally had needed to receive from the parents, he now gave to them. Whereas they had incessantly stirred up his unruly desires, he helped them to control themselves. He bestowed oral gratification upon them, in a symbolic way, to undo starvation and castration.

By this behavior he likewise undid the dangers of passivity. Henceforth compelled to ward off any passive longing, he could not accept help from anyone, ask for anything, etc. Instead, he adopted the strictly "do-it-yourself" attitude traceable to early fantasies about anal-parthenogenetic procreation. Removing himself to a large degree from objects, he now took pride in fulfilling his own and other people's needs by himself alone. The gratification afforded by this pattern was a narcissistic one. In his masturbation fantasy about "union with himself" the deepest core of the pattern was demonstrated most clearly. Its bearing on the problem of "creativity," which drove him into analysis, will be discussed later.

We see that Roger succeeded in *becoming active again,* but in a nonsexual, nonaggressive way. He now enjoyed building, improving, rescuing others, being rational and constructive. Here he was identified with the feeding mother, the strong and protective father. He had cleansed the parental figures of their unacceptable, sexual traits, and reconstructed them within himself in an idealized form. This idealized and internalized image of the united parents, with whom he thus identified, represented an aspect of his superego that could, in contrast to the negative one I described before, be called an ego ideal. An intense form of gratification resulted from living up to this ideal to a large degree. He could vest himself in this way with a good deal of the libidinal cathexis originally directed toward the parents, which yielded a considerable feeling of narcissistic pride.

By being the savior and helper, he succeeded in winning praise and admiration from his objects, so that a nonsexual behavior could replace and gratify the repressed wish to win the mother via phallic exhibition. Thus by being "constructive" he achieved a new form of "union"—again, highly gratifying with a narcissistic undertone. And indeed, by being admirable and outstanding, he fulfilled his mother's deep, narcissistic need: he was magnificent, perfect. She gloated in the glory of her son. His greatness was the only means by which her defects, her castration, could be cured. He was part of her, her penis. Thus, through his success, the longing for mystic union was fulfilled.

I mentioned at the outset that Roger was highly accomplished in his work and generally successful in the role of confidant and altruistic friend. Obviously this success was not based upon his own emotional needs alone, but equally on his ability to understand other people's problems: on his astute, intuitive psychological insight. The coincidence of these two factors raised his behavior from the level of a purely neurotic activity to that of true sublimation.

The genesis of his psychological propensity was significant. It represented yet another method of substitution for the unattainable sexual union with the infantile love objects. That from his wishes for direct participation in the sadomasochistic love play he withdrew into seeing, understanding, thinking, was as decisive as the retreat into exhibitionism. This shift from action to thinking is generally of moment for the development of obsessional characters and, when successful, constitutes an avenue toward important sublimations. In Roger's case its aggressive-libidinal origin could be clearly discerned. Giving up his dangerous objects, he had turned his interest upon himself. Here, too, he "did it himself" and established "the union" with himself.

What this really meant was strikingly demonstrated by his behavior in the analysis. To avoid being analyzed by me, which for him implied all the dangers pointed out before, Roger analyzed himself. This self-analytical action, which he could perform amazingly well, was based upon a very special capacity for self-observation and introspection that had existed long before his contact with analysis. His "communion with himself" had taken the form of constant self-observation and rumination about himself. By introspection he "penetrated" himself, "invaded" his own "privacy." This self-centered and very acute psychological interest thus had the character of a substitute activity replacing the masturbation from which he so conspicuously refrained. During his adolescent years, it was pursued while sitting on the toilet, where to his mother's annoyance he would stay for a very long time.

Thinking about himself represented the desexualized version of exhibiting and at the same time looking at himself. It was thus a derivative of the forbidden phallic wish to show his erection to the mother and to be looked at and caressed by her. He was simultaneously playing both roles here. Furthermore, the act of looking at himself with "sharp eyes" and with "penetrating understanding" corresponded to an aggressive, phallic attack against himself (the sharp eye representing a penis substitute). Thus, in a symbolic form, he was simultaneously active and passive, sadistic and masochistic. This again made him independent of the object, yielded narcissistic gratification, and removed him from infantile dangers.

This transmutation was particularly successful due to the sublimated character of the thinking and observing process. Roger's capability to make correct observations had developed at an early age when his mother, extending her anxieties about herself to the child, would anxiously observe him with regard to health and intactness. In identification with his mother, he observed and admired himself, thereby undoing her feeling of castration and his own. Quite early, his faculty for observation and understanding had become a very keen one, of which he could be proud, as the mother was proud of him. Later on, it came to be extended from himself to other persons; from being able to become aware of his own feeling, he developed an ability to sense what was going on in others.

The libidinal undercurrents of Roger's interest in observing and understanding never interfered with the quality of his performance. He succeeded in developing reality-syntonic capacities for thinking in general and for specifically psychological comprehension. Notwithstanding their closeness to the instinctual sources, there was never an intrusion of one sphere into the other, never a lowering of the standard of his reality testing.

Reality testing is a function of the ego. Yet it seems to me that in this particular situation the superego was involved. Roger, in spite of his rigid defenses, had easy access to his fantasy life; but it was of paramount importance for him to be able to keep reality apart from fantasy. His constant stress upon the "rational" revealed him as being on guard against an intrusion of fantasies. Thus, "rational thinking" and "objective observation" had the character of a superego demand.

This intellectual ability, which played an important role in Roger's professional work, demonstrates nicely how a sublimation is composed of two factors, one of them being a securely desexualized ego component, while the other stems from and merges with the world of instincts. According to Hartmann (1955), irreversibility may be considered the most important characteristic of true sublimation. Roger's psychological propensities were never in danger of reverting to infantile fantasies. Yet, as I described in the beginning, he could not always make as full use of them as should have been possible.

In the course of his analysis, it became clear that, at the deepest level, real and unencumbered intellectual productivity represented the gratification of fundamental infantile fantasies for Roger: it meant creating babies with the mother, fulfilling the longing for fusion with her. But in these fantasies he had taken over the maternal role as well; he now was the object, producing children with himself. Creativity thus represented complete narcissistic fulfillment. It was here that the inhibition took place.

Nevertheless, in view of his history, it seems quite striking that Roger was not sicker. We frequently encounter patients suffering from far more severe pathology, whose childhood histories appear much less traumatic. Likewise remarkable is the absence of childhood objects with whom he could identify directly for the purpose of superego formation, without resorting to idealization or having to take exclusively the converse of the parental figures as his model. Yet he succeeded singularly well in developing defenses the results of which could be used in such constructive form for ego purposes and could be integrated as character traits into the structure of the ego.

A number of factors may have contributed to this success.

1. As has been variously indicated, in spite of all conflicts and anxieties, there was a basic identification with the active, masculine father figure. After puberty, this became positively influenced and strengthened by the example of a young cousin and some masculine, active friends.

2. Roger's ability to melt together defensive patterns with slightly modified instinctual gratification was an unusual one. We have seen that in his case the psychological interest as well as the altruistic behavior pattern was by no means founded exclusively upon reaction formation, but contained a considerable amount of transformed libidinal drive. It may be due to this factor that he remained free of more disturbing pathological symptoms. His ability to fit his adult sexual life into the frame of the curing-healing-giving compulsion may have preserved him from more serious potency disturbances and allowed him to achieve a substantial degree of sexual gratification despite the heavy burden of his early experiences.

3. The considerable ego strength here displayed, particularly the success of the synthetic function in integrating the wealth of pregenital fantasies into the realm of the ego, might be explainable by the assumption that the ego could continually draw energy from

the id, neutralizing it and using it for its own aims. One might say that the ego possessed a particular capacity for sublimation, based on the one hand upon the solid structure of his defenses, and on the other hand upon this free line of access to the id.

4. Furthermore, his ability to solve his problems in a "constructive" way seems to have been rooted in some element of magic thinking, of preserved omnipotence. It was as though these regressively revived features of a primitive ego could be mobilized *at will* for purposes of reconstruction.

13

Further Remarks on Countertransference

(1960)

WITHIN THE last few years, a large number of papers on countertransference have been published, coming from many different parts of the world. It has been claimed that just as transference was at first thought to be merely a disturbing factor, yet was recognized later on as the pivotal therapeutic factor in psychoanalysis, so now countertransference is found to represent not only an interfering agent, but an essential catalytic one needed to achieve the therapeutic goals of psychoanalysis. The purpose of my paper is to discuss this idea and to refute it.

I believe that the increasing concentration on the phenomenon of countertransference can be traced to a number of causes. Modifications of the analyst's technique and behavior are sometimes necessitated by the "widening scope" of psychoanalysis, since we no longer deal only with neuroses, but also with various other forms of pathology. The rising importance of psychoanalysis in psychiatry as a whole, in social work,

Published originally in *The International Journal of Psycho-Analysis*, 41:389–395, 1960.

education, etc., the expansion of "psychoanalytically oriented" psychotherapy, and the ensuing emphasis on "interpersonal relations," all have brought in their wake the danger of a dilution of psychoanalysis, of a confusion between psychoanalysis proper and psychotherapy, and therefore of confusion about the role of the therapist. Besides, it should not be overlooked that our growing experience in the training of student analysts confronts us more and more with emotional interferences in the students, reminding us again of similar difficulties in ourselves.

I believe that the complexity of these problems, with all their implications for analytic theory and technique, justifies me in presenting a critical evaluation of the current ideas on countertransference without attempting to offer any basic new theory about it.

The diversity of motivations for the interest in countertransference manifests itself in a lack of clarity regarding the definition of countertransference. Before going into this, I would like to repeat briefly what I said in a previous paper on the subject (1951, this volume). Countertransference comprises the effects of the analyst's own unconscious needs and conflicts upon his understanding or technique. In such cases the patient becomes an object in relation to whom the analyst experiences past feelings and wishes. The provoking factor may be something in the patient's personality, a particular transference pattern, or a specific analytic situation and material.

These countertransference responses consist in libidinal and/or aggressive strivings, in defenses against such strivings, or in identifications and ego attitudes connected with a specific past conflict of the analyst.

As an intermediate step, unresolved problems of his own analysis and his own transference conflicts may emerge. It is of significance that frequently the analyst is not conscious of the response as such, but becomes aware only of certain consequences, such as anxiousness, inappropriate and often overstrong emotion, inability to understand the patient, boredom, etc.

One of the prevailing misconceptions is the equation of countertransference with the analyst's total response to the patient, using the term to include all conscious reactions, responses, and ways of behavior. This is as incorrect as to call transference everything that emerges in the patient in relation to the analyst during analysis, and not to distinguish between the manifestations of unconscious strivings and reality-adapted, conscious behavior or observations. The analyst is for the patient, and the patient for the analyst, also a reality object and not only a transference or countertransference object. There has to be in the analyst some (aim-inhibited) object-libidinal interest in the patient, which is a prerequisite for empathy. Conscious responses should be regarded as countertransference only if they reach an inordinate intensity or are strongly tainted by inappropriate sexual or aggressive feelings, thus revealing themselves to be determined by unconscious infantile strivings.

The significance of the fact that the analyst is equally a reality object for the patient was correctly stressed by Ferenczi (1919) and various later authors (Balint and Balint, 1939; Benedek, 1953; etc.) Each of us has some particular qualities and an individual style of analyzing; none is completely "neutral." It is important that the patient be enabled to talk freely about any actual observations he may have made or information he may have received with regard to his analyst. If such reality factors can be brought into the analysis, they will become irrelevant for it in the long run. But to prevent all this from being mentioned, or to treat it exclusively as the patient's transference, means to deny the reality of his observations or information about the analyst. Such denial can be considered an expression of a specific countertransference, since the analyst then really behaves like a parent forbidding the child to know anything about his "secret" private life, an attitude which obviously reinforces the patient's defenses.

This failure to differentiate between countertransference and total response, combined with the erroneous assumption that the analysand "is not supposed to be" a reality object for the analyst, leads to the idea that "analytic neutrality" is an impossible and unrealizable task because it can be kept up only through a most unnatural restraint. Hence the whole concept of "analytic neutrality" is thought to be based on a "dishonest" presumption, on the "myth of the analyst's *perfection.*" From these notions, some authors have drawn very far-reaching conclusions. Since perfection in the form of complete neutrality does not exist, they claim, *neutrality should be dispensed with entirely;* the analyst should respond to the patient in whatever way he feels. In fact, there is a frequent misconception that "analytic neutrality" means to behave like a superior being who looks down upon the patient. Thus we are told that solution of transference and termination of analysis have to be brought about by giving up this godlike role and behaving freely and humanly (Weigert, 1952). I believe it is obvious that to renounce the principle of the analyst's neutrality implies a basic lack of understanding about the nature and importance of transference, and therefore about the essence of psychoanalytic therapy.

But even where such grave misunderstanding is avoided, the overemphasis on countertransference entails practical consequences. Besides the demand for greater "honesty" about countertransference, we often hear that its admission to the patient is necessary in the interest of the latter. To be sure, at times it may be unavoidable to admit certain countertransference manifestations to a patient; e.g., that the analyst forgot something or made a slip, etc. Such an admission may be required in order to permit the patient's free verbalization with regard to the analyst. But it is clearly quite a different matter to burden him with the analyst's own affairs and to interfere with the sequence of the analysis by introducing extraneous material that is irrelevant for the patient himself.

Another rampant misconception about countertransference should be noted because it has an undesirable effect upon methods of teaching psychoanalysis. I mean the view which regards *any* wrong interpretation and *any mistake* in handling the analytic situation as an expression of countertransference. This has led to the erroneous idea that the supervisor's main task is to point out the countertransference of the student, or to concentrate on any complications of the relationship between student and instructor, rather than to teach his supervisee how to apply the principles of psychoanalysis to the intricate patterns of clinical material. It is as though there were a tacit assumption that the young analyst was born with an *inherent knowledge* of psychopathology and "correct interpretation," and that mistakes are regularly based on countertransference but have nothing to do with lack of knowledge and experience.

The truth, of course, is that our analytic understanding, which directs our management of an analysis, has its roots in theoretical and clinical knowledge, as well as in intuitive processes. While analyzing, we constantly oscillate between these two methods of gaining insight. In one moment, we integrate our observations into the body of our analytic knowledge; in the next, we listen with free-floating attention (Fenichel, 1938a). We listen with our unconscious or, as Reik (1948) said, with "the third ear." The ability to draw upon the wealth of both these realms is a prerequisite for the good analyst. Therefore we are legitimately concerned about the psychological obstacles that interfere with the intuitive process, as each of us may fall victim to them time and again.

The psychology of analytic empathy has long been a topic of great interest. Insight into the hazards of this process helps us to understand the dynamics of certain countertransference phenomena. On the other hand, just what we know about intuitive understanding tends to lead to further confusion about countertransference.

Intuitive understanding of what goes on in another person is based upon trial identification, a term aptly coined by Fliess (1942) in his excellent paper on "The Metapsychology of the Analyst." Based upon his findings as well as those of Deutsch (1926) and Reik (1937), who preceded Fliess in this psychological investigation, one can say that analytic understanding—

particularly of transference manifestations—comes about as follows. (1) The analyst becomes the object of the patient's libidinal and/or aggressive strivings (or of the defense against them). (2) In a special, transient way, the analyst identifies with the patient and in this way participates in the patient's feelings. (3) He can then recognize these feelings and the underlying instinctual strivings as belonging to the patient, i.e., he again becomes detached from him. Thus, the analyst acquires knowledge about the nature of the patient through an awareness of something that went on in his own self.

Deutsch (1926) points out that the process of empathy is even more complicated. She shows that direct responses (of love or hate) to the patient's instinctual strivings cause the analyst to identify also with the original infantile object of these drives. Through this identification, which Deutsch calls a complementary one, the analyst gains knowledge about the patient's objects by feeling what goes on in himself. This particular aspect of empathic identification is important here, since it plays a major role in the ideas of the British school of psychoanalysis about the interplay between analyst and patient during the analytic process, and about the role of countertransference.

The capacity for empathy is, of course, based upon the fact that in the unconscious we are all endowed with the same strivings: but I must emphasize that what may be a homoeopathic dose for one may be strongly cathected for the other. *In the case of the analyst, the process of identification and externalization is cathected with minimal amounts of energy and must have been preceded by a far-reaching process of neutralization.* He has to forgo any immediate gratification and content himself with the sublimated gratification derived from his ability to understand and to function correctly in an ego-syntonic way.

Furthermore, in trial identification, primitive ego mechanisms of introjection and projection are regressively revived, at will and only temporarily, for the purposes of the ego. A neutralized cathexis of the patient is never relinquished. Thus, the analyst never loses sight of the patient as a separate being and at no time feels his own identity changed. This enables him to remain uninvolved. But this delicate process of trial identification is fraught with many hazards, and its failure manifests itself as countertransference. For instance:

1. The analyst may react to the impact of his patient's instinctual strivings with a direct response. He may return love with love, hate with hate, failing to identify and to detach himself again. Such direct responses, especially when they assume great intensity, represent the commonest and simplest form of countertransference. They arise from the analyst's infantile motivations.

2. The other very frequent form of complication, which stems likewise from the analyst's infantile conflicts, was pointed out first by Deutsch (1926). As she puts it, he may get stuck in some of these trial identifications because they please him too much: he becomes unwilling and unable to relinquish them. Thus, instead of merely going through a transient identification for purposes of understanding, the analyst remains identified with the patient (or the latter's object). He behaves or feels like the patient, which will render him blind to the patient's defenses.

Of course, the manifestations of countertransference here enumerated do not cover the whole range of its possible forms, but only those which are the direct outgrowth of the process of empathy. I discussed this aspect so extensively because certain ideas about the positive value of countertransference can be correlated to the psychology of analytic intuition.

The first of these ideas was originated by Heimann (1950) and taken over by other authors. What she proposed, but without formulating it in this way, was to use the analyst's emotional responses, his countertransference manifestations, as a substitute for empathy. She described how a patient, soon after starting his analysis, suddenly decided to marry a "defective" object, to which the analyst reacted with an emotional response of worry and anxiety. Aware of this response and trying to analyze it in herself, Heimann recognized her patient's decision as a transference acting out based on sadistically tinged fantasies about the analyst, who was seen as a defective object.

Let me try to reconstruct here what had been going on in the analyst. Something interfered with the process of immediate, intuitive understanding. The analyst reacted to the patient's striving with an emotional response of her own. She did not just "know" that the patient was involved in an acting out of his transference, since she failed to identify with him and to detach herself again from such trial identification. For this process she substituted a *retranslation* of her own feelings into those of the patient. We might say that she used a secondary, a roundabout and incomplete way of understanding because the direct path was blocked. This particular detour may be very frequent and sometimes usable. Nevertheless, it is not desirable, for the analyst's own strong involvement always contains the danger of obscuring his objective grasp, particularly of the transference situation, by introducing something that is not inherent in the patient but only in the analyst's own psychology.

The honesty with which Heimann and a number of others have treated this topic contributes very greatly to its clarification. In this respect, I also want particularly to mention Gitelson's (1952) paper. Most pertinent, indeed, is the practical conclusion drawn by many of these authors: that we should be alert to our own feelings, stop to investigate them, and analyze what is going on. For the analyst's awareness of his undue emotional response warns him of an obstacle that interferes with his competent functioning and ought to be removed. *The countertransference as such is not helpful, but the readiness to acknowledge its existence and the ability to overcome it is.*

Sharply at variance with this point of view are a number of other authors, who do not regard the analyst's strong emotional responses merely as a sometimes unavoidable detour to understanding. They claim that *the nature of the countertransference manifestations corresponds to the nature of the impulses and defenses which prevail in the patient at the same time, so that insight into the countertransference opens a direct pathway into the patient's unconscious* (Heimann, 1950). This concept, I believe, results from confusing the special, transient form of identification followed by redetachment, as it occurs in empathy, with identification and projection in their most direct form.

Some analysts of the British school, because of the

emphasis they place on pregenital aggressive conflicts and on the mechanisms of introjection and projection, tend to see the analytic process completely from this angle. According to them, the analytic process consists in a mutual identification and projections between analyst and patient (or part of their respective personalities). To take over the analyst's healthy personality through identification thus is thought to form an important part of the cure, a point to which I shall come back later. Furthermore, using Deutsch's idea, it is reasoned that the analyst has become identical with the patient's infantile objects via "complementary identification" and that analysis of any countertransference reaction therefore reveals the infantile history. Thus, if the analyst feels anger toward the patient, this indicates that the infantile object was angry with the patient. The analysis of the countertransference thus brings to light the development of the transference. Since it is assumed that the analyst's emotional experiences and his responses to the patient are identical with the original models, such interplay of transference and countertransference *replaces recall* of the past or even its reconstruction. To recover the memory of specific events connected with actual objects is not considered important.

The equation of the subtle process of trial identification with such mutual identification neglects an essential fact. Empathic identification, as I mentioned before, is marked by minimal and neutralized cathexis, whereas the countertransference here is evidently charged with intense emotional force. Little (1957), for example, speaks of feeling "real hate of a patient for weeks on end" or being "suddenly flooded with rage," or the great danger of the analyst's "phobic or paranoic" attitudes toward his own unconscious.

Indeed, we are faced here with a striking contradiction. Such a strong emotional cathexis can only stem from the analyst's own unconscious conflicts; thus, it must represent an intrusion of these conflicts into what Little (1951) calls the process of the mutual reflecting each other in the mirror of the other's unconscious. This factor of falsification via the analyst's particular conflicts is disregarded by those who advocate "free countertransference," just as they disregard the specific events of the patient's past. Their concept seems to presuppose a typical content of countertransference. According to Racker (1953, 1957), countertransference is dominated by the law of talion which follows simple rules and allows retranslation of complicated, subtle psychological experiences, as though we were dealing with arithmetic problems that permit only one correct answer.

I would like to mention at this point that ideas about a typical content of countertransference can be found quite frequently in today's literature. Some authors, e.g., Winnicott (1949) and Glover (1955), seem to regard countertransference as consisting predominantly of hate and aggression. Most definite in his statements is Racker (1952, 1953), who claims that for a male analyst any male patient represents the father and any female patient the mother, and that the analytic situation *eo ipso* represents an oedipal one. Spitz (1956) also generalizes too much in assuming that the *typical* countertransference is based on the child's "diatrophic" attitude (meaning the child's behavior when he wants to feed and take care of other children or dolls, in identification with the nursing mother). All such notions about a typical content of countertransference represent schematizations and a narrowing down of the beautiful variety of psychic functioning.

To come back to the review of current theories, thus far, I have described those which consider the analysis of countertransference a valuable method of gaining insight into what goes on in the patient. However, a variety of other important functions is ascribed to countertransference as well.

Some authors advocate the free expression of countertransference feelings, including negative ones, as a method designed to promote identification by the patient with the healthier personality of the analyst. For instance, Little (1957) deems it necessary for very disturbed patients to experience the analyst as a loving, hating, feeling person and to introject him, so that they themselves may become capable of feeling. Identification with the analyst is also viewed by numerous authors as one of the main vehicles of therapy for patients with less serious disturbances. That such identifications frequently do occur in analysis cannot be questioned, but they represent material which should be analyzed, as they often prove to be transference repetitions of infantile identifications. It is not the aim of analysis to transform these temporary identifications into permanent structures. This holds true also for superego identifications. At some time or other in the course of analysis, the analyst becomes a superego figure and the patient tries to identify with him. A regression to a certain phase in superego development has taken place, which makes analysis of the superego possible. Such identifications come about spontaneously in the analytic situation. They need not be promoted by any "acting out" on the part of the analyst, which can result—in the most favorable case—in some educational impact upon the patient, but not in his being analyzed. The therapist's assumption of such an educational role may be of importance, though, for borderline cases or psychotics who were never able to form a stable identification. I shall come back to this point shortly.

Various authors regard countertransference in the form of intense involvement as a requisite to reach difficult patients. Little (1951), who is a most important representative of this group, proposes that where the transference fails, countertransference has to do all the work. For this purpose the analyst must allow the ideas and gratifications derived from his work to regress to an extraordinary degree. She indicates that when interpretation is of no avail, the direct impact of the analyst's emotional response breaks through the walls of resistance. Ineffectiveness of interpretations is similarly alleged by other authors. But these statements must be taken with a grain of salt, as they fail to specify what interpretations are being given and under what conditions. The handling of interpretations is evidently a complicated matter dependent on correct understanding, timing, wording, etc.

In my opinion, when an analyst suggests that a cure can be brought about only through his *acting out* his own emotional experience, he is using what Freud (1915) would call *Suppenlogik und Knödelargumente* ("the logic of soup with dumplings for arguments") in a reversed way (p. 167). The implication is roughly this: *Words are not enough; real—i.e., transference—*

gratifications have to be given to the patient; healing is accomplished by love.

For certain patients the relationship with the therapist indeed represents the first consistent viable relationship, just as identification with him may be the first stable identification. In this instance, any therapeutic improvement may well be due to the nurturing of this relationship; namely, to a loving care given by the therapist and his attempt to substitute for something that never existed in the patient's life. But such therapeutic endeavors are not psychoanalysis, even though they may be based on the fundamental insights of analytic psychology.

Moreover, emotional responses of the analyst are advocated not only for dealing with such deep-seated disturbances of object relations, but with severe neuroses in general. Tower (1956), who goes farthest in this direction, favors the development of a countertransference *neurosis* as a catalyst in the therapeutic process. In an impressive clinical example, she describes how a male patient suffering from the effects of repressed sadism responded to the analyst's acting out of a masochistic submission in diluted form. This resulted in such a deep emotional rapport between analyst and patient that the latter dared, for the first time in his life, to break through his rigid defenses. It so happened in this case that the countertransference neurosis was complementary to the patient's neurosis, a coincidence which is certainly rare. Besides, as Spitz (1956) pointed out in a critical review of Tower's paper, the result of such mutual acting out will be short-lived and unreliable. In this context, he made a penetrating remark: "the rule of abstinence operates for himself [the analyst] as much as it does for the patient" (p. 261).

This emotional interplay represents an ideal instance of what Alexander (1956) has termed the "corrective emotional experience." Alexander counsels the analyst to behave in a way converse to the original parental behavior—either through deliberate role playing or involuntarily, as in Tower's case—and to "manipulate" the transference in this sense. He argues that the *experience* of the "changed interpersonal climate" makes a continuation of the original response to parental behavior pointless, so that the neurosis can be relinquished. Neurosis he understands as a result of the child's faulty adaptation to the original "difficult" family situation, a concept which obviously represents a simplification. It seems to give credit only to the external childhood reality, but to omit the most commonly unrealizable libidinal and aggressive infantile strivings and the ensuing inner conflicts.

In the case of this as well as other divergent schools of psychoanalysis, oversimplification and the omission of essential parts of psychoanalytic theory cause an exaggerated therapeutic value to be placed on the analyst's overactive involvement and the patient's "corrective emotional experience."

At the risk of generalizing unduly, I would venture the opinion that this emphasis on the effect of countertransference and on the analyst's "deep emotional impact," rather than on interpretation, represents a return to the concept of the therapeutic effect of abreaction in the sense in which it was understood by Ferenczi, who apparently had a special capacity for achieving it in his patients by virtue of his particular emotional response.

This powerful, emotionally stirring experience, which is believed to reach the patient's depth and to be promoted by the analyst's emotional participation, consists—I repeat—in transference gratifications or frustrations that are meted out to the patient "not by words alone," i.e., not by means of interpretation. Thus, whether a positive or a negative approach is chosen, the effect of such an experience remains incomplete. The relegation of interpretation to a secondary place implies that ego analysis must be entirely or at least partly omitted. Any differentiated, subtle understanding of the interaction of the various psychic structures, any detailed, careful analysis of defenses, any effort to analyze ego pathology and to correct it is left aside. Instead, there is an attempt to work directly with the id and to exert immediate influence upon object relations. Such an approach disregards Freud's most important formulation concerning the therapeutic aim of analysis: "Where id was, there shall ego be." Therefore, no lasting effect can be expected from these methods.

14

Pathologic Forms of Self-Esteem Regulation

(1960)

S ELF-ESTEEM, in common usage, is defined by Webster as a high opinion of oneself, respect for oneself. This positive evaluation of the self obviously is a precondition for one's well-being.

There are many ways in which human beings attempt to keep up a positive evaluation of themselves. The methods they use may vary according to numerous factors, such as age, character and capacities of the ego, individual nature of conflicts, and so on. My discussion will limit itself to certain abnormal modes of self-esteem regulation which are characteristically found in some types of "narcissistic disturbances." Obviously, disturbances of self-esteem are a frequent symptom in schizophrenic as well as in manic-depressive states. However, I shall not deal with the psychoses but intend to concentrate on "narcissistic neurosis."

I am well aware that Freud used the term "narcissistic neurosis" to designate exclusively psychotic illness,

---

Published originally in *The Psychoanalytic Study of the Child,* 15:215–232, 1960. New York: International Universities Press.

delimiting it from transference neurosis. But it seems to me that narcissistic pathology cannot be viewed as restricted to psychosis. I would like to use this term in a much wider sense. In the course of the last decades, we have become less inclined to regard clinical entities as pertaining exclusively to certain phases of development. We know overlapping of phases to be ubiquitous. There is usually a partial regression to earlier ego and libidinal states mixed with later, more highly developed structures. Even a marked narcissistic orientation need not be completely so; i.e., it need not be characterized by a complete withdrawal of cathexis from objects. Indeed, we now even question the usefulness of a too narrowly circumscribed nosology. We are much concerned with so-called borderline conditions, and we tend to look upon the boundary between psychosis and neurosis as somewhat fluid.

Narcissism denotes libidinal cathexis of the self, in contrast to object cathexis. Without repeating the well-known facts about the development from primary to secondary narcissism, I merely wish to stress that narcissism per se is a normal phenomenon. It becomes pathologic only under certain conditions: (1) in states of quantitative imbalance, e.g., when the balance between object cathexis and self-cathexis has become disturbed, and objects are cathected insufficiently or not at all; (2) in infantile forms of narcissism, which are frequently—but not always—present in the states of quantitative imbalance. Infantile narcissism consists in cathexis of the self at a time of incomplete ego differentiation and insufficient delimitation of self and object world. The absence of the ability, at this stage, to distinguish wish from reality manifests itself in the use of magic to achieve need satisfaction and mastery of reality; thus, the infantile narcissism has a megalomanic character.

Narcissistic pathology becomes especially noticeable in the methods used for self-esteem regulation.

Fenichel (1945), following the ideas of Ferenczi (1913), regards self-esteem as the expression of nearness to or distance from the infantile feeling of omnipotence. With advancing ego development, the values against which the self is measured change and become more realistic; equally, the methods that are used to keep self-esteem on a stable positive level. The longing for omnipotence, obviously, stems from fixation at a still undifferentiated ego level. By using it as a criterion, Fenichel thus framed a static definition leaving no room for the maturation of values. I prefer the more flexible one given by Jacobson in her fundamental paper on "The Self and the Object World" (1954b), which has helped me to clarify many aspects of narcissistic disturbances. Her definition seems to cover the complexities of the problem more adequately. She considers self-esteem to be the expression of discrepancy or harmony between self-representation and the wishful concept of the self.

Or, to put it differently: in the course of growing up, we must learn to evaluate our potentialities and accept our limitations. Continued hope for the impossible represents an infantile wish, revealing a basic lack of ability to face inner and outer reality. Self-esteem thus depends on the nature of the inner image against which we measure our own self, as well as on the ways and means at our disposal to live up to it. That this inner image is influenced by many factors, especially by the particular form of the superego, is obvious. Living up sufficiently to the demands of one's superego is a mature form of self-esteem regulation.

What we loosely describe as "narcissists" are people whose libido is mainly concentrated on themselves at the expense of object love. I shall not speak here of those who without visible conflict entertain an exceedingly high opinion of themselves. Another type of narcissist frequently has exaggerated, unrealistic—i.e., infantile—inner yardsticks. The methods he uses to deal with the resulting inner tension depend on the general state of his ego and often are infantile ones. This is the specific pathology I wish to discuss, concentrating at this time on the forms it takes in men. As a starting point, I shall bring in a few clinical data to illustrate some characteristic patterns of such pathologic self-esteem regulation.

Daniel K. was a very accomplished writer who wrote one book after another, with marked success. But he did not feel gratified by this. Nothing he did was as grandiose as he wanted it to be. He would feel reassured, for a time, when he looked at his bookshelf and counted: "Here are seven books I wrote, six volumes I edited; there are 23 articles I brought out in other people's publications; I am quoted so and so many times:—*There are about two and a half feet of Mr. K. on the shelf.*" The phallic meaning of this little game was obvious. He had to reassure himself that his phallus was not only there, but of extraordinary size.

Daniel's life consisted to a large extent in behavior of this kind; he was constantly preoccupied with attempts to feel great and important. He was active in innumerable civic and cultural enterprises and had attained a leading position in his community. But neither this nor his prolific literary production nor his erotic successes sufficed to make him happy. He was a man of considerable talent, well informed, and rich in ideas. But frequently his writing was careless and superficial, not up to the level of his capacities, because he was driven to produce too fast. He could not *wait* for results, could not stand tension and unpleasure, although he *knew* better. He had an inner standard of quality for his work as well as the gift for it, but was unable to muster enough self-discipline to realize his potentialities. He had to have the immediate gratification of success. This need was so overwhelmingly strong that he had little control over it. He also was touchy, quick to take offense at the slightest provocation. He continually anticipated attack and danger, reacting with anger and fantasies of revenge when he felt frustrated in his need for constant admiration.

Obviously, Daniel overconcentrated on himself. His object relations were weak and apt to be relinquished under pressure. His main aim was to increase his self-esteem and to ward off the underlying danger of passivity by incessant masculine activity.

The narcissistic goal against which he measured himself was most clearly expressed by his fantasies in puberty: he would see himself successively as the Mayor of New York City, the President of the United States, and as the president of the world, until he had to stop with the painful question: "And then what?" Later, he wanted to be the outstanding genius of his time. Of course, no success in reality could measure up to such limitless inner demands, and his state of dissatisfaction was all the more intensified because he had to sacrifice more mature superego demands in reaching out for his illusory aims.

This bottomless need for grandiosity is clearly a compensatory striving. He has to be president of the world, he has to have a symbolic phallus two and a half feet long, because he is under the impact of unbearable castration fears.

Compensatory narcissistic self-inflation is among the most conspicuous forms of pathologic self-esteem regulation. Frequently, the attempt at compensation proves unsuccessful: instead of producing a feeling of "narcissistic bliss," it results in severe symptoms.

Thus Daniel continually felt not only slighted, unloved, unappreciated by others, but also awkward, embarrassed, and "self-conscious." Moreover, he harbored severe anxieties regarding his state of health. He was forever anticipating early death from cancer or heart attack, etc., and anxiously watched himself for signs of disease. "Self-consciousness" and hypochondriacal anxiety both are typical symptoms in persons with narcissistic pathology. They represent, so to speak, the reverse side of the narcissistic self-inflation. I shall have more to say about this later.

Two factors which are characteristic of the pathology in compensatory narcissistic self-inflation were implied in this material: (1) there is a large amount of unneutralized aggression which contributes to the hypochondriacal anxieties; (2) there is a superego disturbance that causes an overdependence on approval from outside, thus contributing to the symptom of "self-consciousness."

It should be stressed that in spite of his low tolerance of tension and unpleasure, Daniel's narcisstic orientation was not combined with a general regression to infantile narcissism. The pathology, in his case, rested predominantly on the megalomanic content of the ideals he had set up for himself. He tried to reach his goal of self-aggrandizement through achievement and did not indulge in regressive confusion between reality and fantasy.

However, owing to the regressive character of the narcissistic orientation, one often finds that the infantile-megalomanic ideal is accompanied by a barely disguised sexualization of originally nonsexual activities. Frequently the ambitious narcissistic fantasy is expressed in the form of sexualized and concrete images, thus revealing features of ego infantilism, deficient sublimation, and primitive thinking. In severer cases of this type, the ego disturbance dominates the clinical picture and is not confined to an isolated area, as it was in the example given here.

Let us now examine the origin of the narcissistic imbalance which determines these compensatory efforts. The need for narcissistic inflation arises from a striving to overcome threats to one's bodily intactness. Obviously, such a threat is ubiquitous in all danger situations; but under favorable circumstances, defenses are mobilized that permit a permanent conflict solution. Anxiety is overcome via modification or relinquishment of instinctual aims, while object cathexis can be retained. The development of reliable, solid defenses presupposes a considerable degree of ego integration. The ego must have the strength, while circumventing violent anxiety attacks and using small amounts of anxiety as a danger signal, to mobilize defenses and to influence the drives in the desired way.

But if a traumatic situation occurs too early and is too overwhelming, at a time when the ego is still in a rather primitive state, the ego will not succeed in binding the anxiety. The impact of such early traumata thus can seriously interfere not only with the formation of defenses, but also with the integration and general development of the ego. States of panic in themselves represent grave disturbances in the balance of cathexis. That is to say, during intense anxiety, there often occurs a *passing* withdrawal of psychic interest from objects to the self. Under conditions of too frequently repeated early traumatizations, the narcissistic withdrawal of libido from the objects to the endangered self tends to remain permanent.

Such early traumatization at a time of ego immaturity creates a predisposition to react in an infantile way to later danger situations. The imagined danger is taken for reality: it is not something that might occur in the future and might still be avoided, but something that has already occurred. In the case of my patient, for instance, the overwhelming castration anxiety stemmed from repeated early observations of primal scenes experienced as violence and total destruction, which had led to a feminine identification, i.e., to a latent homosexual orientation. The personality of the mother, a severe hypochondriac who constantly indulged in dramatic performances of being on the brink of catastrophic death, made a later re-evaluation of danger impossible. Femininity remained equated with complete annihilation. It represented not a threat in the future, but an accomplished fact. Hence the persistent orientation aiming at repair of the damage.

This infantile equation of danger with a catastrophe

that has already occurred seems to be characteristic of such early disturbances. The only possible defense, therefore, consists in methods which were available to the infantile ego, particularly in *magical denial*: "It is not so. I am not helpless, bleeding, destroyed. On the contrary, I am bigger and better than anyone else. I am the greatest, the most grandiose." Thus, to a large extent, psychic interest must center on a compensatory narcissistic fantasy whose grandiose character affirms the denial.

Fantasies, to be sure, always have to do with easy ways of wish fulfillment. But they obviously differ vastly in kind, and they range from the most primitive to highly differentiated forms. Being rooted in magical denial and characterized by primitive features of an early ego state, the compensatory narcissistic fantasies often are poorly integrated into realistic, adult thinking.

The exclusive production of fantasies that aim at one's own aggrandizement reveals a serious disturbance of the narcissistic balance, particularly when these fantasies persist after puberty. For example, I remember a patient whose masturbation fantasies were consistently and exclusively concerned with self-adoration: "I am the greatest general in the world; I am the greatest all-round athlete; I am winning all Olympic ski races," etc. Grandiose fantasies of this type are not just a pleasant pastime whose wishful and unreal character is fully recognized, and which can be "turned off" at will. They have become an intrinsic part of the personality. Indeed, they have become life's main purpose, and the self is being measured against them.

I shall show later that such fantasies are based on

primitive identifications with idealized infantile objects and thus represent primitive ego ideals.

The degree of pathology resulting from the persistence of these archaic ego ideals depends upon the structure of the ego. Ability to function adequately in reality, availability of sublimations, etc., determine whether any attempts can be made to transpose the fantasy at least partially into reality. Sometimes it may be tunéd down to a pitch that is realizable in some degree, sufficiently to keep the self-esteem on a stable high level.

In the predominantly narcissistic personality, however, the withdrawal of interest from reality and object world frequently entails regressive trends. As a result, the wishful fantasy becomes or remains overcathected and the distinction between wish and reality will become blurred. Thus the fantasy is not only a yardstick, but is also experienced as magically fulfilled. The degree of pathology in a given case will depend on the degree of indulgence in such magic gratification and neglect of reality testing.

What is of interest for our special problem is the fact that such regressive abandonment of reality testing with respect to self-appreciation occurs frequently as an isolated lacuna in an otherwise well-coordinated personality. In other words, self-evaluation may remain infantile in certain restricted areas. For instance, the high sense of gratification which arose when the child was able to master certain difficulties may persist throughout later life, even though "objectively" such activity no longer represents any particular achievement. Rather minor activities and productions can thus be experienced as extremely important, sometimes, as though a hidden narcissistic fantasy had been realized. The resulting feeling of increased self-esteem, of exaggerated self-assurance, creates an impression of unwarranted conceit, since others cannot share the archaic value judgments which underlie it.

When an adult still finds magnificence, let us say, in being able to ride by himself in a train, he manifests an infantilism of inner standards. Usually the survival of such infantile values, too, is the end result of compensatory needs; but the intensity of inner conflict is less pronounced in these persons than in those with exaggerated standards. It is likely that their fixations took place on a somewhat higher level of development.

It would of course be artificial to delimit the compensatory narcissistic fantasy too sharply from the superego as the embodiment of "mature" values transmitted by education. Although the superego is the more complicated structure, both may exist simultaneously. They may overlap or may be fused and mixed with one another.

The differences between the two structures are self-evident. Narcissistic fantasies often stand in sharp contrast to superego demands, since they contain many elements of an unsublimated, instinct-fulfilling character. The primitive values comprised in them are expressions of body narcissism.

Overstrong body narcissism is rooted in traumatic experiences, pregenital as well as early genital, which had shattered primitive feelings of pleasure and unquestioned security. These traumata had thus destroyed the infantile feeling of power to subject the disobedient object world, including the own body, to the wishes of the infantile ego. Uncontrollable feelings of helplessness, anxiety, and rage ensued. These represent what we call "narcissistic injuries" that necessitate continous reparative measures. The result is a turning away from love objects to an enormous overvaluation of the body or particular organs: of their intactness, size, strength, beauty, grandiosity. Most glaring here is the overvaluation of the phallus, in contrast to the concept of the female organs as being destroyed, bleeding, dirty, etc.

It should be stressed that castration threats, with ensuing overvaluation of the phallus, represent only the most conspicuous and the most tangible narcissistic traumata. However, any need for repair or restitution may be condensed into fantasies about phallic intactness and greatness. Castration thus is equated with object loss, emptiness, hunger, bowel loss and dirtiness, while phallic intactness also expresses the undoing of pregenital losses and injuries. Most important in this context is the equation of the whole body with a phallus, whose oral background was pointed out by Lewin (1933).

The megalomanic character of the body-phallus equation has to do with fantasies about incorporation of early objects (or of their organs) seen in an idealized way. Thus, to use Jacobson's formulation, fusion has taken place between self- and object images. The grandiosity originally attributed to the object belongs now to the self. Archaic object relations of this kind, with fluid boundaries between self- and object image, represent the matrix of increased body narcissism.

The body-phallus equation usually reflects a narcissistic erotization of the whole body. This fantasy often has an out-and-out perverse quality and may lead to dire consequences.

To give an example: I once treated a professional actor, a handsome fellow, who was in a continual state of self-infatuation. That he really experienced his whole body as a penis was revealed by the fact that he liked to masturbate facing a mirror, with the fantasy that his neck was as thick as his head. This patient's constant preoccupation with his own body had disastrous effects. He became plagued by continuous, severe hypochondriacal anxieties. He was afraid of innumerable fatal diseases, worried that his nose would be disfigured by a chronic eczema, etc.

My other patient, Daniel K., showed the same pattern of self-adoration in a slight disguise when he admired his almost yard-long row of books. This transparent displacement from the body-phallus to his brainchildren was of no avail: he suffered from the same intolerable hypochondriacal fears as the actor.

Frequently, attempts are made to modify the sexual body narcissism and to transform it into something nonsexual and nonobjectionable; these attempts sometimes are on a rather primitive level. Certain tokens of masculinity are used in place of the real thing. I have repeatedly observed this in patients who attached a strong masculine connotation to particular garments or to the pipes they smoked, the cars they drove, etc. This displacement represents a not very successful attempt at desexualization. The thinking remains symbolic, unrealistic, and incommunicable. (I never could establish, for instance, why one suit was regarded as more masculine than the other.)

Successful modification of body narcissism depends primarily upon the ego's capacity for sublimation and, as we shall see, deaggressivization. Unsublimated, erotized, manic self-inflation easily shifts to a feeling of utter dejection, of worthlessness, and to hypochondriacal anxieties. *Narcissists of this type thus suffer regularly from repetitive, violent oscillations of self-esteem.*

It is as though the warded-off feeling of catastrophic annihilation, which had started off the whole process originally, were breaking through the elegant façade again each time. The brief rapture of elated self-infatuation is followed by a rude awakening. Usually the tiniest disappointment, the slightest physical indisposition, the most trifling experience of failure can throw the patient into extreme despair. He does not suffer from a cold: he has lung cancer. He did not meet with a minor setback because a contract fell through: his whole career is ruined; and so on. Thus, the grandiose body-phallus fantasy—for instance, "standing out high above everybody else, like an obelisk"—turns *suddenly* into one of total castration, often with a pregenital coloring: "I am falling apart at the seams," or "I am just a bagful of excrement," "I am full of poison that is going to kill me," etc. It is as though the original castration fear had extended from the penis to the whole body.

This infantile value system knows only absolute perfection and complete destruction; it belongs to the early time in life when only black and white existed, good and bad, pleasure and pain, but nothing in between. There are no shadings, no degrees, there are only extremes. Reality is judged exclusively from the standpoint of the pleasure principle; to evaluate it objectively is still impossible. Nor does a realistic evaluation of the self exist as yet. Like tolerance for others, tolerance for onself is a late achievement.

The amount of aggression, both in the positive and in the negative phase, is conspicuous. The state of self-inflation is intensely competitive as a rule. My patient Daniel's grandiosity, for instance, could be measured in feet and inches, just as others measure theirs in dollars and cents. Such a concretization and oversimplification of values facilitates competition with others: "I am bigger than you—I am better—I am the best." The primitive correlation of value to size is of course a rather common phenomenon; this type of crude comparison easily lends itself to be used for purposes of aggressive competition. The very process of self-admiration involves contempt for others. Undisguised phallic-exhibitionistic impulses of this type generally are combined with unmitigated, primal aggression: the patient "blinds" others with his magnificence; he "rubs in" his successes, as though he were forcing his enormous penis on his audience.

But with the collapse of his phallic grandiosity, this vehement aggression instantly turns back upon his castrated self. Instead of admiring and loving himself the patient now hates himself. A drive diffusion has occurred, which the ego in its state of regression is unable to master. This explains, I believe, the intensity of the hypochondriacal anxieties regularly present in narcissistic disturbances.

In a number of these cases I have found the fantasy that only one grandiose phallus exists in the whole world. When the patient is in possession of it or is identified with it, everyone else is deprived of it and thus totally destroyed. In the negative phase, the tables are turned: the grandiose phallus belongs to somebody else—perhaps to its rightful owner—who, full of contempt, now destroys the patient. Either way, the acquisition of this glorified organ is accomplished through violent aggression.

This fantasy about the single glorified penis shows quite clearly that this and similar primitive forms of self-esteem regulation are based on a persistence of primitive types of object relations, i.e., a fixation on infantile levels of libidinal and ego development.

At that early stage, the ability to perceive reality objectively is but *in statu nascendi*. Instinctual needs are so overwhelming that the sexual characteristics of the object flow together with the object as a person. Drives prevail toward oral—or anal—incorporation of the admired and envied objects; in this way, a feeling of *being* the object is temporarily achieved. But with growing ego differentiation, the child becomes increasingly aware of his own smallness as well as his separateness from objects. Hence the still completely sexualized and glorified object is set up as a primitive ego ideal, as something he longs to be. Under unfavorable conditions, however, the boundaries between this ideal and the self-image become blurred again, time after time.

Reverting to magical identification, the patient who has regressed to this infantile level may feel as though he *were* the magnificent phallus-father, as though he *were* his own ego ideal. Repair is achieved once more via magic fusion. But after a short time, as we have seen, this wishful identification turns into the opposite; it is doomed to break down, as the uncontrollably mounting aggression destroys the glorified object.

To relieve the ensuing intolerable feeling of annihilation, the aggression must be counteracted by a renewed elevation of the object; hence the grandiose phallus is restored to it and the entire process starts all over again. This state of affairs is reflected in the instability of moods, rapid oscillations of self esteem, perpetual shifts from positive to negative feelings about the self, from megalomanic elation to hypochondriacal anxiety.

Let me illustrate this with a case characterized by a particular instability of self-esteem and body image. The origin of the primitive, still completely sexualized ego ideal in severe infantile traumatization can be clearly demonstrated here.

Robert L., a successful lawyer, suffers from repetitive mood swings. For a while he feels strong, victorious, much more creative and intelligent than his peers. He is proud of his slim figure; his whole body, to him, has definitely phallic characteristics. The analyst and everyone else during this period is seen as inferior, old, weak, defective. He feels that he is arousing envy in the analyst. He wishes to dazzle with his brilliance, to overpower by his masculinity. By exhibiting his own greatness he aggressively annihilates all others.

The slightest disappointment, however, or even the mere passage of time, transforms this state of phallic grandiosity into the opposite. Now he is afraid of the consequences of his aggressive wishes. He feels unsuccessful, hopeless, threatened by illness; he is affected by peculiar body sensations, as though he had a hang-over. The analyst and other objects appear changed; they have gained in stature. The analyst looks younger, stronger; she is brilliant, wonderful. Now he wishes to be "adopted" and helped by her. She should give to him of her wisdom and her riches which will help to restore him. During such periods, he cannot evaluate objects at all critically or realistically. He hangs on every word of the analyst as a revelation, and it is as though her mere physical presence could do wonders for him. Now he idealizes the object, clings to it, wishes to become one with it. By this fusion he can participate again in the greatness of the glorified object.

Here we see not only the rapid change from phallic grandiosity to hypochondriacal anxieties and depression, but also a rapid change in the appearance and value of the object. Again, there are only extremes: the object either is glorious or it is nothing. Besides, the object is not experienced fully as a person. Like the patient's own body, it is treated only as a phallus, as a wonderful and life-giving breast, or as a gaping, dirty wound.

This severe disturbance of object relations was caused by a series of early traumatic events. When he was little more than six months old, Robert's obsessional mother started toilet training by means of regularly given enemas. For years to come, this interfered with his development of the sense of being a person separate from his mother: it was she who had power over his body. At the same time he experienced himself as an open bag full of excrement: things were put into him and came out of him. He could have no control over his body content. An operation early in his third year confirmed the feeling that the intactness of his body was constantly threatened. Then around the same time, his parents' marriage broke up. With the loss of his father he lost all security of permanent object relations, particularly as the mother soon became involved with a series of lovers of whom Robert was intensely jealous.

Somewhat later, the little boy learned to retain his stools. He would sit for hours by himself, playing aggressive fantasy games in which he would kill and destroy tin soldiers, at the same time pushing and withholding a fecal column in his rectum. This gave him a feeling of mastery and of being completely solid and intact within his body, as though he had a powerful, aggressive anal phallus inside himself. In identification with his father, who was considered an aggressive monster by the mother, he became now "Freiherr von Richthofen," the German war pilot, seen as a murderous giant able to destroy the whole world. But this aggressive, anal-sadistic game led to a state of constipation which he could not overcome any more. It led to feelings of being sick and full of poison, to a new series of enemas, so that his sense of helpless annihilation broke through again.

These pregenital traumatic experiences were condensed with the child's envious admiration of his father's large penis and the simultaneous, terrifying awareness that the mother lacked this organ.

All this necessitated magical restitution. As we have seen, infantile states of elation persisted into adulthood in a slightly disguised form. They prevail for short periods, to be abruptly displaced by the sense of being worthless and destroyed. The peculiar "hang-over" feeling, which assails the patient at the same time, can now be understood. By the destructive incorporation of everything that had caused his envy before, he destroyed the very power he acquired. He feels poisoned from within: he has incorporated something bad.

To repeat, the attempt at repair through primitive identification becomes intolerable due to the intensely aggressive feelings that may emerge at any moment. By destroying the object, the patient likewise destroys himself. Seeking to restitute himself, he again must endow the objects around him with ego-ideal qualities; and so the cycle is endlessly repeated.

This material throws into sharp relief that if the archaic character of the ego ideal has persisted, it invariably results in a complete failure of such attempts at self-esteem stablization. Indeed, it is the primitive, crudely sexual quality of the ego ideals, conditioned by a fixation on the primitive levels where traumatization had occurred, that represents the quintessence of this pathology.

In the course of a more normal development, identifications with other than openly sexual aspects of the objects acquire importance. Hence the identifications lose their magical character. They bring about real changes in the structure of the ego, or they become more sublimated ideals to be incorporated in the superego. Primitive ego ideals may survive, nevertheless, while maturation of the personality progresses. In the "simpler" forms of self-esteem pathology I described before, their persistence expressed itself predominantly in a narcissistic orientation of the inner standards. The condition was not complicated by a reprojection of ego ideals onto the object world.

However, it should be stressed that a reprojection of ego ideals onto external objects need not by itself imply a greater degree of pathology. Ego ideals of a more sublimated nature may be so reprojected, and restitutive merging with real love objects may become a method of self-esteem stabilization. In my paper on "Narcissistic Object Choice in Women" (1953, this volume), I showed how the attempt to undo narcissistic injuries via identification with the partner's greatness may effect a rather stable solution if it is undertaken by a mature ego.

I would like now to come back briefly to another sympton which frequently occurs, as I mentioned before, in persons of the narcissistic structure here described, namely, "self-consciousness." This excellent term, as far as I know, exists only in the English language. Webster defines self-conscious as follows: "prone to regard oneself, as an object of the observation of others; embarrassed or stagy because of failure to forget one's own self in society." *Self-consciousness* thus describes an accentuated state of awareness of the own self and also indicates the assumption that the same exaggerated amount of attention is paid to one's person by others.

The remarks which follow are somewhat tentative. The symptom of self-consciousness is not restricted solely to the compensatory narcissistic personality. Structure and dynamics may be different under different conditions.

To be the object of admiring attention is frequently sought for as a means to undo feelings of insufficiency. But the imagined fulfillment of this wish can be experienced as extremely unpleasant. The attention desired from others is contained in and replaced by the ego's concentration upon the own self. The ego thus plays a double role: it is the observer and simultaneously the object of observation. What is relevant in pathologic cases of this kind is that cathexis has been shifted to the self not only from objects, but also from normally neutralized ego activities, to a degree which is intolerable.

Here the hypercathexis of the self is accompanied by a disturbance of sublimation, i.e., by a (voyeuristic-exhibitionistic) sexualization of ego activities. This reflects itself in the fact that any activity—any thought or feeling—exists not for its own sake, but exclusively for the purpose of narcissistic exhibition. It is as though the person would say: "Look, I am walking, speaking, thinking. Look, I have such beautiful feelings, deep interests, important thoughts." Normally such activities are invested not only with neutralized energy, but also with aim-inhibited "love" for some particular field, subject, etc. This type of "thing-love" or interest is precluded by the accentuated self-concentration we describe as "self-consciousness." The ensuing narcissistic imbalance generates disturbances of the sense of reality, ranging from feelings of emptiness or ungenuineness to severe depersonalization.

In addition, we must take into account the aggressive components of the narcissistic exhibitionistic strivings. Self-conscious people seek to undo feelings of inadequacy by forcing everyone's attention and admiration upon themselves, but they fail in this defensive attempt. They feel that attention is indeed focused on them in a *negative* way: as though others, instead of being dazzled, were discerning the warded-off "inferiority" behind the false front. The exhibitionistic drive contains contempt for those whose admiration is needed. Due to the re-emergence of inferiority feelings and to the concentration of cathexis on the self, the direction of the aggression changes: hence the contempt for others turns into self-contempt, which is experienced as shameful exposure.

The painfully increased self-awareness of self-conscious persons thus results from a shifting back onto the self of resexualized and reaggressivized cathexis which can no longer be bound in a stable way by attachment to objects or ego activities.

Not rarely, the symptom of self-consciousness becomes further complicated by a deficiency of the self-evaluating functions. It is as though such persons were unable to form any independent moral judgment about themselves, but needed "public opinion" as a yardstick. Their superego is not fully internalized or, frequently, has become reprojected onto external objects. Here the impairment of ego functions, which is so often seen in narcissistically oriented persons, includes also a superego defect.

When the self-conscious person imagines himself being judged by an outside observer, who stands for an externalized superego, he makes an unsuccessful attempt to get rid of inner conflicts, of unacceptable strivings, by means of projection. This contributes to the feelings of unreality and estrangement. It is as if he were saying: "I am not the one who wants to exhibit himself aggressively, but other people aggressively observe and judge me." Self-consciousness thus is a first step in the direction of a paranoid pattern, and this feature is in keeping with the disturbance of object cathexis which I described before.

It is obvious that the oscillations of self-esteem in compensatory narcissism bear similarities to cyclothymic states, but there are considerable differences. These mood swings are of shorter duration than the true cyclothymic ones. Notwithstanding the severity of the disturbance, large areas of the personality usually remain intact and are not involved in the pathologic process. Most noticeable is the difference of the role played by the superego. The sadistic intolerance of the superego, so predominant in the depressive phase of cyclothymia, is absent in the cases here described. The phase of lowered self-esteem is characterized preponderantly by anxiety and feelings of annihilation, not by guilt feelings. Thus, it is not the dissolution of an over-strict superego that brings about the positive phase, but a compensatory narcissistic fantasy of restitution via fusion with an archaic ego ideal. And while object loss causes regression to narcissistic identification in melancholia, these patients react with permanent vacillations between libidinal and aggressive hypercathexis of the self to an infantile traumatic situation necessitating endless attempts at repair.

15

Masturbation
and Self-Esteem

(1964)

Oᴺᴇ ᴅᴀʏ many years ago, I received a telephone call from the school which my daughter, then aged fourteen, was attending. I was asked to come and fetch her home, for something terrible had happened there: a boy the same age, a very good friend of hers, had committed suicide by throwing himself out of a fifth-floor window, without any apparent motive. Later on it emerged, from notes in his diary and a letter addressed to my daughter, that he had been racked by intense masturbation guilt; driven to despair by his feeling that he was unworthy of her, unworthy of the "pure virgin," he had decided that he could no longer live.

I know nothing more about this boy's history, nor what were the contributing factors that raised his feelings of guilt to the pitch of cruel self-destruction. But from many instances in which analysis could avert

Read in Vienna, 1964, before the Vienna Psychoanalytic Society. Translated from the German by Paula Gross.

such merciless self-punitive acts, we know how easily masturbation in adolescence or childhood can lead to extreme feelings of inferiority, of intolerable unworthiness, and to the severest fears of damage to health, especially when all attempts to give up the "vice" have ended in failure. Insanity, illness, death, are expected to occur in retribution. The most senseless countermeasures may be taken, such as 300 push-ups 10 times a day, for example, and every variety of masochistic self-flagellation. All kinds of neurotic symptoms develop, which represent ways of undoing the fateful consequences of masturbation. We also know that these anxieties and guilt feelings ensue, in particular, from the incestuous, oedipal fantasies which underlie masturbation. The masturbation complex is mostly responsible for those impairments of self-esteem which we describe as a sense of inferiority.

The tragic incident related above occurred almost a generation ago. I do not think that it came to my mind by chance, as I cast about for an example with which to begin my presentation. Adolescent suicides because of guilt feelings about masturbation still occur, but are certainly less prevalent today. On the other hand, things have become more complicated. Young people nowadays are apt to know that masturbation is not harmful; besides, sexual activity with partners is far more common among adolescents now. There is no longer a simple distinction between "good" and "bad." To be sure, the underlying incestuous fantasies exist, just as they did before, and lead to guilt feelings exactly as before. The psychic consequences are more blurred, however; often they take the form of complicated character neuroses and not, as formerly, of clear-cut neurotic symptoms. Indeed, the observable shift in clinical manifestations over the last three or four decades is an interesting subject, but one I cannot deal with here.

What I want to discuss are other alterations of self-esteem connected with masturbation: not inferiority feelings, but changes in an opposite, positive sense, which often affect the whole personality in a very significant way. In addition, they include oscillations between pathologically heightened and pathologically lowered self-esteem, which themselves must be regarded as severely morbid. Such oscillations, when they reach extreme intensity, are frequently accompanied by grave disturbances of the sense of reality and of object relations, based on ego defects of the order encountered in the psychoses. However, even otherwise well integrated personalities may manifest partial and milder narcissistic disturbances, namely, pathologically heightened self-esteem, intermittent transitory feelings of grandeur, and corresponding reactions of hypochondriacal fears and temporary near-psychotic feelings of nothingness. Such "narcissistic neuroses" have engaged my special interest for many years. I am aware that my use of the term "narcissistic neuroses" to describe these conditions runs counter to Freud's, who preferred to reserve this term for manic-depressive psychosis. Today I shall limit myself to relatively milder disturbances of this kind, in connection with masturbation.

Self-esteem depends upon the relation between one's wishful self-images and one's self-representation, that is to say, on the consonance of what one wants to be with what one is and how one perceives oneself to be.

I propose to examine the problems of masturbation from this perspective, without going further into the complex interrelations which determine self-esteem in general. It suffices to note, therefore, that inferiority feelings arising from masturbation reflect severe tensions between the wishful ideal image, the ego ideal, which usually dates from early childhood, and the actual self-image or self-representation which is often distorted as a result of masturbation-castration anxiety and guilt feelings.

These tensions become exacerbated when the patient's narcissistic wishful images (ego ideals) are too grandiose and his self-demands too stringent. In some of my papers, I described narcissistic disturbances characterized by particularly grandiose, infantile wishful images that had arisen in compensation for early infantile traumata. Impairments of ego development, due to the same trauma, may lead to temporary fusions between the wishful image (ego ideal) and the self-representation. At times, or in a part of their personality, such individuals feel themselves to be as grandiose and as exceptional as they felt in their wishful childhood fantasies. As Freud (1914) noted in "On Narcissism," they see themselves as being what they had wished to be.

In this way the original trauma is undone. There is a special factor, however, which should not be overlooked: in such persons, *certain transient features of normal sexual excitement become increased and play a particular role.*

In normal states of sexual excitement, thinking becomes global, less and less abstract, less and less objective; fantasies predominate; there is a regression to "image thinking," and emotions hold sway over thought. With intensive excitement, thinking virtually comes to a stop; perception is shifted from external reality to physical sensation, from the outside world to the own body. The ultimate degree of this state is what the French call *la petite mort.*

The orgastic experience often is accompanied by a psychic experience which might best be described as ecstasy. Deutsch (1927), describes the ecstatic experience as characterized by the fantasy of fusion with the primary, admired, omnipotent object: the mother. In narcissistic individuals the ego ideal and the remnants of self-perception become merged, and the boundaries between self and object disappear. Probably this fantasy explains why, in such persons with weak object relations, the orgastic state approximates megalomanic states.

But even when the regression is not as deep, and when orgasm results from masturbation and the masturbation fantasies revolve around instinctual aims of later phases, there frequently occurs in such individuals a significant modification of the sense of reality, a suspension of reality testing that is peculiar to many fantasies. The instinctual aim will then be fantasied as *attained,* and this sudden wish fulfillment is always associated with an elevation of self-esteem, a transitory sense of omnipotence. The distinction between wish and reality at such times is suspended. Often this inflated self-esteem becomes drastically reversed by a rapid onset of guilt feelings once the excitement has subsided. But in other instances, self-criticism is inadequate, the fantasy too strongly cathected with libido, the pleasure premium too great, and distortion of the underlying wish too successful, to permit such abrupt reversal to reality. No feeling of guilt sets in, no disillusionment. The wish-fulfilling fantasy images and concomitant feelings of grandeur persist, and color the person's entire life.

We can thus distinguish two different mechanisms in grandiose feelings based on sexual excitement: (1) The ecstatic experience arises from a transitory, complete obliteration of the ego boundaries, and a total fusion of the self with the infantile object. (2) Certain masturbation fantasies, not quite as ecstatic in kind, are marked by the temporary experience of wishes as being fulfilled; this constitutes a somewhat less far-reaching ego regression. The two phenomena are obviously related, representing different degrees of the same regressive-narcissistic condition.

This temporary withdrawal from reality is characteristic not only of masturbation in the pubertal period, but also of childhood masturbation with its long, drawn-out, forepleasurelike type of excitation. Although it does not usually lead to actual orgasm, it produces similar effects: withdrawal of attention from the external world, weakening of reality testing, turning toward inner experience, heightened self-esteem, and the taking-for-true of the fantasy which ends in wish fulfillment. I shall give an example later on of a case of infantile orgasm, and describe the particular consequences which this experience had for the total personality. This example will also illustrate the distinction between the two forms of narcissistic regression.

The contents of masturbation fantasies vary widely, of course. They may be more or less object-oriented, or more or less narcissistic-aggressive. Residual elements of the earlier, pregenital phases may predominate to a greater or lesser extent. Particularly narcissistic-pregenital-aggressive forms are often associated with the ego regression I described before, and may have very significant effects on character and behavior. In some cases the physical act of masturbation has been given up, but the fantasy is acted out in some distorted form, for example, in delinquent behavior. It is important to note, in this connection, that the frequently reported megalomanic character of the masturbation fantasy stamps the entire behavior and the personality as a whole. Traces of this megalomanic attitude adhere sometimes also to the simultaneously present measures of defense against masturbation and measures of undoing. We then find, as is so often the case, that the return of the repressed manifests itself in the defense. The megalomanic infantile attitude, which had marked the original masturbation fantasy, now regressively determines the defensive reactions of the ego, and hence both self-esteem and behavior.

Therefore, in these instances, we also find a combination of inferiority feelings with ideas of grandeur, or an oscillation between the two, which is decisive for the eventual clinical picture. I should like to give you a case example of this type, which illustrates a not unusual combination of grandiose fantasy with excessively severe, unrelenting attacks on a helpless ego. This constellation, which is prevalent in adolescence, can often be overcome with the onset of adult sexual life and the concomitant maturation of the ego. In the case I am about to describe, it appeared only in adulthood.

The patient was a man of forty, successfully engaged

in an intellectual profession, happily married, the father of two children, and in good financial circumstances. This life situation, however, which was regarded by others as extremely favorable, failed to satisfy him. He was particularly distressed because he was not writing important scientific papers or books; he continually compared himself unfavorably to colleagues, and this always to the most outstanding among his rivals. He was perennially in debt, because his demands always exceeded his very sizable income. For example, he would go on expensive trips at the same time as building a house in the country. Driven by various fears, he took out excessively high life insurance in order to provide security for his family. Time and again, he had to satisfy sundry concurrent needs of various relatives, so that he would borrow both on his country estate and on his policies, never considering that these loans would have to be repaid, with interest. This peculiar way of conducting his financial affairs was connected with a childhood fantasy about his father. The father, so he thought, possessed limitless riches—all he needed to do was to sign a check. The little boy did not know that his father first had to deposit his hard-earned money in the bank before he could issue a check at all.

If the patient expected omnipotence of himself in matters financial, he likewise expected to be gifted with unlimited capacity for work. Besides doing work, he wanted not only to produce important scientific writings, but also, and at the same time, to learn several foreign languages, to pursue studies in an unlimited number of difficult fields of knowledge, and to engage in various forms of creative art as well as in various active sports. He expected, in addition, to have time for his wife and children, and to perform all repairs in his city apartment, country house and garden with his own hands.

At the same time he carried on an unsuccessful battle against smoking, which he regarded as an addiction. He constantly tried, without success, to keep some special diet. He could never find enough time to sleep, chronically felt sleepy and tired. Unable to concentrate on a single one of his magnificent plans, he wanted always to do everything at the same time. Stacked on his bedside table were 15 books which he had commenced to read. He made programs sufficient for three lifetimes. But instead of carrying out any of these, he would read mystery stories or could not tear himself away from the television set. This waste of his time he also felt to be an addiction.

It is obvious that this patient was desperately struggling with a number of "vices," all of which had a character of wastefulness, extravagance, and addiction, with vices, that is, which were akin to masturbation—descended from it, so to speak. He exhausted himself in "unsuccessful" countermeasures which could all be reduced to the common denominators of "constructive achievement" and of ever-ready, "omnipotent" assistance to others.

Interestingly enough, he came of a family where he had already been taught at an early age that masturbation was harmless, and he remembered no struggle against masturbation in his adolescence. On the contrary, he had masturbated freely, with a fantasy of conquest over beautiful girls who admired him. Apparently the transition to adult sexual activity had not been too difficult, but masturbation had not been discontinued completely; nor had it stopped, later on, when he married a beautiful, entirely suitable girl. The analysis revealed that he did not feel sufficiently admired by his somewhat perfectionistic wife, and that he continued to masturbate occasionally with the fantasy of being adored by other, unknown, girls—clearly recognizable as a new version of the original fantasy, the core of which was to be admired by many girls.

Whereas in earlier years he had harbored no conscious guilt feelings on account of masturbation, his life now was absorbed by defensive measures against the dissipation of money, time, bodily strength; it had become an incessant struggle against disorganization and against being overwhelmed by temptations. He endeavored in vain to be doing something "constructive" at all times. Everything "constructive," so it transpired, was associated with the father, who had been a pioneer in his field and the author of several scientific works. In an infantile, idealizing way, the father was seen as a "genius," and the wish to emulate him had an infantile, grandiose quality. This was the core of the fantasy which consumed the patient: to become a "genius," to create something utterly magnificent, to be, *de facto*, omnipotent—to have unlimited strength, time and money for everything. The patient's plans, of course, were entirely irrational. Not only did he splinter himself, not only did he squander time on "masturbatory things," such as television and detective stories, smoking and overeating, but in truth he was interested only in himself, his own stature and achievements, and lacked sufficient true, sublimated interest in his pursuits of the moment. In his childhood and youth, too, he had merely "played around," doing only what was fun, and never worked in earnest, in contrast to his father who had been an indefatigable worker and a truly productive person.

The patient would feel, "After all, I am still young"—"it will come, all right"—"I will become a genius, all right, like my father"—"I still have time, after all." These ideas were intimately connected with the masturbation fantasy, "the girls admire me." This fantasy was likewise connected with the father, who had continually had extramarital affairs and had been greatly admired by his mistresses as well as by the son. The idea that one day, quite of oneself, without labor and without some quite ardent, intense interest, one could become a "genius"—that is, the father—represented, without much disguise, the original childhood wish to take the father's place. Predominant in the masturbation fantasy was the narcissistic aim to replace the admired father. The love object—the girl—was almost unimportant, a fact probably indicative of the patient's ambivalent attitude toward his constantly weeping, depressive mother. From the mother, all sorts of pregenital fears derived. The mother was given to threats and admonitions; the child had to deliver his anal products with regularity. The mother was always worrying that the child did not eat enough, anxious lest his health be endangered. The boy's whole interest veered away from the threatening, horrible, contemptible mother, and was concentrated on the wonderful father.

As he grew older, and with the father's sudden death, he became assailed by doubt: would he be able to realize his fantasy? It was only now that the struggle with masturbation set in, and the feeling of inferiority. Although he was adult at this time, in his middle twenties, he behaved like a typical adolescent: every week he expected that he would be able to realize his "constructive" plans; "*every Monday the new life was starting.*" Now he was full of good intentions and had more plans than could be carried out in a lifetime. Only now did he remember a frequent remark of his father: "I am sure you still have not done your homework today."

To neglect **his** duties now became a sin. Old fears rose up in **him**, based on his pregenital anxieties and **his** masturbation-castration fear—fears for life and limb, of which he had never until now been conscious. The restitutive measures he devised were of such number and variety as to make superhuman demands on him. As a result, the patient was consumed by the strongest feelings of inadequacy. None of his real achievements, such as his good functioning in professional life, seemed to be of account. On the other hand, the multiplicity of his self-demands was megalomanic, showing how grandiose was the ideal which he had set up for himself, how terrible the damages he had to undo. His sense of reality and his reality testing were disturbed only in a specific way, namely, with regard to his self-condemnation and to evaluation of the future. As a young man, he had thought: "I shall turn out to be as great some day, surely, as I long to be." Now he was thinking: "Some day I shall still achieve the fulfillment of the demands which I make on myself." "I shall suddenly become a 'genius.' " The megalomanic idea was displaced to the future. It was a restitutive fantasy, and thus alternated with his deep feelings of inferiority. The original sexual fantasy, which one might paraphrase: "I am being admired, like father," still persisted unchanged, but was secondary in importance to the restitutive fantasies.

It is characteristic that in the original sexual fantasy a wish could be experienced as fulfilled, whereas the restitutive fantasy—which was closer to reality, being based on the recognition that he could not measure up to the aggrandized image of his father—took the form not of fulfillment, but of hopeful expectation of future fulfillment. In the sexual fantasy, he *was* the father; in the fantastic self-demands and expectations, he *would become* the father. At the same time he was flooded by anxiety. These grandiose demands left no room for self-tolerance and for a positive evaluation of his real capacities, and prevented him from limiting himself to realistic, attainable goals.

It is an interesting question why the patient's wish to be like his admired father led not to true ego identification and sublimation, but merely to idealization of the father and identification with an ego ideal. One might wonder whether an ego regression or a disturbance of ego development had ensued from the fact that he indulged in uninhibited masturbation, contented himself with gratification through fantasies, avoided any fight against masturbation and had not been compelled to turn to reality. The wish was equated with reality, and this had highly undesirable consequences. One is reminded here of "progressive" education, which through overpermissiveness and insufficient demands has not infrequently led to ego disorders. But the preconditions for successful sublimation are probably far more complicated. However it may be, the narcissistic character of the original fantasy breaks through in a distorted form in the defense, preventing any realistic solution. It seems to me that this endless, retrogressive compensation for adolescent struggle against masturbation is a rather frequent phenomenon.

I would like to submit clinical material from another case, which exemplifies even more strikingly the influence of masturbation and sexual excitation upon self-esteem.

The patient, a woman of 45, was a highly gifted, successful, and creative scientist. She had been divorced twice, and came to analysis because of the difficulties she had encountered in living with her husbands. She was plagued by all sorts of guilt feelings. She was too "narcissistic," she felt, too "bisexual," and "bad" in general. Both her marriages had foundered because she was unable to tolerate moral defects in her partners. She was strict toward herself and could not love anyone who was not.

Both parents manifested pathological sexual behavior which the patient found intolerable. The mother was overtly perverse and homosexual. It became clear to the little girl very early that the genital inspections, to which she was subjected since early babyhood, and which were intended to guard her against masturbation and its evil consequences, had a perverse homosexual, voyeuristic undertone. The child felt profoundly guilty because of her masturbation and believed herself to be bodily impaired by it. She soon became aware that the regular scrutiny of her genital by the mother also served the latter's pleasure, and she hated her mother for being a liar and hypocrite. She was not mistaken: the mother later had an overt homosexual affair. The father was a distinguished scientist in a highly prominent position. He carried on numerous secret affairs with women of a lower class, domestic servants, prostitutes, etc. The moral strictness of the patient probably was connected with these circumstances. Her disappointment in the parents facilitated projection of her own guilt feelings which became conscious rather late. The damage to her object relations, however, was lasting.

The patient's infantile masturbation, which was clearly recalled since the third year of life, had the following remarkable features. It was attended by an unmistakable orgasm, which is a rarity, as far as my experience goes. It consisted in friction of the vulva, accompanied by steadily mounting excitement which culminated in a "pointed," overwhelming sensation. This was followed by a pleasant languor and tranquillity. In her analysis, the patient described the climax as a tremendous *inner light*—a transcendent *illumination*. The fantasy, as she recalled it, had always been the same: she was a circus acrobat in flesh-colored tights, who could perform such marvelous stunts that all men admired her and could not tear themselves away from her.

Although her overt masturbatory activity branded her as "bad" in the eyes of her family, the child felt that masturbation and orgasm were *precious possessions,* which she was neither willing nor able to relinquish. Already at an early age, the orgastic feeling—the "illumination," as she called it—merged with all sorts of scientific and religious ideas which were made known and explained to her by the father, as well as by a much older brother. With an intellectual capacity far beyond her years, the little girl absorbed these ideas; and she reacted to them, particularly during early adolescence, with a degree of enthusiasm and excitement inextricably linked to the feeling of "illumination." There was no conscious guilt at this time.

Throughout the latency period, she persisted in this masturbation which was associated with such a wealth of "higher feelings." It made her feel "rich, elevated, and special." In the prepubertal period, various symptoms began to appear, particularly ideas of impairment. She feared that her nose was too big, that her teeth would fall out, that her body as a whole was asymmetrically built, etc. Under the impact of these anxieties, she finally gave up masturbation; but from then on she was tormented by feelings of guilt.

Also from then on, masturbation substitutes grew more and more frequent. These could be described essentially as states of *intellectual or spiritual ecstasy*. Stimulated by a rich artistic and intellectual milieu, and especially under the influence of her father and older brother, the child had developed "higher interests" at a very early age. She was capable very early of "abstract thinking," a precocious acquirement that soon became established and gave her superiority over her classmates, but which also served as a defense against homosexual seduction by the mother. She was interested predominantly in philosophy, religion, music, science, and mathematics. Absorption in problems of this kind could transport her into states of utmost enthusiasm and rapture, states of ecstasy that were more precious to her than anything else in life.

Much later, we came to understand that what she

call her "spiritual" higher interests, her penchants for mysticism and Christian theology, had to do with the "inalienable essence," the "inner core of the soul," which could easily be recognized as the "inner light"—the pulsating clitoris in orgasm. Whatever befell her in life—illness, poverty, the loss of her home, loss of love objects, and so on—this "innermost essence" could never be lost. Transported to ecstasy when she was reading about some new theory, thrilled with excitement by scientific thoughts, she would reach the same "illumination" which the four-year-old child had experienced in orgasm.

This fantasy of the "inner essence," of the "true, spiritual inner core," which was concomitant with that of the admired circus star, meant that she possessed an internal, indestructible phallus, a phallus that could never be lost, despite all the inspections and threats of her mother, and which manifested itself anew in each orgasm, in each "illumination." "Is it possible," she asked, "that God is identical with this inner core?" She thus equated God, omnipotence and the phallus. The phallus was inside her; thus she was *not* damaged and castrated.

In the course of the analysis, it became clear that this phallus belonged to the admired father and brother. She was identified with them both, and had internalized the paternal phallus. Possession of this admired organ gave her a feeling of strength, of power, which tremendously heightened her self-esteem and negated any feeling of insufficiency.

The fantasies connected with her acquisition of this phallus had many layers; they were deeply rooted in sadistic, pregenital strivings, and had to remain repressed. The phallus was obtained through oral incorporation; it was bitten off and eaten. Also, her whole body was identical with it, since on that primitive level one becomes what one eats. She was the circus star, able to perform wondrous feats which correspond to erection. Analyzed at the deepest level, this internal phallus led to an omnipotent, phallic mother whom she had incorporated and with whom she was fused. Her profound feeling of guilt, which broke through in the prepubertal period, was linked to this sadistic, pregenital component of the fantasy.

Despite this infantile prehistory of the internal phallus fantasy, however, the patient had achieved a solid ego identification with her father and brother. She succeeded in combining the strongly sexualized feeling of ecstasy with correct scientific thinking, and was able to retain sufficient common sense, i.e., reality testing, not to lose herself in speculative mystical ideas.

The ego regression concomitant with the orgastic experience resulted in a grandiose expansion of the ego and in a fusion of the self with the omnipotent, phallic mother and the admired paternal phallus, this gave rise to the patient's enhanced self-esteem, but went hand in hand with a permanent disturbance of object relations. It seems to me that the essentially unshakable narcissistic foundation of her character could be attributed, despite all her feelings of guilt, to this heightened self-esteem which was linked up with the experience of infantile orgasm.

I am aware that infantile sexual excitation does not always lead to feelings of omnipotence. I believe that the particular character of the fantasy, and especially the greater or lesser admixture of aggression against

the objects, which may turn back destructively upon
the self, determine whether feelings of grandeur or of
annihilation will preponderate. In the case of this patient, the feeling of grandeur was combined with an
intense sense of guilt, with a fear of being unable to
love, of being homosexual or evil, and with a feeling of
being damaged by the recoiling hatred toward her
hypocritical parents. However, these guilty feelings did
not impair the patient's productivity.

Her impressive sublimatory achievements were
based on intact reality testing; fostered by the ecstatic
experience, they became the most important thing in
her life. The decisive difference between the grandiose
feeling of this patient and the wish to be a "genius,"
in the case mentioned before, might be described as
the presence or absence of objective contents. Her ecstasies related to "thought," to "concepts," to "the
world," whereas the first patient was concerned exclusively with his own person and stature.

His fantasy was, so to speak, more primitively narcissistic than hers. On the other hand, it was precisely
the excitation, the "illumination," which made her
thinking so rich and productive. It would seem that in
favorable cases, under the influence of excitation, inhibitions are abolished, more ideas are conceived, a productivity springs up which flourishes only under these
particular conditions. It is as though the excitation
supplied fuel whose energy can be used for other, nonsexual purposes. Speaking in general, this compound of
sexual and substantive motives seems to be one of the
most decisive factors in creative achievements, and the
most important prerequisite for productivity.

The patient's admiration for father and brother,

and—probably stemming from a very early time—her love for the mother, outweighed the ambivalence toward the latter which developed later. These positive elements enabled her to establish interests in ideas like the father's and brother's, and a similar mode of thought; her capacity for theoretical thinking was connected with this. Thus, in spite of everything, love prevailed over aggression. It is *always* the solidity of object relations and identifications that determines the reliability of the sense of reality and of reality testing. In this case it also caused the grandiose feeling to preponderate over the negative influence of the feeling of guilt.

In both patients the guilt and inferiority feelings, on one hand, and those of grandeur, on the other, were mutually opposing concomitants and corollaries of masturbation. It is interesting to note also that in the second patient, the elevated self-esteem arose from identification with an idealized, infantile love object. However, as I have shown, in her this identification had led to a true ego identification and not merely to a narcissistic fantasy. To attempt an examination of the fundamental difference between these two structures would overstep the limits of my topic. At any rate, an excess of guilt feelings, which is indicative of particularly intense aggression, is unfavorable to the development of stable ego identifications. Likewise decisive is the greater or lesser faculty for sublimation. It seems likely that elements not entirely comprehensible to analysis, such as intelligence, endowment, and constitutional disposition, play a substantial role.

The orgastic experience evidently is of great moment also in the self-esteem of normal persons, who have progressed from masturbation to object-directed sexual activity. Several factors contribute to its importance. First, the physiological effect of periodic tension reductions through sexual gratification obviates the need for neurotic regressive reactions to dammed-up tension that cannot be discharged. The second is a rise of self-esteem based on the perception of one's satisfactory, normal sexual functioning. Furthermore, in most instances, there is a feeling of being loved or desired by the partner. But besides all this there are often normal regressive trends, so to speak, in the orgastic experience.

We expect that the normal sexual act of the adult proceeds without fantasies, and that the content of consciousness, in so far as it exists, revolves around the partner. But also the sexuality of the normal person has a prehistory of masturbation fantasies. Frequently, a residue of this prehistory may be preserved, that is to say, a residue of that fantasy world. With the orgastic modification of mental activity, ecstasylike phenomena may appear which are often plainly characterized by specific residues of old masturbation fantasies. Viewed in this way, the orgastic experience is essentially a narcissistic process. At the moment of highest excitement, the object and reality vanish, so to speak, and an ancient longing for fusion with the object, for disappearance of the ego boundaries, is fulfilled. This fulfillment is marked by a fleeting sense of omnipotence. The process concludes with the normal sequel of the act, natural sinking into sleep which represents a temporary regression to primary narcissism.

Normally this temporary, narcissistic regression leaves no traces behind; neither does the nightly regression into sleep, as such. But I am inclined to think that the rare phenomenon of infantile orgasm leaves indelible traces in the whole personality, most important among them, a narcissistic, grandiose foundation of personality structure.

16

Special Types of Resistance in Training Analysis

(1965)

T HE TOPIC of training analysis has been discussed over and over again during the last few years. The opinion has been expressed by many, including Anna Freud, that training analysis presents *insurmountable* obstacles, creates *insurmountable* defenses, and is therefore a practically impossible endeavor, doomed to failure. I am in disagreement with this view; I think the difficulties are widely overrated.

To be sure, institute procedures should be reduced or redesigned so as to minimize interference. Written reports by the training analyst, in particular, should be kept to a minimum, and information about contents of analyses should be eliminated as completely as feasible. When serious problems endanger the positive outcome of a candidate's analysis, perhaps a discussion should take place with the chairman of the educational committee or student committee (or whatever the competent authority may be called), in order to arrive at necessary decisions. Otherwise, only routine reports on the prog-

Presented at the Annual Meeting of the American Psychoanalytic Association, New York, May 1965.

ress of the analysis should be given. Such reports would not need to be kept secret from the student; rather, they should be worked through in the analysis, and should be acceptable to him as a part of reality. One can work with this, as with anything else.

Of course, there are many factors which complicate the training situation, and which appear to be completely rational. For example, highly competitive attitudes may prevail toward the analyst as well as toward the student's own peers, who are, after all, his competitors. This is understandable. The student is in the same field as the analyst and is vying with his fellow students. His future career does, to a degree, depend on his analyst. It seems quite rational that the student may be very concerned with the analyst's judgment and evaluation of his person. A student may be exposed to his analyst as a teacher in class, he may know too much of the analyst's private life, to mention only a few of the many situations which may arise. In general, our students are, in a way, put into a grade-school position in the institutes, which many of them obviously resent. All these, and many more, are reality factors which have to be watched and carefully brought up in the analysis. Since the analyst meets the student more frequently outside the analysis than the ordinary patient, he must make sure that these encounters are worked through, lest they become unanalyzed resistances. The numerous facts which the student knows about the analyst must equally be brought up and analyzed. They do become serious obstacles if not dealt with. One also has to be aware of the student's frequent attempts to identify with the analyst: with his special ideas and interests, his behavior, his particular analytic technique. These flattering identifications should not be accepted at face value. They always cover some other, deeper analytic content which has to be understood. The analyst must not allow himself to be seduced into accepting them without attempting to analyze them. They reflect important transference elements and give valuable clues to character and personality development. Such identifications, by the way, are to be found not only in students. They can be seen quite frequently also in patients who come for therapeutic analysis. The training and learning situation merely provides a solid rationalization for them.

In general, I would say, it is certainly true that manifold reality factors play a disturbing role in training analysis. But when such reactions are particularly disturbing, one can be certain that these reality factors also become the expression of special problems of the specific individual; that is to say, the apparent reality problems are only being used to conceal deeper ones. It is precisely when the complications of a training analysis present inordinate obstacles, which seem to be insurmountable, that they constitute only superficial screens hiding the real problems. This is the main point which I want to stress. The apparently realistic factors, to which inordinate importance is attributed, are used for the expression of deep-seated transference problems or the defense against them. The most important features of the particular individual, serious character difficulties or thinly disguised neurotic symptoms, thus emerge in the guise of seemingly rational reactions to the training situation. If one has occasion to analyze the same person after conclusion of his training analysis, one can see quite frequently that the basic personality is not essentially different without these handy rationalizations and externalizations.

The purpose of these rationalizations is obvious. Emotional and irrational elements need not be faced when they can be understood as "rational" responses to the training situation, i.e., to outside reality. It is the task of the training analyst to recognize such behavior as resistance and not to be fooled by the reality situation, but to find the transference element behind the frequently well integrated façade of resistance.

A general example is the ubiquitous, "understandable" attitude of the student who wishes to show himself from his best, most brilliant side and endeavors to display all his intellectual faculties. Behind this, one will often discern the reluctance to reveal his "deficiencies," his infantile libidinal and aggressive fantasies, on which he avoids focusing.

Of course this is a very elementary example. It shows, nevertheless, that in an analysis nothing is simply "understandable" and exists, so to speak, only in one layer. In the analytic situation, with a student as with an ordinary patient, everything is under the impact of transference. One must not overlook that in the training situation, in the special circumstances given by the institute, transference may often be split. Adviser, teacher, and supervisor can be the recipients of certain transference aspects, particularly when there are deeper reasons to keep these aspects out of the analysis. Not infrequently, conflicts with supervisors and critical attitudes toward them express negative feelings toward the analyst. This is not meant to deny that critical attitudes toward supervisors are realistic sometimes, but the intensity of feeling originates most frequently in the analytic situation as such.

One of the salient differences between the training analysis and the usual therapeutic one can be found in the different motivations with which students and ordinary patients come to analysis. The patient usually has an awareness of his pathology, for which he needs treatment, whereas the student, at least consciously, comes for the purpose of training. The essential motivating factor in his case may be scientific psychological interest, or a wish to understand and help other people, and similar reasons. But it may also be of a more narcissistic nature, and there may be various ulterior motives, such as prestige, social position, financial expediency, etc. There is usually a good deal of intellectual knowledge about psychoanalysis, acquired through previous hospital training or reading. This frequently represents one of the major obstacles to effective work in analysis. For many students it is not easy to break through the wall between intellectual, theoretical knowledge and emotional experience, to reach fully intuitive self-awareness and eventually to uncover memories.

Intellectual knowledge thus often serves as the most tenacious resistance, and is used for narcissistic and other secondary gratifications. As we know, this holds true not only for our students in training, but also for persons in a variety of related fields, such as teachers, psychologists, social workers, and so on. Many people, especially if they suffer from obsessional neurosis or obsessional character problems, are driven to read psychoanalytic literature—driven by the need *to cure themselves*. The half-knowledge being spread by all kinds of lectures and college courses may often be used in the same way. I remember a young patient who was a student in one of the fashionable girls' colleges, where they "studied" *The Interpretation of Dreams* for one week. She was very much helped by this to substantiate her resistances. In short, intellectualization is rather a ubiquitous form of resistance, in others as well as in candidates.

The essential difference lies elsewhere. It has to do with the difference in motivation, which I just mentioned, and a difference of goals. The future analyst does not look predominantly for cure, but wants to become capable of analyzing others. He wants to learn not only to understand the unconscious of others, but also to respond to it in a specific way. He has to acquire the particular attitude which we call "free-floating attention." He also must develop the special combination of intuitive understanding and ability to remain uninvolved emotionally, which is the most important precondition for functioning as an analyst. But in order to fulfill the difficult demands which his future analytic work will dictate, the student must meet certain criteria of suitability. Among the most important of these we consider the capacity for being in contact with his own unconscious and the ability to face himself honestly. "Know thyself" is, so to speak, the basic rule as far as the analyst is concerned. Intellectualization as a resistance shows that this prerequisite for becoming a good analyst is lacking. Candidates who persist in intellectualization do not want, or are unable, to replace intellectual knowledge about themselves with real self-knowledge. They are incapable of probing beyond their intellectual understanding and the surface of good functioning. Tenacious resistance against real introspection and genuine analytic experience is often deeply rooted in a need to hold on to one's "normalcy" at all costs. Such a candidate feels his "normalcy" threatened and therefore has to perpetuate the attitude that infantile, neurotic behavior can be found only in others, but not in himself; in this way, he can feel superior.

It has been frequently asked whether a "normal" person can be analyzed. This question seems to me based on a wrong assumption. Who is completely normal? Even the so-called normal person has an unconscious, has dreams, makes a slip occasionally, produces a transference, has fantasies, and so on. If approach to fantasies, to childhood in general, is completely shut off, if there are no fantasies, if one's inner life is completely "rational," one can suspect that free communication with one's own unconscious is blocked, that this degree of "normalcy" is a rigid defense—and a defense which does not promise any particular suitability for the psychoanalytic profession. The narcissistic cathexis of one's own perfect functioning, intellectually and otherwise, seems to be connected with a tendency to project undesirable qualities onto the outside, onto others, which necessarily must result in all kinds of difficulties with respect to the ability to analyze. In general, we may say: *who cannot be analyzed, cannot analyze others and should not become an analyst.*

For instance, if a student does not get over the feeling that analysis represents an insurmountable homosexual danger, to which he cannot "give himself" because this would mean intolerable submission, how can one expect that he will be able to analyze others? Such resistances are not inherent in the training situation, but they indicate that this particular student lacks the most important attributes which would make him suitable to become an analyst. Students who cannot stand the complications of the training analysis are often merely people who cannot be analyzed, and these complications serve only as rationalizations.

I am afraid that in this respect I am much stricter than many of my colleagues. I would say that the difficulty does not arise from a specific complication of training analysis, but from the simple fact that not every bright young man, who for some reason wants to be a psychoanalyst, is fit for this complicated kind of work. Not infrequently, one discovers, in bright students who find the training situation unbearable, a more serious pathology of narcissistic (e.g., paranoid) nature.

Weigert (1965) gives an impressive description of the social influences of a certain milieu in which our students quite frequently find themselves. Such a student has worked himself up from a very limited background. He has become the one who is destined to fulfill the frustrated hopes of his parents, and has concentrated upon himself not only his own narcissistic images, but those of the whole family. At the same time, he is plagued by guilt feelings with regard to his less successful siblings, and with regard to his shame and contempt for his background. Dr. Weigert convincingly describes the impact of this situation. Such individuals have a strong need to hold on to their "elevated" personality and their "normalcy." The wish to become an analyst is often not based upon genuine interest, but on the need to live up to narcissistic fantasies which emanate from their social background. Their resistances can be understood as the result of their past, and are so rigid that they cannot be breached. Such and similar complications and resistances sometimes cause the training analyst to become too involved with a particular candidate, and to feel overly concerned that the institute might refuse to graduate this student.

This sentiment illustrates very clearly one of the most important problems, not of the training analysis, but of the training analyst. Indeed, the training analyst is faced with two contradictory goals. He must seek to help and cure his patient, yet he is under obligation to his institute to train and prepare a suitable person to become an analyst. In the situation just described, is it likely that the training analyst will be able to promote in a young man the development of those faculties which are prerequisites for becoming a good analyst? Students who could not be analyzed—not because they were in training analysis, but because they were not analyzable—often are graduated, although they should not be. To graduate these people is a disservice not only to their future patients and to our profession as a whole, but even to them. They will not be successful in their work and, in the long run, they will not be happy in it. Discontented, they will look for shortcuts and invent new deviations in analytic theory and practice; they will discredit our science, and will distort and dilute it. Not even from a practical standpoint are they being helped by their graduation. There are many fields of psychiatry today where one need not work with one's unconscious, where one can succeed without being so deeply analyzed. Persons who are not analyzable might be able to do much better in such areas as drug therapy, psychotherapy, and the like. They would be happier that way, more highly esteemed, and financially more successful. Thus our pity for the student whom we dare not drop is really misplaced.

To sum up, I would like to stress again that the much-discussed negative elements of training analysis can often be revealed as inherent resistances of the particular individual. Our students are human beings, after all. When such defenses cannot be breached, it is not due to the training situation, but frequently means that the student in question cannot be analyzed. Of course it is possible that a particular training analyst may fail in a special case where another may succeed, but very often the second one comes to the same result as the first. In general, we should not lose sight of the fact that the training analysis presents particular problems not for the student, but for the training analyst who often finds himself in conflict over his twofold task of helping a human being and fulfilling his duty toward his profession.

17

Empathy
and Countertransference

(1966)

M ANY YEARS ago, in a paper on countertransference
(1951, this volume), I described the process of
analytic understanding of the patient and his material
as a sudden momentary event, that comes not by deliberate, conscious thinking but like a sudden insight, a
sudden knowledge from within. Suddenly one compre-
hends.

The topic of this paper is to bring together what is
known about this process of sudden understanding and
also to investigate factors that interfere with comprehension.

Analytic understanding obviously is based on insight
emerging from the analyst's unconscious. This process
has been, for a long time, the focus of interest of many
analysts, who tried to analyze the mechanism of analytic comprehension; but there are still many open
questions. Freud himself, Ferenczi, Deutsch, Sharpe,
Fliess, Fenichel, Reik, and others made important contributions to this problem.

Freud (1912), in his paper "Recommendations to

Physicians Practising Psycho-Analysis," has pointed out the most essential preconditions for analytic understanding. The analyst is supposed to listen to the free associations with "evenly-suspended attention" (p. 111).

He should withhold all conscious influences from his capacity to attend, and give himself over completely to his "unconscious memory" [p. 112].
. . . the most successful cases are those in which one proceeds, as it were, without any purpose in view, allows oneself to be taken by surprise by any new turn in them. . . . The correct behaviour for an analyst lies in swinging over according to need from the one mental attitude [free-floating attention] to the other [intellectual evaluation], in avoiding speculation or brooding over cases while they are in analysis, and in submitting the material obtained to a synthetic process of thought only after the analysis is concluded [p. 114].

This is intended to create for the doctor a counterpart to the "fundamental rule of psycho-analysis" which is laid down for the patient. Just as the patient must relate everything that his self-observation can detect, and keep back all the logical and affective objections that seek to induce him to make a selection from among them, so the doctor must put himself in a position to make use of everything he is told for the purposes of interpretation and of recognizing the concealed unconscious material without substituting a censorship of his own for the selection that the patient has forgone. To put it in a formula: he must turn his own unconscious like a receptive organ towards the transmitting unconscious of the patient. He must adjust himself to the patient as a telephone receiver is adjusted to the transmitting microphone. Just as the receiver converts back into sound waves the electric oscillations in the telephone line which were set up by sound waves, so the doctor's unconscious is able, from the derivatives of the unconscious which are communicated to him, to reconstruct that unconscious, which has determined the patient's free associations.

But if the doctor is to be in a position to use his unconscious in this way as an instrument in the analysis, he must himself fulfill one psychological condition to a high degree. He may not tolerate any resistances in himself which hold back from his consciousness what has been perceived by his unconscious; otherwise he would introduce into the analysis a new species of selection and distortion. . . . It may be insisted, rather, that he should have undergone a psycho-analytic purification and have become aware of those complexes of his own which would be apt to interfere with his grasp of what the patient tells him [pp. 115, 116].

It is thus Freud's basic conviction that the analyst has to eliminate his own resistances by analysis in order to be able to have direct access to the unconscious of the patient. One could call this type of comprehension a special form of empathic understanding. Freud stressed that the analyst's personal conflicts would interfere with comprehension.

Many of Freud's later followers have tried to work out these problems in detail. Deutsch (1926), in a paper on "Occult Processes Occurring during Psychoanalysis," states that in analyzing the patient's transference, the analyst identifies simultaneously with the patient and the latter's object. The analyst thus experiences in himself the patient's impulses towards and against the object and the object's response toward and against the patient. These identifications have to be relinquished after a short time and exposed to intellectual evaluation by the analyst. She mentions that if the material touches too much the analyst's personal conflicts, these identifications may become "stuck." This is one of the mechanisms of what we call countertransference. I will come back to this point later.

Fliess (1942), in a brilliant paper, "The Metapsychology of the Analyst," stresses that the analyst recognizes in himself the patient's instinctual material and conflicts, which he has acquired by "transient identification." He believes that analytic understanding is based on the analyst's self-observation. The ego's capacity for perception is increased by a cathectic shift from the superego to the ego, the cathexis becoming free as the superego gives up resistances against insights into the own conflicts. The "transient identification," which is an emotional experience, has to be of short duration and has to be replaced by reprojection of the material onto the patient. The analyst has to become the observing, evaluating, analyzing outsider again.

Thus it has been stressed that an oscillation between intuitive understanding and an evaluating, intellectual attitude has to take place. This oscillation represents an essential element of analytic comprehension.

Kohut, in his (1966) paper, on "Forms and Transformations of Narcissism," and in his earlier (1959) paper on "Introspection, Empathy and Psychoanalysis," sees empathy as a primitive form of communication or outcome of the feeling of oneness of the infant with the mother, a primitive form of feeling to which one regresses in specific situations, for instance under the impact of a crowd situation and also when analyzing. A healthy, not too rigid ego can return to this primitive form of communication at will. Elasticity of the ego as an important precondition for the ability to analyze was already stressed by Ferenczi (1919).

Schafer (1959) believes that empathy is based on the fact that the analyst at some time or other also felt like the patient, that the analyst can understand only what he has felt himself at some time. I believe this to be a too limited approach.

It is the essence of empathy that something which is not directly inherent in the own experience and history can also be understood. As early as 1937, Reik, in his book, *Surprise and the Analyst,* pointed out that the analyst, for a moment, experiences a change of personality. He *becomes* the patient and thus is able to perceive for himself what he might have felt and done in the patient's place. This becoming the patient is based not only on the patient's verbal communications, but also on all the little expressive movements, alterations in tone of voice, change of tonus, which represent nonverbal expressions of what is going on in the patient's mind.

Fenichel pointed out that observation of the patient's expressive movements *(Ausdrucksbewegungen)* helps the analyst to experience the same emotions. He feels the impulse to repeat the same movements, and understands their meaning with his own body. This is an important source of analytic understanding.

Thus, the mechanism of analytic understanding is not seen by all investigators in the same way. Deutsch, Fliess, and Fenichel conceive of it as a temporary identification; Reik sees it as temporarily becoming the patient, stressing that this process is to be differentiated from identification, though it is obviously very much related. Kohut sees empathic understanding as a regression to a primitive form of communication. Freud, himself, pointed out that the analyst's unconscious, when he is tuned in with a patient and free from his own resistances, can make immediate contact with the derivatives of the patient's unconscious which are presented to him, his own unconscious serving as an "analytic instrument."

Isakower takes up this idea and speaks of a "near-identical constellation with the patient." He stresses that this "analytic instrument" is something quite specific, not to be confused with usual empathy and not based on identification. He believes that by paying special attention to the ways and means of functioning of this "instrument," its acuity can be sharpened. Thus, its use is teachable. He shows that the analyst's reaction to the material, when he is deeply immersed in the process of analyzing, when he is listening "with evenly hovering attention," frequently shows signs of thinking closer to that of the unconscious. To be specific: words frequently give way to visual images. Isakower refers here to Freud (1900), who, in *The Interpretation of Dreams,* brings out that thoughts that emerge in a state that is close to the unconscious, such as falling asleep, tend to be transformed into visual images, just as in dreams. Paying attention to these images increases the analyst's comprehension of what is going on in his "analytic instrument," and betters his understanding of the patient.

In a verbal communication, Isakower (1963) related a convincing example of such an interaction between patient and analyst by giving a report of a supervision hour in which the student analyst suddenly visualized, in connection with a dream of the patient, the inscrutable smile of the Mona Lisa. When this was transmitted to the patient, a great deal of relevant, new material came to light. This image thus served like an interpretation that confirms its correctness by stimulation of new material. In this way, we obtain proof that the analyst was tuned in with the patient and that his association was not an intrusion of private material of his own that was unrelated to the patient.

What is relevant in Isakower's method is that these images are produced by that part of the analyst's unconscious that belongs to the special conflicts of the patient. The analyst who is open to response can be expected to produce the right material. It may not always be easy, though, to become aware of the special modes of functioning of this analytic instrument, and it may be hard to understand. Others believe that the analyst can be too entangled in conflicts of his own, that he may be distracted and his images may not be patient-centered.

Ross and Kapp (1962), misunderstanding Isakower's method, believe that the images emerging in the analyst are not the most important tool for analytic understanding, but represent a distracting preoccupation with the analyst's own conflicts—the countertransference—which should be recognized and transmitted to the patient.

All investigators agree that the tool for understanding is to be found in the derivatives of the analyst's own unconscious. Whether the analyst's associations to and images of the patient's material represent just a resonance in the therapist which promotes comprehension or are motivated by the turning loose of unrelated private concerns is not always easy to distinguish. Therefore, there is confusion between empathy and countertransference.

Arlow (1963) shows that the impact of the patient's material may lead not to images, but to a kind of imitative identification with the patient. This came to the fore during supervision. Consciously, the student analyst did not know what was going on, but he suddenly behaved like the patient by imitating her way of speaking. Thus it became obvious that, in deeper layers of his mind, he had responded. According to Isakower, his analytic instrument used this imitation of the patient as a hard-to-understand language. This nonverbal expression had to be pointed out to the therapist by the supervisor. It did not lead to immediate comprehension. This is in contrast to what Reik and Fenichel postulate, although the latter speak only of reacting to the patient's expressive movements which represent a trial innervation as a reaction to the observed. The analyst, following them, can feel what he would have felt if he had made the same expressive movement. It seems to be that this way of understanding is based on the saving of cathexis, which comes about when the motion is not performed in reality. In this way, the cathexis of the action which is not executed can be used up in intellectual understanding. Arlow's candidate had to have his behavior pointed out to him. It may be more difficult to realize, and to confront oneself with, one's own performed action that with an imagined one, or with images.

Arlow presents a second case in which the student analyst identifies with the patient's instinctual strivings and symbolically acts out the patient's fellatio fantasy by suddenly giving his supervisor a cigarette. Here, Arlow speaks of sharing the patient's fantasies.

Arlow's example may be useful to point out the difference between empathy and countertransference. As it was stressed, analytic understanding always occurs with the help of the analyst's own unconscious. Whether this instrument can work properly or not is dependent on special conditions. The analyst has to be tuned in with the patient; he has to be in a state of resonance, where something in him is just touched and responds in such a way that inner awareness and comprehension is possible. The translation of this "echo" may not always be easy. If, for private reasons, the analyst's receiving apparatus is too charged with his private problems, too many conflicts will be mobilized, too many inner resistances stirred up, or some instinctual impulses too near to breakthrough will threaten. The result, then, will not be a signal useful for analytic understanding in the form of immediate insight, spontaneous association, or visual image; instead, some form of positive or negative (resistive) acting out or blocking, leading to failure to understand, will emerge. It seems to me that Arlow's second case belongs to this latter category; the student is motivated by countertransference.

Implicit in the countertransference, there is always a tendency to act out. Just as the expressions of transference, unless the patient learns in analysis to sublimate them into self-observation and understanding, exert an imperative pressure toward acting out, likewise, countertransference pushes the analyst to act out in a positive or negative way. These impulses or conflicts are not sublimated into comprehension. They are not charged with only minimal cathexis, but carry the full charge of repressed impulses suddenly bursting out from the depth. Thus, they lead either to real action, to overstrong emotion, or to the opposite, to rigid defenses or blank spots.

Countertransference may be caused by the patient's transference, by special material, by the patient as a person or the analytic situation as a whole. Feelings and conflicts are stirred up in the analyst, which are always related to persons in the analyst's past. The analyst's working ego, the comprehending, analyzing ego, becomes disturbed and malfunctioning. There are innumerable forms of countertransference, and the analyst does not always respond with the simplest one. He does not necessarily return love for love and hate for hate, nor does he respond with the opposite emotions and defenses against them. More frequently, we find identifications with the patient in which, as Helene Deutsch puts it, the analyst is "stuck." Often the analyst is not free of transference feelings of his own, not only to his infantile objects, but to their later representative, his former analyst. It is as though he felt: "I shall" or "I shall not treat you [the patient] as my former analyst treated me." To give an example, he might think: "My former analyst did not permit me to divorce my wife. I shall push you [the patient], into the opposite direction; I shall, on the contrary, encourage you to divorce your spouse." I remember, for instance, a former analyst-patient who came to a second analysis because he regularly fell in love with his women patients. It turned out that he had not worked through his homosexual attachment to his former male analyst. In identification with his women patients, he wanted to be loved now by a male analyst, by himself. He was identified with his former analyst.

Blank spots frequently reflect the feeling that the patient mirrors the analyst's unacceptable conflicts. It is as though the analyst felt: "Here, but for the grace of God, go I," whereupon he becomes angry, bored, sleepy, fails to understand, or experiences vague anxiety.

One should not overlook, though, that the failure to understand is by no means always a symptom of countertransference. Particularly when teaching, one should not overlook the fact that one is not born with a complete knowledge of psychoanalysis, that such knowledge has to be acquired by learning and experience. Frequently it is not countertransference that should be pointed out to students, but lacking instruction that should be given.

I have in the past tried to distinguish between acute and chronic countertransference. I now believe this is not altogether correct. The chronic attitudes, not stirred up by something specific to the case, represent neurotic behavior patterns not solved in the previous analysis. They occur not only when analyzing, but in many life situations, and should not be considered countertransference. For instance, many narcissistic patterns belong here, such as narcissistic overvaluation of patients, using them for purely narcissistic purposes, e.g., allaying one's guilt or anxiety or proving one's abilities by magically curing and being able to understand everything, even when the objective basis for comprehension does not yet exist. I shall not attempt to enumerate all the possible faulty patterns which would represent the whole range of neurotic behavior in the analyst.

Acute countertransference is based on special situations. I remember, for instance, the case of an analyst who was plagued, during a certain hour, by a toothache. On this day, he became angry˙about the oral, demanding attitude of a patient, which otherwise did not disturb him. This day the threshold of the analyst's tolerance was lowered. The analytic material may touch on some specific problem of the analyst and he becomes overemotional. I remember, for instance, a young analyst who was suddenly struck by a resemblance between a patient with paranoid behavior patterns and the analyst's own nagging mother. Without realizing what was going on, the analyst fell out of his analytic role, became intensely impatient, and reacted with anger.

In all relevant situations, the intensity of conflict interferes with understanding. Sublimation fails. Real action, overstrong emotion, misunderstanding, blocking, etc., occur. Where minimal amounts of energy should lead to thought, that is, to trial action, real action occurs. Real identification takes place instead of trial identification. The "analytic instrument" fails to function correctly because it is overwhelmed by inner conflict. In such situations, the analyst's associations will refer only to himself and not to the patient.

Of course, one must not forget that the analyst for

the patient, as well as the patient for the analyst, is not only a transference or a countertransference object, but also a real one. For instance, the analyst may like or dislike a patient; this is by no means always a matter of countertransference. The patient is not always a replica of a person in the analyst's past. I remember, for instance, a woman patient who was especially loud, aggressive, used vulgar language, and in general behaved like a fishwife. She certainly was not very likeable. Only after the deeper meaning of this behavior emerged and the whole transference significance of this pattern became understandable did the rudeness cease to matter. In general, the analyst's dislike of a patient does not interfere with his understanding unless repressed elements in the analyst reverberate. When comprehension is reached, these superficial responses of dislike are usually eliminated.

Unless there are special reasons for the contrary, the analyst is usually interested in and likes the patient with whom he is working. The analyst, after all, spends many hours with him, and becomes aware of the patient's conflicts and difficulties; the patient becomes the object of the analyst's efforts and is thus the center of certain narcissistic interests of the analyst. Unless his liking is based on real countertransferences and, therefore, becomes unduly intense, it is, I believe, a completely natural occurrence.

While it is true that absolute, mirrorlike neutrality does not exist, the rule of abstinence should apply to both analyst and patient.[1] This does not mean the analyst's real personality has to be denied or hidden

[1] See also Reich (1951, 1960), this volume.

completely, which is impossible. The Balints (1939) pointed out that every analyst brings certain realities to the analytic situation, such his mode of talking, interpreting, furnishing of his office, and so on. All these things will and should come into the analysis, at some time; they should not be taboo. If it is made possible to speak about them, they do not matter very much, or may even contribute important material to the analysis. One also should keep in mind that not everything the patient says about the analyst is transference; it may be reality, too. But even reality may be used for transference purposes. Exaggerated aloofness from the patient constitutes a prohibition to the patient to think about the analyst in reality, and represents a kind of countertransference.

There is recently a trend to treat countertransference not as a disturbance that should be avoided as much as possible, but as something that occurs unfailingly and of which particular use should be made, as it is, for instance, expressed in the paper by Ross and Kapp (1962). Particularly those groups which cannot accept transference as the reliving of feelings and impulses that originally belonged to infantile objects, but who believe that interpersonal relations and reactions to current emotions are manifested in the transference, believe in the positive value of countertransference. One should not only recognize and analyze it, but also inform the patient of its occurrence and its contents. In this way, they believe, the analyst becomes human. I firmly believe that this means burdening the patient with extraneous material that will interfere with the development of his transference and the spontaneous progress of his analysis, to say the least.

Of course, it happens that one makes a slip, an error in the bill, a mistake in time, that one forgets some of the patient's material, or makes an error in interpretation. Such things should be admitted freely, but I do not see any reason why the patient should analyze the analyst. The analyst, however, should try to see for himself what is behind his parapraxis.

The one who is most vociferous about countertransference is neither a Horneyite nor a Sullivanite, but a Kleinian. Margaret Little (1951, 1957) sees analysis as the mutual reflection of the patient and the analyst in a kind of mirror, which the unconscious of each of them is presenting to the other.

The idea that the analysis of the countertransference should be used as a tool for understanding is based on the idea that any response of the analyst is a proper response to what is emerging from the unconscious of the patient, and by understanding the response one can always grasp what is going on in the patient, as though every response were typical and revealed the content of the patient's unconscious. For instance, Racker (1953) believes that any patient of the same sex as the analyst represents the parent of the same sex, and any patient of the other sex, the other parent. Accordingly, what played out is always the Oedipus complex, and one can figure out, like following a multiplication table, what is going on in countertransference and in transference. This is sheerest mythology and much too schematic.

One cannot deduce from the emotion the analyst is feeling, what is going on in the patient. The analyst's anger cannot be understood as just the "natural" response to aggressive impulses in the patient. The patient's violence may be pseudo aggression, by which he wants to provoke punishment. There is no simple translation from the analyst's emotion to the concealed meaning of what takes place in the patient. On the contrary, any strong emotion of the analyst will confuse the picture.

It was pointed out that comprehension is acquired via direct contact between the patient's productions and the analyst's receiving instrument, or by transient identification. It seems to be quite different when the analyst is disturbed by his own inner conflicts. Any strong emotion is a sign that the "receiving instrument" is contaminated. The analyst's response will then be too specific, too personal, too private; it will not be patient-centered but too much concerned with himself, and will make correct understanding impossible. A misunderstanding that is typical only for himself will take place. At worst, direct action will occur. Then the analyst's response is not only awareness of what the patient feels and what he means, but the analyst is carried away by very specific reactions to his own individual past which need in no way correspond to the patient's past.

To give an example of the misuse of countertransference which was reported to me recently: an analyst became annoyed about the patient leaving the door open. He understood this as the patient's impulse to manipulate him, to which the therapist reacted with anger for reasons of his own. But the need to leave the door open was based on claustrophobic fears of the patient. The analyst's emotional reaction thus was completely inadequate; he reacted to something in himself and not in the patient. His reaction distracted the patient from what would have emerged spontaneously, and disrupted the natural sequence of events.

As to dealing with countertransference, I have nothing new to say. An analyst has to be constantly watchful and discover his own countertransferences and try to use some self-analysis in order to cope with them. In case of need, he should go into analysis himself when he becomes aware of some undue involvement, preferably before he has acted out with the patient. If he first gives in to countertransference wishes and later sends his patient to another analyst, I am afraid the second analysis begins under unfortunate circumstances.

To sum up, there is an essential difference between the empathic use of one's unconscious and acting out in countertransference. Empathic understanding represents an ego activity, while countertransference is based on the breakthrough of id impulses which have to be warded off with more or less neurotic defenses. Whether it is possible to transform these impulses into comprehension, which is a real sublimation, seems to depend on quantitative factors. The analyst's emotions, impulses, or defenses must not be too strong. The possibility of gliding from a controlled, aim-directed use of one's unconscious, into being run by it, is always there. Who is so free of guilt that he may throw the first stone?

References

Abraham, K. (1924), A short study of the development of the libido, viewed in the light of mental disorders. In: *Selected Papers of Karl Abraham*. New York: Basic Books, 1953, pp. 418–501.

Alexander, F. (1956), *Psychoanalysis and Psychotherapy*. New York: Norton.

Arlow, J. A. (1963), The supervisory situation. *J. Amer. Psychoanal. Assn.*, 11:576–594.

Balint, A. (1936), Handhabung der Ubertragung auf Grund der Ferenczischen Versuche. *Internat. Zeitschr. Psychoanal.*, 22:47–58.

———— & Balint, M. (1939), On transference and countertransference. *Internat. J. Psycho-Anal.* 20:223–230.

Benedek, T. (1953), Dynamics of the countertransference. *Bull. Menninger Clin.*, 17:201–208.

Bibring, E. (1929), Klinische Beiträge zur Paranoiafrage. II. Ein Fall von Organprojektion. *Internat Zeitschr. Psychoanal.*, 15:44–66.

———— (1953), The mechanism of depression. In: *Affective Disorders*, ed. P. Greenacre. New York: International Universities Press, pp. 13–48.

Brunswick, Ruth Mack (1940), The preoedipal phase of the libido development. *Psychoanal. Quart.*, 9:293–319.

Cohen, M. B. (1952), Countertransference and anxiety. *Psychiat.*, 15:231–243.

Crowley, R. M. (1952), Human reactions of analysts to patients. *Samiksa*, 6:212–219.

References

Deutsch, H. (1926), Occult processes occurring during psychanalysis. In: *Psychoanalysis and the Occult*, ed. G. Devereux. New York: International Universities Press, 1953, pp. 133–146.

———— (1927), Uber Zufriedenheit, Glück, und Ekstase. *Internat. Zeitschr. Psychoanal.*, 13:410–419.

———— (1942), Some forms of emotional disturbances and their relationship to schizophrenia. In: *Neuroses and Character Types*. New York: International Universities Press, 1965, pp. 262–281.

Eissler, K. R. (1953), The effect of the structure of the ego on psychoanalytic technique. *J. Amer. Psychoanal. Assn.*, 104–143.

———— (1958), Remarks on some variations in psychoanalytic technique. *Internat. J. Psycho-Anal.*, 39:222–229.

Federn, P. (1928), Die Wiener Diskussion aus dem Jahre 1912. *Zeitschr. psychoanal. Pädagogik*, 2:106–112.

—–—— (1952), *Ego Psychology and the Psychoses*. New York: Basic Books.

Fenichel, O. (1926), Identification. In: *The Collected Papers of Otto Fenichel*, 1:97–112, New York: Norton, 1953.

———— (1928), Organ libidinization accompanying the defense against drives. In: *The Collected Papers of Otto Fenichel*, 1:128–146. New York: Norton, 1953.

———— (1931), The pregenital antecedents of the Oedipus complex. *Internat. J. Psycho-Anal.*, 12:141–166.

———— (1936), The symbolic equation: girl=phallus. *Psychoanal. Quart.*, 18:303–324, 1949.

———— (1937), Early stages of ego development. In: *The Collected Papers of Otto Fenichel*, 2:25–48. New York: Norton, 1954.

———— (1938a), *Problems of Psychoanalytic Technique*. New York: Psychoanalytic Quarterly, 1941.

———— (1938b), Theoretical implications of the didactic analysis. Mimeographed Topeka, Kansas: Menninger Foundation, n.d.

———— (1939), Trophy and triumph. In: *The Collected Papers of Otto Fenichel*, 2:141–162. New York: Norton, 1954.

———— (1945), *The Psychoanalytic Theory of Neurosis*. New York: Norton.

References

Ferenczi, S. (1912), On onanism. In: Sex in Psychoanalysis. New York: Brunner, 1950, pp. 187–192.

────── (1913), Stages in the development of the sense of reality. In: *Sex in Psychoanalysis.* New York: Brunner, 1950, pp. 213–239.

────── (1919), On the technique of psychoanalysis. In: *Further Contributions to the Theory and Technique of Psycho-Analysis.* New York: Basic Books, 1952.

────── (1926), Organneurose und ihre Behandlung. In: *Bausteine zur Psychoanalyse,* 3:294–301. Bern: Huber, 1939.

────── (1927), The problem of termination of analysis. In: *Final Contributions to the Problems and Methods of Psychoanalysis.* New York: Basic Books, 1955, pp. 77–86.

Fliess, R. (1942), The metapsychology of the analyst. *Psychoanal. Quart.,* 11:211–227.

────── (1953), Countertransference and counteridentification. *J. Amer. Psychoanal. Assn.,* 1:268–284.

Freud, A. (1936) The ego and the mechanisms of defense. *The Writings of Anna Freud,* Vol. 2. New York: International Universities Press, 1966.

────── (1948), Certain types and stages of social maladjustment. In: *Searchlights on Delinquency,* ed. K. R. Eissler. New York: International Universities Press, pp. 193–204.

Freud, S. (1894), On the grounds for detaching a particular syndrome from neurasthenia under the description 'anxiety neurosis.' *Standard Edition,* 3:90–117. London: Hogarth Press, 1962.

────── (1900), The interpretation of dreams. *Standard Edition,* 4 & 5. London: Hogarth Press, 1953.

────── (1905a), Jokes and their relation to the unconscious. *Standard Edition,* 8. London: Hogarth Press, 1960.

────── (1905b), Three essays on the theory of sexuality. *Standard Edition,* 7:130–245. London: Hogarth Press, 1953.

────── (1908), Character and anal erotism. *Standard Edition,* 9:167–175. London: Hogarth Press, 1959.

────── (1909), Notes upon a case of obsessional neurosis. *Standard Edition,* 10:155–249. London: Hogarth Press, 1955.

────── (1910), The future prospects of psycho-analytic therapy. *Standard Edition,* 11:141–151. London: Hogarth Press, 1957.

References

_____ (1911), Psycho-analytic notes on an autobiographic account of a case of paranoia (dementia paranoides). *Standard Edition*, 12:9–82. London: Hogarth Press, 1958.

_____ (1912), Recommendations to physicians practising psychoanalysis. *Standard Edition*, 12:111–120. London: Hogarth Press, 1958.

_____ (1912a), Contributions to a discussion on masturbation. *Standard Edition*, 12:239–254. London: Hogarth Press, 1958.

_____ (1913), The disposition to obsessional neurosis. *Standard Edition*, 12:311–326. London: Hogarth Press, 1958.

_____ (1914), On narcissism: an introduction. *Standard Edition*, 14:73–102. London: Hogarth Press, 1957.

_____ (1915), Observations on transference-love (further recommendations on the technique of psycho-analysis III). *Standard Edition*, 12:157–171. London: Hogarth Press, 1958

_____ (1915–1917), Introductory lectures on psychoanalysis. *Standard Edition*, 15 & 16. London: Hogarth Press, 1963.

_____ (1917), Mourning and melancholia. *Standard Edition*, 14:243–258. London: Hogarth Press, 1957.

_____ (1921), Group psychology and the analysis of the ego. *Standard Edition*, 18:69–143. London: Hogarth Press, 1955.

_____ (1923), The ego and the id. *Standard Edition*, 19:12–66. London: Hogarth Press, 1961.

_____ (1924a), The loss of reality in neurosis and psychosis. *Standard Edition*, 19:182–187. London: Hogarth Press, 1961.

_____ (1924b), Neurosis and psychosis. *Standard Edition*, 19:149–153. London: Hogarth Press, 1961.

_____ (1926), Inhibitions, symptoms and anxiety. *Standard Edition*, 20:87–175. London: Hogarth Press, 1959.

_____ (1931), Female sexuality. *Standard Edition*, 21:225–243. London: Hogarth Press, 1961.

_____ (1933), New introductory lectures on psycho-analysis. *Standard Edition*, 22:5–182. London: Hogarth Press, 1964.

_____ (1937), Analysis terminable and interminable. *Standard Edition*, 23:216–253. London: Hogarth Press, 1964.

Frosch, J. (1952), *The Annual Survey of Psychoanalysis*, Vol. 3. New York: International Universities Press, 1956.

Gitelson, M. (1952), The emotional position of the analyst in the psychoanalytic situation. *Internat. J. Psycho-Anal.*, 33:1–10.

References

Glover, E. (1955), *The Technique of Psychoanalysis*. New York: International Universities Press.

Greenacre, P. (1947), Vision, headache and the halo. *Psychoanal. Quart.*, 16:177-194.

———— Ed. (1952), *Trauma, Growth and Personality*. New York: International Universities Press, 1969.

Hart, H. H. (1947a), Narcissistic equilibrium. *Internat. J. Psycho-Anal.*, 28:106-114.

———— (1947b), Problems of identification. *Psychiat. Quart.*, 21:274-293.

Hartmann, H. (1939), *Ego Psychology and the Problem of Adaptation*. New York: International Universities Press, 1958.

———— (1950), Comments on the psychoanalytic theory of the ego. In: *Essays on Ego Psychology*. New York: International Universities Press, 1965, pp. 113-141.

———— (1952), The mutual influences in the development of ego and id. In: *Essays on Ego Psychology*. New York: International Universities Press, 1965, pp. 155-181.

———— (1953), Contribution to the metapsychology of schizophrenia. In: *Essays of Ego Psychology*. New York: International Universities Press, 1965, pp. 182-206

———— (1955), Notes on the theory of sublimation. In: *Essays on Ego Psychology*. New York: International Universities Press, 1965, pp. 215-240.

———— (1960), *Psychoanalysis and Moral Values*. New York: International Universities Press.

———— Kris, E., & Loewenstein, R. M. (1949), Notes on the theory of aggression. *The Psychoanalytic Study of the Child*, 3/4:9-36. New York: International Universities Press.

Heimann, P. (1950), On countertransference. *Internat. J. Psycho-Anal.*, 31:81-84.

Isakower, O. (1963), Minutes of Faculty Meeting, New York Psychoanalytic Institute, Nov. 20, 1963.

Jacobson, E. (1947), Primary and secondary symptom formation in endogenous depression. Paper read at the Midwinter Meeting of the American Psychoanalytic Association, New York, December 16, 1947.

———— (1953), Contribution to the metapsychology of cyclothymic depression. In: *Affective Disorders*, ed. P. Greenacre. New York: International Universities Press, pp. 49–83.

———— (1954a), Contribution to the metapsychology of psychotic identifications. *J. Amer. Psychoanal. Assn.*, 2:239–262.

———— (1954b), The self and the object world: vicissitudes of their infantile cathexes and their influences on ideational and affective development. *The Psychoanalytic Study of the Child*, 9:75–127. New York: International Universities Press.

Jones, E. (1913), The God complex. The belief that one is God and the resulting character traits. In: *Essays in Applied Psycho-Analysis*, 2:244–265. New York: International Universities Press, 1964.

Klein, M. (1928), Early stages of the Oedipus conflict. *Internat. J. Psycho-Anal.*, 9:169–180.

———— (1932), *The Psycho-Analysis of Children*. New York: Norton.

Kohut, H. (1959), Introspection, empathy and psychoanalysis. *J. Amer. Psychoanal. Assn.*, 7:459–483.

———— (1966), Forms and transformations of narcissism. *J. Amer. Psychoanal. Assn.*, 14:243–272.

Kris, E. (1938), Ego development and the comic. *Internat. J. Psycho-Anal.*, 19:77–90.

———— (1950), On preconscious mental processes. *Psychoanal. Quart.*, 19:540–560.

Lampl-de Groot, J. (1933), Problems of femininity. *Psychoanal. Quart.*, 2:489–518.

———— (1950), On masturbation and its influence on general development. *The Psychoanalytic Study of the Child*, 5:153–174. New York: International Universities Press.

Lewin, B. D. (1930), Kotschmieren, Menses und weibliches Über-Ich. *Internat. Zeitschr. Psychoanal.*, 16:43–56.

———— (1933), The body as phallus. *Psychoanal. Quart.*, 2:24–47.

———— (1950), *The Psychoanalysis of Elation*. New York: Norton.

Little, M. (1951), Counter-transference and the patient's response to it. *Internat. J. Psycho-Anal.*, 32:32–40.

———— (1957), "R"—the analyst's total response to his patient's needs. *Internat. J. Psycho-Anal.*, 38:240–254.

References

——— (1958), On delusional transference (transference psychosis). *Internat. J. Psycho-Anal.*, 39:134-138.

Malcove, L. (1933), Bodily mutilation and learning to eat. *Psychoanal. Quart.*, 2:557-561.

Nunberg, H. (1932), *Principles of Psychoanalysis. Their Application to the Neuroses.* New York: International Universities Press, 1956.

——— (1936), Homosexuality, magic and aggression. *Internat, J. Psycho-Anal.*, 19:1-16.

Ophuijsen, J. H. W. Van (1920), Uber die Quelle der Emfindung des Verfolgtwerdens. *Internat. Zeitschr. Psychoanal.*, 6:68-72.

Orr, D. W. (1954), Transference and Countertransference: a historical survey. *J. Amer. Psychoanal. Assn.*, 2:2:621-670.

Racker, E. (H.) (1952), Observaciones sobre la countratransferencia como instrumento tecnico. *Rev. Psicoanal.*, 9:342-354.

——— (1953), A Contribution to the problem of countertransference. *Internat. J. Psycho-Anal.*, 34:313-324.

——— (1957), The meanings and uses of countertransference. *Psychoanal. Quart.*, 26:303-357.

Rado, S. (1928), The problem of melancholia. *Internat. J. Psycho-Anal.*, 9:420-438.

Reich, W. (1926), Uber die chronische hypochondrische Neurasthenie mit genitaler Asthenie. *Internat. Zeitschr. Psychoanal.*, 12:25-39.

——— (1932), Der masochistische Charakter. *Internat. Zeitschr. Psychoanal.*, 18:303-351.

Reik, T. (1937), *Surprise and the Psycho-Analyst.* New York: Dutton.

——— (1939), Characteristics of masochism. *Amer. Imago*, 1:26-59.

——— (1948), *Listening with the Third Ear: The Inner Experience of a Psychoanalyst.* New York: Farrar, Straus.

Ross, D. W. and Kapp, F. T. (1962), A. technique for self-analysis of countertransference. *J. Amer. Psychoanal. Assn.*, 10:643-657.

Sachs, H. (1928), Der Witz. In: *Das psychoanalytische Volksbuch*, 1, ed. P. Federn & H. Meng. Stuttgart: Hippocrates, pp. 100-110.

References

Schafer, R. (1959), Generative empathy in the treatment situation. *Psychoanal. Quart.*, 28:342–373.

Simmel, E. (1930), Zum Problem von Zwang und Sucht. Bericht über den fünften allgemeinen ärztlichen Kongress für Psychotherapie in Baden-Baden, 1930.

Spitz, R. A. (1956), Countertransference: comments on its varying role in the analytic situation. *J. Amer. Psychoanal. Assn.*, 4:256–265.

Stärcke, A. (1919), The reversal of the libido-sign in delusions of persecution. *Internat. J. Psycho-Anal.*, 1:231–234, 1920.

Tauber, E. S. (1952), Observations on counter-transference phenomena: the supervisor-therapist relationship. *Samiksa*, 6:220–228.

Tausk, V. (1919), On the origin of the "influencing machine" in schizophrenia. In: R. Fliess, Ed., *The Psychoanalytic Reader*, 1:52–85. New York: International Universities Press, 1948.

Thompson, C. M. (1952), Countertransference. *Samiksa*, 6:205–211.

———— (1956), The role of the analyst's personality in therapy. *Amer. J. Psychother.*, 10:347–367.

Tower, L. E. (1956), Countertransference. *J. Amer. Psychoanal. Assn.*, 4:224–265.

Vienna Psychoanalytic Society (1912), *Die Onanie.* Vierzehn Beiträge zu einer Diskussion der "Wiener psychoanalytischen Vereinigung." Wiesbaden: J. F. Bergmann.

Weigert, E. (1952), Contribution to the problem of terminating psychoanalysis. *Psychoanal. Quart.*, 21:465–480.

———— (1965), Contribution to Panel on "Special Types of Resistance in Training Analysis." Presented at Annual Meeting, American Psychoanalytic Association, New York.

Winnicott, D. W. (1949), Hate in the counter-transference. In: *Collected Papers.* New York: Basic Books, 1958, pp. 194–203.

Name Index

Name Index

Subject Index

Subject Index

Subject Index

Superego, 164
  analysis of, 283–284
  in comic performance, 118–120
  development, 200–201
  early identifications in, 209–235
  as distinguished from ego ideal, 188–190
  and ego pathology, 236–249
  in narcissistic neuroses, 293–311
  in paranoid schizophrenic, 80–82
Symptoms
  conversion, 217–231
  neurotic, 158–159

Talent, nature of, 99–100
Thinking
  "image," 316
  magical, 49–50, 270
Training analysis, 275–276
  resistance in, viii, 129, 132, 334–343
Transference, 271, 279–280

and countertransference, 136–138, 284
positive, 84
in terminal phase of analysis, 121–135
in training analysis, 337–338

Unconscious
  of analyst as tool for interpretation, 136–137, 147, 345–346, 349–352
  fear of, 143–144
Unio mystica, 87–88, 92, 186

Voyeurism, sublimated in analyst, 148–154

Wishes
  exhibitionistic, 261, 265
  passive homosexual, 27
  phallic-oedipal, 259–260
  rape, 8
Withdrawal, narcissistic, 260–261
Women, psychology of, 85–98

DATE DUE			
DE 01 '89	DEC 6 '89		
DE 01 '89	DEC 6 '89		
GAYLORD			PRINTED IN U.S.A.